*Staged Narrative*

The Joan Palevsky  Imprint in Classical Literature

In honor of beloved Virgil—

"O degli altri poeti onore e lume . . ."

—Dante, *Inferno*

# Staged Narrative

*Poetics and the Messenger in Greek Tragedy*

James Barrett

UNIVERSITY OF CALIFORNIA PRESS

*Berkeley    Los Angeles    London*

The publisher gratefully acknowledges the generous
contribution to this book provided by Joan Palevsky.

University of California Press
Berkeley and Los Angeles, California

University of California Press, Ltd.
London, England

© 2002 by the Regents of the University of California

Library of Congress Cataloging-in-Publication Data

Barrett, James.
    Staged narrative: poetics and the messenger in Greek
tragedy / James Barrett.
        p.      cm.
    Includes bibliographical references and index.
    ISBN 0-520-23180-5 (acid-free paper)
    1. Greek drama (Tragedy)—History and criticism.
2. Messengers in literature.    3. Narration (Rhetoric).
4. Rhetoric, Ancient.   I. Title.
PA3136 .B36   2002
882'.0109352—dc21                              2001005017

Manufactured in the United States of America
10   09   08   07   06   05   04   03   02   01
10   9   8   7   6   5   4   3   2   1

The paper used in this publication is both acid-free and
totally chlorine-free (TCF). It meets the minimum require-
ments of ANSI/NISO Z39.48-1992 (R 1997) (*Permanence of Pa-
per*). ♾

*For Otto*

## Field of Vision

I remember this woman who sat for years
In a wheelchair, looking straight ahead
Out the window at sycamore trees unleafing
And leafing at the far end of the lane.

Straight out past the TV in the corner,
The stunted, agitated hawthorn bush,
The same small calves with their backs to wind and rain,
The same acre of ragwort, the same mountain.

She was steadfast as the big window itself.
Her brow was clear as the chrome bits of the chair.
She never lamented once and she never
Carried a spare ounce of emotional weight.

Face to face with her was an education
Of the sort you got across a well-braced gate—
One of those lean, clean, iron, roadside ones
Between two whitewashed pillars, where you could see

Deeper into the country than you expected
And discovered that the field behind the hedge
Grew more distinctly strange as you kept standing
Focused and drawn in by what barred the way.

Seamus Heaney

# CONTENTS

# ACKNOWLEDGMENTS

This book has been a long time in the making, and many people have lent a helping hand, knowingly and unknowingly. The initial impetus that set me on this path came from a graduate seminar at Cornell University, taught by Patricia Easterling. I thank her for sharing her inspired approach to Greek tragedy and for pointing the way. The ideas originally spawned in that seminar eventually led to a dissertation from which the present book took shape. I owe a debt of gratitude to Pietro Pucci for supervising that earlier work. I have benefited greatly from his vast learning, helpful criticisms, and generous spirit. I thank also those whose paths crossed mine in the Cornell Classics department: Fred Ahl, Kevin Clinton, Gregson Davis, Judy Ginsburg, Ralph Johnson, David Mankin, Phillip Mitsis, and Jeffrey Rusten; their expertise and insight proved helpful on many occasions. I count myself lucky to have spent time in the charmed company of those who frequent the Centre Louis Gernet in Paris. In particular, Nicole Loraux, Jesper Svenbro, and Pierre Vidal-Naquet encouraged my work on this project. I thank as well members of the CorHaLi group who have often inspired me: Jean Bollack, David Bouvier, Pierre Judet de la Combe, Gregory Nagy, Philippe Rousseau, and Froma Zeitlin. Those who first taught me Greek some years ago at

UC Santa Cruz provided a sympathetic guiding hand as well as stimulation that has been a constant companion ever since: Norman O. Brown, Mary Kay Gamel, Gary Miles, and Laura Slatkin. Colleagues at Colby have provided a friendly and stimulating atmosphere, and they have improved this work in a variety of ways; I thank Jill Gordon, Kerill O'Neill, Hanna Roisman, Yossi Roisman, and Anindyo Roy. I thank also friends and colleagues who have contributed in ways great and small: Herta Blaukopf, Kurt Blaukopf, Peter Boffey, Tom Falkner, Nancy Felson, Franz Gruber, Peitsa Hirvonen, Paul Allen Miller, Jo(h)n Robinson/Appels, David Rosenbloom, Thomas G. Rosenmeyer, Seth Schein, Harry Walker, James C. White, and Nancy Worman. I have been fortunate to find myself in the able hands of Kate Toll, editor for the Press, quae acrius viam ad astra perlucida cernit. I thank the anonymous reviewers of the Press who saved me from error and improved this study with their astute criticisms and valuable comments. Lorraine Barrett and Robert Barrett have been loyal, true, and constant in the face of my incessant wandering. Finally, I thank Mary Beth Mills, without whom this book might never have come into being. Her talent for lucid analysis and elegant solution is paralleled only by her unending patience and uncanny good sense. Through all, she has encouraged and sustained me.

Parts of this study have been presented at various meetings of the American Philological Association, the Classical Association of the Middle West and South, the Comparative Drama Conference, the Classical Association of the Atlantic States, and CorHaLi. I thank the members of those audiences for their many helpful remarks. Research support was provided by grants from the University of Mississippi. Portions of the introduction and chapter 1 have appeared in "Narrative and the Messenger in Aeschylus' *Persians*," *American Journal of Philology* 116 (1995) 539–57. An earlier version of chapter 3 appeared as "Pentheus and the Spectator in Euripides' *Bacchae*," *American Journal of Philology*

119 (1998) 337–60. This material is used courtesy of Johns Hopkins University Press.

"Field of Vision" from *Opened Ground: Selected Poems 1966–1999* by Seamus Heaney, copyright © 1998 by Seamus Heaney. Reprinted by permission of Farrar, Straus and Giroux, LLC. Permission also granted by Faber and Faber Ltd. to reproduce Seamus Heaney's "Field of Vision" from his *Seeing Things*.

# ABBREVIATIONS

Abbreviations of Greek and Latin authors and their works follow *The Oxford Classical Dictionary*, 3d ed., edited by Simon Hornblower and Antony Spawforth. In addition, the following abbreviations are used:

| | |
|---|---|
| D-K | Hermann Diels, ed. 1951–52. *Die Fragmente der Vorsokratiker*. 3 vols. 6th ed. Edited by Walther Kranz. Berlin: Weidmann. |
| Kassel-Austin | R. Kassel and C. Austin, eds. 1983–. *Poetae Comici Graeci*. Berlin: de Gruyter. |
| *PMG* | D. L. Page, ed. 1962. *Poetae Melici Graeci*. Oxford: Oxford University Press. |
| Radt | Stefan Radt, ed. 1985. *Tragicorum Graecorum Fragmenta*. Vol. 3. |
| *TrGF* | Bruno Snell, ed. 1971–. *Tragicorum Graecorum Fragmenta*. Göttingen: Vandenhoeck and Ruprecht. |
| Voigt | Eva-Maria Voigt. 1971. *Sappho et Alcaeus*. Amsterdam: Athenaeum—Polak and Van Gennep. |
| West | M. L. West. 1989. *Iambi et Elegi Graeci*. Vol. 1. 2d ed. Oxford: Clarendon Press. |

# PREFACE

The messenger of Greek tragedy is a curious figure. It is a messenger's narrative *(angelia)* that informs us about the death of Jocasta and the blinding of Oedipus in Sophocles' *Oedipus Tyrannus*, for example. Such narratives likewise report the madness of Herakles, the slaughter of Aigisthos, the death of Hippolytus, and the dismemberment of Pentheus in the plays of Euripides. Aeschylus's *Persians* recounts through an *angelia* the defeat of the Persian fleet at Salamis. Appearing, in fact, in more than three out of four tragedies, the messenger is a familiar inhabitant of one of the most-studied forms of ancient Greek literature. Nonetheless, this conventional figure has received relatively little critical attention. Besides a handful of dissertations, only two monographs devoted to this figure have appeared in more than one hundred years.[1] This neglect, I suspect, derives principally from the status of the messenger-speech as a conventional element thought to be rigidly fixed and uninteresting. This study will argue, however, that the convention in question is quite fluid and has much to teach. The pages that follow will make the case that the messenger speaks with a voice that is unique on the tragic stage and

1. Di Gregorio 1967 is an evolutionary and formal study; de Jong 1991 is a narratological reference work.

that this figure offers important testimony about tragedy's identity as a genre and about fifth-century experimentation with modes of speech.

Like most drama, Greek tragedy confronts the spectator directly with a multitude of voices, each with an equal claim, in principle, to truth and authority. The absence of a narrator renders all speech onstage equally authoritative or suspect, equally bound by its status as a rhetorical creation. This particular form of drama, however, augments and complicates this fundamental quality in a variety of ways. As John Herington (1985) has shown, Greek tragedy represents a bold experiment in mixing what were otherwise separate generic forms. Elements of epic, lyric, elegiac, and epinician poetry along with speech clearly marked as belonging to the spheres of oracles, prayer, and lament, for example, all co-exist on the same stage. The result, therefore, is not only a multitude of individual voices, but also a plethora of types of speech. Perhaps more than other forms of drama, Greek tragedy exploits such encounters of differing voices as a means of producing opacity and ambiguity in the language of the plays. This multiplicity of generic forms and voices thus conspicuously reproduces what occurs in other avenues of public discourse at Athens, perhaps most of all in the political arena, where debate among "equals" *(isēgoria)* was a fundamental premise of democratic systems as they evolved throughout the fifth century B.C.E.

At the same time, critics have long treated the messenger-speech as effectively untouched by the rhetorical atmosphere onstage. It makes a modicum of sense that the messenger's narrative should pass as a virtually transparent account unmarked by signs of motivation or partiality: the tragedian needs a reliable vehicle for incorporating offstage events. But the tragic texts themselves display an interest in the functioning of this figure and manipulate our expectations in ways that draw attention to the problematic status of such a figure. Working from these cues, I ask how it is that this figure manages to speak with a voice that, on the whole, has gone unquestioned and unexamined by critics.

I argue that typically the tragic texts endow the messenger with a narrative voice that closely resembles that of epic, and that this explains his success on two grounds.[2] First, the approximation to Homer in itself carries a powerful authority that resounds uniquely in the Greek literary tradition. The voice of epic narrative transmits that of the Muse, and its adoption by the messenger brings with it something of that divine authority. Second, in appropriating the narrative voice of Homer, the messenger employs a number of narrative strategies that work to claim a privileged status. Most important of these is his tendency within his narrative toward self-effacement that appears as virtual disembodiment. While there is, on the whole, a strong identification of speaker and speech in tragedy, the messenger, in sharp distinction, offers a narrative that in general is conspicuously disassociated from any particular point of view. His narrative, in short, often appears to "tell itself."[3] These practices distinguish the messenger from the others onstage, while freeing his narrative to a considerable degree from the partiality that defines the speech of the other *dramatis personae.*

Regarding these unusual qualities of the messenger as a serious challenge to fundamental premises of the tragic genre, this study takes as its principal subject the epistemic and discursive status claimed by this figure largely through his adoption of epic narrative strategies. The messenger, that is, typically makes (implicit) claims to a secure form of knowledge, while his report presents itself as an unproblematic—and nonrhetorical—account of events offstage. In examining both the practices of tragic messengers and the commentary on these practices in the tragic texts themselves, this study seeks to address the rather far-reaching import of tragedy's use of and interest in this figure. This study also contributes to our knowledge of tragedy's borrowings from earlier generic forms, as it clarifies a confused debate more than a century old about the

2. Among tragic messengers, only the Nurse in Sophocles' *Trachiniae* and the servant in Euripides' *Alcestis* are female. As a generally representative form of shorthand, I here speak of the messenger as male. I discuss below in chapter 2 the problem of defining who is and who is not a messenger.

3. I borrow this phrase from Benveniste 1971, 208.

status of the messenger-speech as an epic element.[4] The present study explains the epic affiliation of the messenger-speech on the basis of clues in the plays themselves. Tragedy shows itself to be indebted to epic not only for its characters and plots, but also for its successful functioning as theater. Most important, the rich rhetorical and discursive experimentation of tragedy asks to be viewed against its reliance upon an authoritative "epic" voice and against the genre's own commentary on this reliance.

This study, then, combines several critical approaches, offering a synthetic view of the messenger and of the phenomenon he embodies. Drawing on narrative theory, genre study, and rhetorical analysis, I situate the messenger at the intersection of these domains. In doing so, I rely upon an intertextual approach in reading the tragic messenger with and against Homeric texts in particular. As a result, the messenger's generic affiliation proves to be a guide to understanding his narrative practice. These various axes of interpretation together illuminate the epistemic claims implicit in the messenger's account of events offstage. Finally, I show through metatheatrical readings that the tragic texts themselves corroborate my claims in their commentary on the messenger as a theatrical institution.

Although this study concentrates on the narratives of tragic messengers, it is not a narratological work in the narrow sense. Indeed, Irene de Jong (1991) has provided us with an admirably systematic account of the messenger in narratological terms. Nonetheless, I consider this study to be largely compatible with and complementary to that of de Jong, even though our interests are quite different. I devote my attention principally to identifying typical practices and examining these for their rhetorical content and for what they have to teach about generic and epistemic issues. Given that the tragic *angeliai* constitute the genre's most sustained attention to extended narrative, studies of the messenger can not only address the strictly narratological workings of these narratives;

4. On generic borrowing in tragedy see Herington 1985, Nagy 1990b, 400–403, and Rutherford 1994/95; cf. Ober and Strauss 1990.

they can also ask what use the genre makes of such narratives. This study takes up this latter possibility, inflecting the question in terms of genre and the epistemic status these narratives claim. In short, I draw on narrative theory with my sights set largely elsewhere.

My interest in turning the tragic texts' use of the messenger toward epistemic issues derives from two concerns. First, analysis of narrative inevitably hinges on such issues insofar as every narrator claims knowledge of some form. What and how a narrator knows, and consequently how she or he is able to provide the account offered, is therefore central to all narrative. Such a concern is addressed in the opening lines of both the *Iliad* and the *Odyssey*, for example, where the narrators in question identify the divine Muse as the source of their stories. Inasmuch as I argue that the tragic messenger forges his own authority along the lines established by the epic narrator, the messenger's epistemic status proves to be central to understanding this conventional figure in a particularly urgent way.

Second, this study follows the lead of those who have shown that Athenian tragedy—if not all tragedy (see Reiss 1980)—attends at nearly every turn to questions about language and knowledge: the discursive and epistemic status of the characters onstage—inextricably linked in such a medium—prove to be at issue in perhaps all of our extant plays.[5] The messenger, then, *qua* narrator, invites questions about his epistemic status, but his identity as a familiar figure on the tragic stage renders those questions even more pressing and more potent. For such questions speak not only about the messenger; they speak also about the genre's attention to epistemic issues more broadly. As such, the messenger proves to be a familiar, yet little-understood, figure who promises to illuminate some of the genre's most persistent concerns.

Drawing on a variety of critical approaches, then, this study consists largely of close readings of tragic texts. The introduction explains the

5. See, for example, Goldhill 1986, chap. 1, and Segal 1986, chap. 3.

conundrum represented by the messenger by offering an overview of critical attention to this figure. Chapter 1 takes up our earliest play, Aeschylus's *Persians*, as a case study that suggests the value of epic narrative as a model for the messenger. Here, generic affiliation and intertextual rewriting combine to produce a nearly paradigmatic messenger-speech. Chapter 2 reviews the literary background of the tragic messenger in epic and lyric poetry. This literary genealogy allows us to make sense of the attention devoted to the messenger in ancient literary criticism, which this chapter then takes up. I argue here that both Aristotle and Philodemus address the question of the messenger as an epic element in tragedy. This section concludes with a survey of tragic texts that demonstrate the messenger's typical strategies. Chapter 3 turns to the metatheater of Euripides' *Bacchae* and its commentary on the messenger. What Aeschylus's *Persians* displays at length, Euripides' play scrutinizes as a theatrical institution. Chapter 4 takes up the only fictitious *angelia* among extant plays, that in Sophocles' *Electra*. This fictitious messenger-speech constructs an incisive metatheatrical commentary on the tragic messenger in large measure by exploiting the Homeric texts. Both the *Iliad* and the *Odyssey* figure prominently in Sophocles' play, culminating in the Paidagogos's false *angelia*. I argue here that this fictitious messenger-speech reproduces much of the *Odyssey*'s literary sophistication as it offers a provocative commentary on the impact of the *angelia* in the theater. Chapter 5 then turns to the remarkable messenger-speech of the charioteer in *Rhesos*. This figure's performance appears to contradict my argument at nearly every moment, as it violates virtually all of the "principles" that enable messengers to succeed elsewhere. I argue that this comic messenger confirms my larger argument in demonstrating precisely what happens when a messenger departs too much from conventional practice. This play also provides a telling commentary on the workings of myth, and it does so largely through the charioteer's unique performance. Finally, chapter 6 takes up the play that perhaps more than any other addresses discursive and epistemic issues, Sophocles' *Oedipus*

*Tyrannus.* I argue that this play makes telling use of its messengers, enlisting them in the service of its larger, more philosophical interests. In so doing, Sophocles' play affirms the centrality of discursive and epistemic questions in the constitution of the messenger, as it highlights the theatrical conventions that underpin this figure's privilege.

In making this argument, I hope to show that the texts of Athenian tragedy offer fertile ground for further study of related issues. The implications of what follows here for the genre more broadly, that is, extend beyond the messenger himself. Given that this form of tragedy borrows from a great variety of generic forms and types of speech, and that the extant texts again and again formulate questions about language and knowledge, the results of this study, I hope, will suggest the value of inquiry along related lines into the epistemic and discursive status of other forms of speech in our texts.[6] Similarly, in discussing tragic borrowings from Homer, I hope not only to bring to light some allusive moments, but also to show how tragic texts can use, comment on, and even rewrite familiar Homeric passages. By reading tragedy with and against earlier texts, this study will also demonstrate some ways in which tragic texts can revise and evaluate the tradition of myth itself.

This study suggests as well that the role of the messenger bears not only on issues relevant to the history of tragedy. Inasmuch as the messenger plays an important role in tragedy's ongoing investigation into the problems of language and knowledge, he also offers testimony relevant to early philosophical investigations into these matters. Indeed, the experimentation represented by the tragic messenger covers some of the same ground as do a number of these philosophical texts. From Xenophanes to Plato (and beyond), there is continuous engagement with the question of how to construct an authoritative, philosophical voice. Although there are various solutions to this problem, several of these texts

6. Bushnell (1988) points the way for such a consideration of divine speech in tragedy.

incorporate a divine voice.[7] Most, however, face the task of speaking "truth" without divine aid. When disavowing such authority, the early Greek philosophers struggle to legitimate their individual voices.[8] And this project, I suggest, bears an affinity to tragic experimentation with the messenger. Indeed, a similar problem confronts the historian, perhaps most in evidence in Thucydides.[9] These nominally separate traditions prove to be valuable *comparanda* for one another and thereby demonstrate that tragedy's use of the messenger forms part of a much larger current of intellectual investigation from the archaic period through classical times.

In confronting the rather broad territory inhabited by the tragic messenger, I have had to limit my study in a number of ways. I address what I consider the principal and most urgent questions surrounding this figure. I do not, for example, attempt to provide a comprehensive account of the messenger's presence onstage, generally bypassing questions such as those about social positioning (gender, ethnicity, age, etc.; I do, however, address some of these issues generally in chapter 2). I have little to say about strictly formal issues, one aspect of the messenger that has been particularly well-studied. Similarly, I pay relatively little attention to nonnarrative passages involving or relevant to the messenger.[10] I also

7. Most notably, Parmenides and Empedocles.

8. An illuminating commentary on this problem appears in Heracleitus fr. 50 D-K.

9. On Thucydides see Hartog 1982 and the studies of Crane (1996) and Allison (1997). On Herodotus see Dewald 1987; on both Herodotus and Thucydides, and for a survey of literature on related issues in the historians, see Dewald 1999.

10. Messengers almost always engage in some dialogue before, generally after, and sometimes within the more strictly narrative sections. I will address such nonnarrative passages on occasion, however. Inasmuch as I argue here for the peculiar privilege often attained by messenger-speeches, any account of nonnarrative sections that serves to underscore a messenger's characterization and consequent partiality, for example, would only render his success

generally ignore issues of performance in the theater per se: costume, mask, movement, and so on. Instead I focus on what I take to be the most important aspect of the messenger's performance: the narrative itself. Once this form of narrative is better understood as a central participant in tragedy's use of generic forms and in its attention to discursive and epistemic issues, other aspects of the messenger can be more fruitfully addressed. While much work still remains to be done on the messenger—and I expect that all of the areas mentioned above would prove to be productive sites of investigation—it is beyond the scope of any single study to provide a comprehensive treatment of this figure. My hope is that this book will serve as a guide to some of the work that has yet to be carried out. If, then, readers come to feel the need for such further studies, it will be some indication of the present work's success: for in part my aim here is to stimulate critical interest in the messenger and all that the presence of this conventional figure on the tragic stage implies.

In transliterating Greek names, I have generally used forms close to the Greek ("Polybos" rather than "Polybus," for example), although I have used the Latinized forms for the more familiar characters such as Achilles, Electra, and Oedipus. This compromise is designed principally with nonspecialists in mind. I hope that purists will be tolerant. When citing from tragic texts, I provide both the Greek and my own trans-

_____

at claiming impartiality via his narrative more remarkable. Indeed, it is not uncommon for tragic messengers to offer a "coda" that makes clear their feelings about what they have reported, as they summarize their reports. Similarly, the narratives are not uncommonly introduced by expressions of grief, horror, awe, and so on. De Jong 1991 does a good job of showing that even the narratives themselves offer ample evidence of the messengers' sympathies and allegiances that serves to underscore the partiality that inevitably shapes these narratives. Dialogue, then, might well corroborate or extend such characterization of the messengers, but it does little to alter the dynamics at work in the narratives themselves.

lations. Making no claims about the virtues of these renderings into English, I hope that they will be found both helpful and faithful to the originals. I cite from the Oxford Classical Text series: Denys Page for Aeschylus (1972), Hugh Lloyd-Jones and Nigel Wilson for Sophocles (1990), and James Diggle for Euripides (1981–94), unless otherwise noted.

# Introduction

εἰ καὶ τυραννεῖς, ἐξισωτέον τὸ γοῦν
ἴσ' ἀντιλέξαι· τοῦδε γὰρ κἀγὼ κρατῶ.

Even if you are king, the right to contradict at equal length,
at least, must be shared. I, too, have a claim to this.

Teiresias to Oedipus, Sophocles *Oedipus Tyrannus*\*

Shortly after the *Iliad* begins it becomes virtual drama for more than 100
lines: beginning with Kalkhas's plea to Achilles for protection (74–83),
the narrator speaks only single lines introducing the characters as they
speak in turn (with the exception of one 5-line passage, 101–5).[1] Fol-
lowing Kalkhas's plea and Achilles' pledge to protect him, Achilles and
Agamemnon trade insults and threats for nearly 70 lines. At line 188,
however, these two fall momentarily silent, and the "drama" gives way
to the voice of the narrator (188–92):

Ὣς φάτο· Πηλεΐωνι δ' ἄχος γένετ', ἐν δέ οἱ ἦτορ
στήθεσσιν λασίοισι διάνδιχα μερμήριξεν,

---

\*All translations are mine, unless otherwise noted.

1. On the dramatic quality of this scene see Scully 1986, 137 and 146–
47; Edwards 1987, 179. Cf. Arist. *Poet.* 1448b35, 1460a9.

ἢ ὅ γε φάσγανον ὀξὺ ἐρυσσάμενος παρὰ μηροῦ
τοὺς μὲν ἀναστήσειεν, ὃ δ' Ἀτρεΐδην ἐναρίζοι,
ἦε χόλον παύσειεν ἐρητύσειέ τε θυμόν.

So he spoke. Peleus's son became angry, and his heart in his hairy
chest was divided, whether he should draw his sharp sword from be-
side his thigh, push back those in his way and kill the son of Atreus,
or put an end to his rage and hold back his anger.

No longer are we left alone face-to-face with Achilles and Agamemnon.
When Achilles begins to unsheathe his sword (194) we know that this is
no mere threat to Agamemnon: he is pondering whether or not to kill
him, the narrator tells us. This silence between the protagonists, mark-
ing a break with the "dramatic" form, allows us to see into the mind of
Achilles, as the narrator divulges his thoughts. The voice of the narrator
here concisely exhibits its role in defining one of the key constituents of
epic narrative as it interrupts the dialogue to disclose what dialogue alone
cannot reveal.

But this aposiopesis accomplishes something else. During this silence
of more than 30 lines Athena appears to Achilles and urges him to leave
his sword in its sheath. She tells him that he will be compensated for
Agamemnon's outrage, and Achilles relents. We learn from the narrator
that none of the others saw Athena (198), and we may deduce that none
heard either her or Achilles, for that matter. This dialogue between
Athena and Achilles supplants that of Achilles and Agamemnon, audible
only to the interlocutors and to us, the audience. And yet when Achilles
speaks again to Agamemnon nearly 40 lines later, he continues virtually
where he left off.[2] Just as Athena's appearance and her dialogue with
Achilles go unnoticed by the others, so the silence leaves no trace on the

---

2. Kirk (1985 *ad* 1.215–18) remarks: "The whole episode, indeed, after
Akhilleus' initial violent impulse, is kept severely in place, presumably so as
not to detract from the dramatic force of the main argument between the
two leaders."

"stage" of action inhabited by the Greek chiefs. This moment of authorial interruption and explicit manipulation remains invisible in this sense. As such, it silently offers us a privileged view and guides our witnessing of the scene. No longer do the characters themselves control the development of the poem, its range and pulse; now the narrative voice reasserts its authority, allotting the characters their places.[3] In short, the narra-

---

3. This is not to say that we must always acquiesce in the Homeric narrator's guidance. If in *Iliad* 1, for example, he reveals Achilles' thoughts, he does not do the same for Agamemnon, and this discrepancy offers purchase for a critical view. Robert Rabel, for example, distinguishes between the narrator and the "implied poet" of the *Iliad*. He argues that the narrating voice itself is a creation of the implied poet, the latter speaking, for example, lines 1–7 of book 1: "Homer has contrived . . . the emancipation of the poet from the narrator of the poem, thus winning for himself ironic distance from the interests of the storyteller as well as from the interests represented by the characters within the story. Furthermore, he has freed the speech of his characters from the overall control and mediating power of the poem's narrator, allowing it to become the direct and immediate self-presentation of thought and feeling of the sort otherwise found only in the later drama" (1997, 20). Yet even if we grant that the narrator is part of the poem's fiction, it is clear that he does not inhabit the same realm as the (other) characters. Although we may see some ironic distance between implied poet and narrator—with a degree of critical judgment weighing against the ultimate authority of the narrator—it remains true that this narrator wields substantial control over the lives of the poem's characters. Rabel's claim, then, that the speech of the characters is freed from the "mediating power of the poem's narrator" overstates the case. Although we are free to doubt the judgments of this narrative voice, we cannot avoid the fact that it decides when and what we hear. Cf. Richardson 1990, 4. On the term "implied poet" see Rabel 1997, 24–25. De Jong, too, distinguishes between poet and narrator, although for her the poet does not speak (see Chatman 1978, 148, on the "implied author" as one who "has no voice"; cited by Rabel 1997, 25). De Jong argues that every narrator, including the Iliadic, is a focalizer, and she speaks—along with Wayne Booth—of the narrator's "rhetoric" (1989, 97–98). This narrator, she writes, is "a *creation* of the poet like the characters"

tor's voice is extradiegetic, or outside the world of the characters who inhabit the narrative.[4]

The narrator is, of course, always present, if only as the one through whom the characters speak. And in performance the bard's voice serves as the medium for all of the characters as well as for the narrator. This narrator, of course, is not an individual; it is rather the vehicle of a tradition of song in any given instance. As such, the narrator in principle chooses at each turn who speaks. The temporary autonomy of Achilles and Agamemnon, like the narrative voice's act of reclaiming its "privilege," is illusory. The trajectory from narrative to dialogue and back is, of course, entirely the plan of the tradition at work.

By contrast, when we turn from Homer—even a scene "close to the theater" (Edwards 1987, 179)—to Greek tragedy things change substantially. Although it might seem equally obvious that dramatic characters speak only at the command of the author, tragic authors do not have recourse to an extradiegetic voice. Tragedy appears starkly as a genre without the privileged views, clear ordering, and interpretive guidance offered by the epic narrator. As a consequence the characters themselves create their own narrative context, and we must navigate the many voices on our own. Charles Segal defines this aspect of tragedy in relation to epic:

> Tragedy . . . is full of elusive details, missing pieces, unexplained motives, puzzling changes of mood, decision, or attitude. Instead of the oral poet who tells us in person of the will of Zeus, we have the absent poet who has plotted out every detail in advance. And we have the feeling, at times, that we have been plotted against, that we are the victims of a calculated counterpoint between surface and depth, appearance and reality, seeming and being. (1986, 79)

---

(45, her emphasis), "an agent who orders and interprets the events of the fabula" (42).

4. On the term "extradiegetic" see Genette 1980, 228–31.

Segal's "absence" is precisely that of the narrator.[5] As a measure of how widely accepted such a view of tragedy is, it is worth noting that a recent companion to Greek tragedy tells us that "the multiple voices of tragedy can all claim their own truth" because the genre "lacks the single, authoritative voice of a bard" (Burian 1997, 191).

The *Iliad* itself, in fact, already points in this direction. In book 9 with Achilles having withdrawn from battle and the Greeks suffering badly in the fight against the Trojans, Agamemnon agrees to send an embassy offering gifts to Achilles in recompense for his earlier transgression of taking Briseis, Achilles' captive war-booty. Nestor orders Phoinix, Ajax, and Odysseus, along with the heralds Odios and Eurybates, to take the message to Achilles. After a libation, a drink, and some final words from Nestor, they start on their way. Suddenly, at line 182 the text turns from speaking of this group in the plural to a series of duals. Wolfgang Schadewaldt called this "the greatest problem in the whole of the *Iliad*."[6] To date there is no scholarly consensus about why the shift to the duals occurs, nor about whom these duals refer to.[7] Departing from the terrain of philological argument, Michael Lynn-George discusses these problematic duals as part of what he calls "epic theatre" and in so doing illustrates something of the relation between narrative and drama, as contained in the poem. Referring to lines 182–96 of *Iliad* 9, Lynn-George attributes the uncertainty about the duals to the "silence" of the text in its refusal to reveal the identities of those to whom the duals refer. Speaking of "the theatre to be staged within the tent of Achilles," Lynn-George continues:

> If the drama is created by the relative absence of an authority which
> sets everything firmly in place through naming and identifying, it is

5. This "absence" is not unique to tragedy, of course. See, for example, Szondi 1987, 8; Pfister 1988, 2–6.

6. Schadewaldt 1966, 137 (cited by Griffin 1995, 51).

7. See Griffin 1995, 51–53, for a concise survey of views.

that very absence which has always disconcerted critics in their approach to book IX of the *Iliad*. What they object to is thus the fundamental condition of the drama. (1988, 54)

Following Aristotle in his qualification of Homeric poetry as "dramatic," Lynn-George identifies the uncertainties produced by the duals in book 9 as a function of the poem's dramatic aspect. In so doing, he places in sharp relief not only the "fundamental condition of the drama" of *Iliad* 9, but also the fundamental condition of drama more generally.[8]

If fifth-century tragedy shares with many other types of drama the formal property of the "absence of an authority which sets everything firmly in place through naming and identifying," it also exploits this property in idiosyncratic ways. Greek tragedy takes as one of its primary concerns the collisions of various points of view, the incommensurability of different kinds of speech, and the semantic ambiguity of its language. These various cleavages are all intensified in tragedy by its formal exclusion of an authoritative, organizing voice. In an influential essay, Jean-Pierre Vernant speaks of "shifts in meaning" as the dialogue "is interpreted and commented upon by the chorus and taken in and understood by the spectators." Speaking of Sophocles' *Antigone*, he goes on to say that "the various heroes of the drama employ the same words in their debates but these words take on opposed meanings depending on who utters them" (1988b, 42). Although he remains optimistic about the spectator's ability to sift through the ambivalence, Vernant maintains that

> the tragic message . . . is precisely that there are zones of opacity
> and incommunicability in the words that men exchange. Even as he
> sees the protagonists clinging exclusively to one meaning and, thus
> blinded, tearing themselves apart or destroying themselves, the spec-

8. Tonelli remarks: "Theatre is, in fact, the locus of a performance where, in the end, there is no privileged discourse" (1983, 289). On Aristotle and Homer see Lynn-George 1988, 50 (with references); cf. Rabel 1997, 8–21.

tator must understand that there are really two or more possible meanings. (1988b, 43)[9]

Tragedy, then, is replete with contestation not only for formal reasons necessitated by the absence of a narrator: the tragic poets consistently build their dramas around themes of conflict and dispute as they exploit the semantic range of the vocabulary they employ. The formal condition of drama thus becomes a principle of its thematic construction. This coincidence of form and theme may be no accident. One critic, in fact, argues that it is precisely in periods of epistemic and discursive instability, with doubt cast on the ability of language to express truth, that tragedy arises.[10] If the *dramatis personae* exist in a world of relation, in Lynn-George's terms,[11] rather than nomination, if they alone in relation to one another agonistically construct the language(s) of tragedy, so too does this relational process become a theme to a greater or lesser degree in nearly every play.[12] Indeed, if Timothy Reiss is correct, it could hardly be otherwise.[13]

Consequently, the ensemble of voices onstage requires the audience to negotiate the many competing claims to authority. Additionally, the juxtaposition of different and competing voices emphasizes the partiality of each speaker. And of course such a quality is only more pronounced in performance than it is for a reader: the partiality of all speech is physically enacted in its vocalization. But for readers as well, tragic language not only becomes a demonstration of (overcoming) the barriers to communication; it also rehearses the inseparability of the

9. See also Segal 1986.

10. Timothy Reiss claims that tragedy is "a discursive type that performs a specific role within the totality of discourses . . . at certain moments of seemingly abrupt epistemic change" (1980, 2).

11. Lynn-George 1988, 54.

12. Cf. Goff 1990, esp. chap. 4.

13. Cf. Else's comments on tragedy's "double vision" and the concomitant " tension which is of its essence" (1965, 44).

connection between the speaker and the spoken, and thus the partiality of all speech.[14]

One may, then, productively consider tragedy as a central participant in the fifth-century examination of language. The expansion of democratic and legal institutions along with the concomitant importance of persuasive speech, the growth of interest in rhetorical theory, and the increasing popularity of studying the art of public speaking must be understood as forming part of the context in which most surviving tragedy was produced. As often noted in recent years, tragic performances were an important constituent of public life at Athens. An important part of tragedy's participation in this life, of course, is constituted by its atten-

---

14. Such a view of tragic language supports the widely embraced view of tragedy as an institution in which "notions which are important to the city and the development of civic ideology are put through profound questioning" (Goldhill 1986, 77). Indeed, Vernant has argued that in tragedy "the hero has ceased to be a model. He has become . . . a problem" (1988a, 25). Insofar as the formal properties of drama, together with the thematic interests of Greek tragedy as a whole, serve to render conclusive judgments difficult, the genre generally encourages the sort of questioning spoken of by Goldhill. Nonetheless, these two aspects should not be confused. As Mark Griffith has shown, one can appreciate that the audience's "point of view shifts incessantly and unpredictably back and forth with the different 'focalizers' of the action" (1995, 72) and yet maintain that "the verbal, musical, gestural, and spatial structures of an Athenian tragic performance do impose certain patterns of response on the whole body of onlookers" (75). One can, in the end, accept that the tragic performances exploited the absence of an authoritative narrator in producing Vernant's "zones of opacity" without conceding that (therefore) these plays offer no answers to the questions they raise This is, of course, a large issue. Goldhill, for example, sees the Great Dionysia as displaying "the strength of the democracy and its civic ideology" while "tragedy explores the problems inherent in the civic ideology" (1986, 77). Griffith seeks to modify such a view by showing that an important function of tragedy is "to negotiate between conflicting class interests and ideologies within the polis" in such a way that "both classes can wind up feeling their own interests and ideology validated" (1995, 109–10).

tion to intellectual and philosophical issues. And one sign of this participation lies in the attention paid to examining and experimenting with various forms of speech.[15]

In addition to exploiting the absence of an authoritative voice, tragedy draws upon another of its characteristic features as a means of investigating the problems and possibilities of various speech forms. As John Herington has demonstrated, Greek tragedy is a genre composed of many poetic forms: by the middle of the fifth century, "almost every metrical element known to the pretragic tradition of poetry" had been absorbed by tragedy (1985, 125). This is important in the present context for two reasons. First, this daunting variety of metrical forms reinforces the sense of multiplicity produced by the array of speaking subjects onstage by contributing a further means of distinguishing among the voices. Second, the various metrical forms are often closely associated with differing speech forms. This variety makes tragedy "a poetry that is able to carry and metrically reinforce every mode of discourse, from narrative and argumentative in the iambic dialogue passages, to emotional in the anapaestic, to the language of our dreams at the lyric level" (Herington 1985, 103). As such, tragedy is capable not only of "conveying all aspects of the human experience in words" (103), but also of marking the varieties of verbal expression as distinct types of speech. This generic variety, then, adds a further layer to tragic experimentation with language.[16]

Tragedy borrows not only meter, however. Besides its many metrical borrowings, Herington discusses tragedy's use of stylistic elements taken from "epic, choral lyric, personal lyric, and iambic" poetry as well as from the speech of the law courts (1985, 126). In other words, he identifies a variety of sources for tragic speech types, from the realm of tra-

---

15. The bibliography here is immense. A few guideposts: Pl. *Grg.* 502b1–d9; Buxton 1982, 10–18; Goldhill 1986, 1–3, 232–43; Lloyd 1992, 19–36; O'Regan 1992, 9–21.

16. See also Michelini 1982, 3–15.

ditional poetic genres as well as from nonliterary speech. Even if there is no metrical connection, then, between a given passage in tragedy and another (earlier or contemporary) type of speech, we may discover stylistic borrowings. Herington not only shows that the inheritance from the poetic tradition that went into the making of tragedy was rich; he also points the way toward studying tragedy's use of other literary genres and speech forms.[17]

By way of example, I turn to a passage of Aeschylus's *Agamemnon* that exhibits some of these properties. Following the herald's report that Troy has fallen, Clytemnestra rebuffs the herald as news-bringer and leaves the stage. The chorus then ask the herald for news about Menelaos. Although hesitant, the herald eventually recounts the battering of the ships that separated the two brothers and may, for all he knows, have led to Menelaos's death. He concludes his account by saying (680):

τοσαῦτ' ἀκούσας ἴσθι τἀληθῆ κλύων.

Having heard this much, know that you have heard the truth.

The herald then exits, and the chorus immediately begin to sing the second stasimon. Their first lines address the naming of Helen (681–87):

τίς ποτ' ὠνόμαζεν ὧδ'
   ἐς τὸ πᾶν ἐτητύμως,
μή τις ὅντιν' οὐχ ὁρῶμεν προνοί-
   αισι τοῦ πεπρωμένου
γλῶσσαν ἐν τύχᾳ νέμων,
τὰν δορίγαμβρον ἀμφινει-
   κῆ θ' Ἑλέναν;

---

17. Aside from Herington, some of this work has been done. Much remains. On political rhetoric and tragedy see Ober and Strauss 1990, esp. 247–49, 259–63. On tragedy's use of the paean see Rutherford 1994/95. Cf. Pl. *Leg.* 700a–701a with Nagy 1990b, 400–403.

Who ever named her so truly in every way? Someone whom we do
not see perhaps? Someone who, knowing what was fated, accurately
spoke the name of that bride of war and strife, Helen?

The chorus then famously etymologize Helen's name as containing the
root ἐλ- found in ἐλένας, ἕλανδρος, and ἐλέπτολις ("ship-destroyer,"
"man-destroyer," and "city-destroyer"). She was named "truly in every
way" because her name reveals the destruction that followed in her wake.

Although their vocabularies differ, both the herald's report and the
name of Helen are said to contain "truth" (ἀληθῆ, ἐτητύμως). The shared
claim to truth allows us to examine the differences between them as in-
dicative of the variety of speech forms in tragedy. The herald's conclu-
sion suggests, for example, that the truth in his account resides in a mat-
ter of quantity (τοσαῦτ', "this much"). And his report about Menelaos
confirms this: it is a narrative of approximately 30 lines. The truth that
he brings is inseparable, and perhaps indistinguishable, from the accu-
mulation of words that make up his account. One hundred lines earlier he
says much the same thing in concluding his first report about the fall of
Troy (582): πάντ' ἔχεις λόγον ("You have the whole story"). Although
in the later passage he does not claim to have told everything, he does con-
tinue to base the value of his report on its quantity. The model of truth-
ful speech he employs here is one predicated upon fullness of descrip-
tion based on his own status as an eyewitness observer.[18]

The act of naming Helen, by contrast, is said to be truthful for no
such reasons. In fact, the chorus express uncertainty about how it could
have happened. Perhaps, they say, it was on the basis of foreknowl-
edge. They also suggest that there was an element of chance involved (ἐν

18. It is worth noting that as she rejects the herald in his professional ca-
pacity and dispatches him with a message for Agamemnon, Clytemnestra
asks rhetorically why he should report to her the bulk of details (τὰ μάσσω,
598). The term she uses is a comparative meaning "greater" or "more." His
mission is implicitly defined as the delivery of an extensive report.

τύχᾳ).[19] There is also a theological element here inasmuch as access to knowledge of the future is controlled by the gods. There is a distinction between what mere mortals can know (and say), as epitomized by the herald, and what lies within the realm of the gods.[20] This prophetic and enigmatic act of naming, in fact, stands as the virtual opposite of the herald's report: it is brief in the extreme, contains no description, requires no observation, speaks of the future rather than the past, and escapes explication. Like the herald's account, however, it is "true."

There is, finally, a third speech form here. The original act of naming Helen is not itself part of the text, having taken place some years earlier. But in "explaining" the cledonomantic property of her name, the chorus in effect name her again. It is they who give to the name the power to signify the multiple forms of destruction. It is they who provide the etymology. While the two namings of Helen are not the same, they share a substantial amount. The first I have described, and it is important to say that this description applies badly if at all to the song of the chorus. They do, however, perform a nearly incantatory act of naming as they etymologize the name. And while explicitly identifying the original act of naming as prophetically true, their own song implicitly claims yet another kind of truth. To be sure, they offer their act of etymologizing as a form of explanation; but it is clear that without their song the "true" meaning of her name would remain unknown.

For the herald's report and the chorus's song, at least, we can see the importance of Herington's claim that tragedy can contain and "metrically reinforce every mode of discourse" (1985, 103). We are free, of course, to accept or reject any of these claims to truth. It has, in fact, been argued that both the herald's report and the signifying abilities of Helen's

19. On the role of chance in cledonomantic utterances see Peradotto 1969, 2.

20. The word for "truly" (ἐτητύμως) here repeats its use earlier at 166 where the gap between mortals and immortals (Zeus) is decisive. The chorus again at 1296 use this word of Cassandra's prophetic knowledge.

name are hedged about with uncertainty and suspicion, leaving both claims to truth in doubt.[21] However we judge this matter, we cannot avoid encountering this variety of claims to truthful speech and considering the implications of these claims juxtaposed with one another so conspicuously as they are. For my purposes here, what matters is precisely the insight of Herington that I take this passage from Aeschylus to exemplify.[22]

Finally, it is perhaps not enough to say that tragedy is characterized by such a multiplicity of voices, semantic registers, metrical forms, and speech types. It is important to add that prior to the emergence of the genre as we know it nothing of this sort existed. This range of mixing what had hitherto been separate would have sounded, says Herington, to the archaic ear as "disconcerting as, say, a trombone in a string quartet" (1985, 74). The novelty of tragedy's accomplishment marks its departure from previous tradition even as it plunders all that precedes it. This practice of joining trombones and cellos is no mere adornment, however. It is rather "one of tragedy's mightiest achievements" (75). As such, this practice is both an indication of tragedy's "modernity" as well as one of the attributes that define the genre. Without these multiplicities, together with the brilliance and the difficulties

21. Goldhill 1984b, 59–61.

22. It is true that competing claims to truth, for example, are not the exclusive province of tragedy. (Nor, for that matter, is metrical variety.) What is significant and unique about these phenomena in tragedy is that they are central to the genre's broader interests. Tragedy typically, and *Agamemnon* in this case specifically, marks the discrepancies between competing voices as central to its larger purposes, often by linking the interference and interaction between such voices to the play's thematic interests. (On the thematic links to this passage of *Ag.* see Goldhill 1984b, esp. chap. 1.) So, for example, here the shared vocabulary of truth in these juxtaposed utterances throws into relief the differences between them, thus inviting us to examine the various forms that claims to truth can take and the uses they can be put to. In short, these differences are not only a feature of tragic form; they are also an important part of what the genre generally takes to be its subject matter.

they bring, Greek tragedy would not merely change; it would become unrecognizable.

## THE MESSENGER

> Greek tragedy is not a form of theatre which is easily accessible to everyone. . . . In the last decades some of its formal and ritual characteristics have found new appreciation, but among these conventions there is one in particular, which is generally found rebarbative or at best puzzling: viz. that important events are never shown and acted, but reported.[23]

With these thoughts about the "rebarbative or at best puzzling" conventional messenger, J. M. Bremer begins an article in which he offers some answers to the question that forms its title: Why messenger-speeches? His question is a good one, and his answers provide a guide to many of the formal constraints of the tragic stage that give rise to messenger-speeches. Although he concludes that the three tragedians make creative use of the convention, the *angelia* remains, in his view, a "necessity" (1976, 46). Only by means of a messenger is the tragedian able to incorporate "events that happen elsewhere" (since the presence of the chorus makes a change of scene impossible), as well as crowd scenes, miracles, and death (30). The difficulties and/or impossibilities involved in staging these matters give rise to the genre's dependence on the narration of these off-stage events.

Having offered these explanations of the formal constraints, Bremer presses the matter further and asks why the tragic poets did not "arrange their material in such a way that most of this reporting was avoided?" (1976, 42). Arguing that the *angelia* was an important part of tragedy in its earliest days, Bremer answers that the large number of messenger-speeches in extant tragedy is due to a conservatism on the part of the poets. He offers the retention of Doric elements in the choral lyric of

23. Bremer 1976, 29.

tragedy as a *comparandum:* conventional features of the genre display a remarkable persistence.

If Bremer's assessment that the messenger-speech "is generally found rebarbative or at best puzzling" has any merit, it is precisely because critics have often seen the messenger as merely functional. Indeed, the messenger's conventionality militates to some extent for this view. Aside from his suggestion that the persistence of the *angelia* reflects a conservatism on the part of the poets, Bremer's explanation of the role of the tragic *angelia* invokes functionality at each turn: the *angelia* allows the playwright to incorporate offstage events into the play, events that could not be accommodated onstage. It is clear that to a great extent tragic *angeliai* do perform the functions he describes. There can be no doubt, for example, that we learn how Pentheus meets his end from the messenger who reports it in Euripides' *Bacchae*. But to the extent that we treat the tragic *angelia* as simply a functional device we miss the inherently problematic status of such a device in this context. If, as I have argued above, tragedy is fundamentally committed to the partiality of all speech and its indissociability from the speaker, if the genre is both formally and thematically grounded in an emphasis on the rhetorical quality of all speech, then no verbal account onstage of events offstage will unproblematically succeed in overcoming the restrictions outlined by Bremer.[24] Every such narrative itself, that is, must become a member of the thoroughly rhetorical world onstage.[25]

24. Bremer does not seek generally to efface the gap between offstage events and the report of them. In the case of Euripides, however, he does just this: "Messenger-speeches as e.g. in *El., H.F.* permit a factual assessment of all that has happened; the gruesome facts are present for everyone to be grasped, and challenge the audience's critical reflexion—one is free to make one's own judgment" (1976, 46).

25. There are other, more general, theoretical grounds for making this claim, of course, as narrative theory (e.g., de Jong 1991) makes evident. I will return to this below.

I have introduced the issue of the messenger's functionality by way of Bremer's essay because this essay concisely sets forth the governing conditions of the theater that give rise to tragic *angeliai*, and points to the "puzzling" nature of these narratives. But his is by no means the most extreme position, and he is far from alone. Occasionally articulated explicitly, a view of the tragic *angelia* comparable to Bremer's characterization of Euripidean messenger-speeches has historically, at least, been quite common. Since the nineteenth century, critics have viewed the messenger-speech as comparable to epic in offering a narrative that presents the events as though through an invisible screen. Domenico Bassi, for example, states that in an *angelia* the "events themselves" should speak and that the style of such a narrative approximates that of epic.[26] More recently, Thomas G. Rosenmeyer has written that the "messenger is, as far as his message is concerned, omniscient. He is the equivalent of the epic bard" (1982, 197), and Ann Michelini has called the messenger-speech in Aeschylus's *Persians* a "transparent window upon the truth" (1982, 75).[27]

That such a view of messenger-speeches has been commonly held by critics is suggested by Malcolm Heath. He addresses critical assessment of the messenger "as a mere functionary . . . a neutral vehicle for oblique dramatisation; this is implied by the apparently widespread view of the Messenger as an unengaged, unindividualised figure." (1987, 44). Though Heath himself argues against such a view of the messenger, his

26. "Gli avvenimenti stessi debbono parlare . . . Lo stile del racconto arieggia quello dell' epopea" (1899, 88–89); Wilamowitz concurs: "Ein Botenbericht ist episch und soll vorgetragen werden wie eine homerische Rhapsodie" (quoted in Fischl 1910, 39 n. 1). I will return to the issue of the *angelia*'s status as an epic element in chapter 1.

27. Howald (quoted by Di Gregorio 1967, 19) calls messenger-speeches "films parlati" and Groeneboom (1930 *ad* 429) speaks of the messenger in the same terms. See also Löhrer 1927, 29; Collard 1975, 75; Lacroix 1976, 231. This view has not, however, been uncontroversial. See below.

formulation suggests just how common this view has been. One indication of how widespread such a view has been lurks in Heath's use of the term "apparently." That is, he must surmise that this is the case from the absence of any substantial discussion of the messenger as a tool of the poet and the problems such a role entails. This absence of discussion, accompanied by the frequent, silent equation of the messenger's narrative and what happens offstage, surely suggests at least an implicit acceptance of the tragic *angelia* as a "transparent window."[28]

More than one critic has cited Shirley Barlow's formulation of such a view as exemplary. She writes:

> Where imagery in monody conveys the irrational and subjective attitudes which characterise the singer of that monody, that of the messenger must seem to convey a rational account of objective fact, the existence of which has nothing to do with him personally, except in the sense that he has happened to observe it. . . . Since the messenger is concerned with narrative of "fact," there are no intuitive revelations for him, no visions through a haze of sunlit cloud, no incoherent passion. . . . The dilemma of the poet is to create through this narrative medium the illusion of undistorted information, while at the same time presenting this "fictive fact" in such a persuasive way that it is accepted by the audience without question.[29]

28. Perhaps most telling of the extent of the functionalist view's dispersion is de Jong (1991), whose second chapter is explicitly devoted to rebutting what she calls the "objectivity claim" (63). In a weaker sense, her entire book can be seen as having a similar purpose, inasmuch as she analyzes Euripidean *angeliai* as narratives produced by the messengers as characters of the drama. See also Goldhill's comment that "the messenger in tragedy is normally treated by critics and characters alike as if he brought a clear and certain record of events—if in somewhat heightened language" (1986, 6). Lowe (2000, 167) calls the tragic messenger "not a supplement for primary action, but a richly functional *substitute*" (emphasis in original).

29. Barlow 1971, 61; cited approvingly by Collard 1975, 275, and Bremer 1976, 46; critically by de Jong 1991, 63.

Although Barlow succinctly expresses what many presume, she is careful to qualify the project of the poet as the "dilemma" of creating "the illusion of undistorted information." This language acknowledges something of the conundrum represented by the conventional messenger, although Barlow does not formulate it in these terms.[30]

Bremer's puzzlement concerning the tragic messenger contains a keen insight into this figure. It is indeed puzzling that narrative should somehow "replace" the staging of the events reported. But while answering the question "Why messenger-speeches?" with reference to the unstageable, Bremer ignores a more profound puzzle. How is it, we must ask, that the tragic *angelia* is able to perform the functions Bremer outlines? How does this common tragic element succeed in making "the gruesome facts present"? How does an inhabitant of the rhetorical world of tragedy manage to produce a narrative in which the "events themselves speak"?

There are several possible avenues of response to these questions. The first, and perhaps most elegantly simple, is to deny that this figure in fact does produce such a narrative. If critics since the nineteenth century have seen the messenger-speech as a transparent medium, so have others since then seen it as a very opaque one. Speaking of Euripidean messenger-speeches, J. Fischl boldly states that the entire narrative reveals the character of the messenger, telling us not so much what actually transpired as what the messenger experienced and what he saw.[31]

---

30. De Jong quotes at length from Barlow "because . . . [she] formulates in detail the objectivity claim" (1991, 63), but she ignores Barlow's qualification. It will be seen below that my approach parallels that of Barlow, although her emphasis is on imagery and her approach lacks a comprehensive view of the messenger. Nonetheless, her statement provides a key to understanding the messenger in the terms that I will elaborate below.

31. "Euripides operam dat, ut totam rem narratam ad nuntii personam revocet, scilicet nuntium minus, quid factum sit, quam, quid sibi acciderit, quid viderit, narrantem facit" (1910, 40). Rassow traces indications of emotional expression or opinion on the part of Euripidean messengers (1883, 34–40); cf. Henning 1910, 24.

Most recently and thoroughly, Irene de Jong has argued against the functionalist view. Her careful analysis of Euripidean *angeliai* demonstrates quite clearly that these narratives bear marks of their enunciation that reveal (often subtle) characterizations of the messengers. Far from transparent accounts, she argues, the messenger-speeches are clearly produced by individuals, all of whom have loyalties and judgments that are evident in their narratives. In de Jong's view, those who assume or argue for a transparency in the messenger-speech are simply mistaken.

De Jong is surely right that the tragic messenger, like every narrator, is also a focalizer and that "his role as focalizer is constant" (1991, 74).[32] In other words, "no narrative is ever objective" (65). Although de Jong's study is the first to pay attention to the workings of messengers' narratives and admirably charts the waters, it too quickly bypasses a telling conundrum evident in critical response to these narratives. In attributing the functionalist view of the messenger to critical error alone, she ignores the aspects of the *angeliai* themselves that induce such a view. While at this point, in the wake especially of de Jong, it appears virtually impossible any longer to operate on the assumption of the messenger's simple functionality, it remains to explain how it is that such a view became so widespread. It may well be that many critics have been inattentive to the intricacies of tragic *angeliai* and that they have made unwarranted assumptions about what goes on in these narratives. Nonetheless, the question still remains: Why did they read these *angeliai* as transparent? Why have so many critics taken this form of speech to be fundamentally nonrhetorical? In short, what is it about the tragic *angelia* itself that produces this response? What is it that creates (in many eyes, at least) an aura of transparency?

There are, as I have suggested, several avenues of responding to this question. Simple denial—the insistence that the tragic *angelia* does not in fact acquire an aura of transparency—fails to account for a large amount of critical response. There is, however, another way of answering this

---

32. On narrative and focalization see de Jong 1989, 29–40.

question that is perhaps more enticing to some. Appearing in twenty-six of the thirty-two surviving tragedies, the messenger is among the more persistent conventional features of the genre.[33] As we saw above, in fact, Bremer takes this persistence to be a sign of the poets' fundamental conservatism. And not only does such a figure appear frequently, but these appearances themselves are highly formalized.[34] When a messenger appears, then, the spectator/reader familiar with the genre will understand certain markers to be cues that what is about to follow is a conventional performance. And, it might be argued, part of what this convention entails is precisely the kind of narrative that I postulate as problematic. In other words, so continues the argument, there is nothing problematic at all given that it is the convention itself that decrees by fiat, so to speak, that the messenger's narrative shall be accepted as a "transparent window" through which to view the events it reports.

Although this reply may in principle be right, it does little to explain how such a convention actually functions. In other words, it ultimately begs the question. If the retort "It's conventional" is shorthand for an analysis that explains the workings of the convention, there can be little quarrel. In fact, I hope to make the case that aspects of the convention have been overlooked, and in so doing I will argue, in effect, that it is the "convention" to an appreciable degree that enables the messenger to function. But I also hope to show that there are specific strategies adopted by tragic *angeliai* that make the convention what it is. If, on the other hand, the retort "It's conventional" is shorthand for an attempt to dis-

33. One may, of course, reckon this ratio differently. In coming to these figures I borrow largely the criteria of de Jong (1991, 179–80 and vii n.5) for determining what constitutes an *angelia*, with two exceptions. I include Euripides' *IA* 1540–1612 as well as the messenger speeches in *Rhesos*. See the more extensive discussion of this issue below in chapter 2. For my own list, see the appendix.

34. A substantial amount of attention has been paid to the formal features. See Keller 1959; Erdmann 1964; Di Gregorio 1967; Stanley-Porter 1968; Rijksbaron 1976.

miss inquiry into the workings of the convention, it seems self-evident that we can only reject this reply.

But there are perhaps more compelling reasons to be unsatisfied with simply attributing to convention what is anomalous about the messenger. Simon Goldhill, for example, takes the conventionality of the messenger-speech as one sign of tragedy's "special focus on language," and the convention itself as ripe for exploitation by the genre in its attention to matters of language (1986, 3). While addressing aspects of tragedy that have nothing directly to do with language per se, Goldhill directs our attention to the fact that this conventional figure performs his principal function—the narration of offstage events—in a context otherwise strongly marked by an interest in the act of communication onstage. The messenger's conventional status and the idiosyncrasies of his narrative, that is, should be understood as part of a genre devoted to an examination of the problems and practices of various speech forms.

Given, then, that a "transparent" messenger-speech violates one of the defining characteristics of tragedy, such a convention would seem to carry a (perhaps impossibly) large burden. Other conventional elements of the genre—the wearing of the mask, speaking in verse, compression and dilation of time, and so on—certainly require a degree of acceptance inasmuch as they are nonnaturalistic. (Of course Greek theater on the whole is nonnaturalistic. We should not expect otherwise.) Yet none of these elements stand in direct contradiction to what might be called a fundamental premise of the genre. For this reason, in part, I suggest, interrogation of the conventional messenger is in order.

As a kind of corollary to this view, Klaus Joerden's formulation of the genre's use of events offstage deserves mention. He claims that by rejecting the physical enactment of many events and limiting themselves to the realm of speech, the tragic poets manage to transgress certain boundaries.[35] If the *angelia* as an important part of this phenomenon in-

35. "Durch den Verzicht auf die 'leibhaftige' Vorführung vieler Vorgänge und durch weitgehende Beschränkung auf das Medium der Sprache

dicates a more general interest of tragedy, so might it be a clue to the boundaries of the realm of the possible as conceived by the genre. If, that is, tragedy shows itself able to do in speech what it cannot do on-stage, we are encouraged to ask just what it is capable of doing in speech. And the answer to this question, I will argue, requires an understanding of the tragic messenger.

Finally, as I will show, the tragic texts themselves are clearly not content simply to make use of this conventional figure. The plays express a surprising amount of interest in the status of the messenger and the workings of the convention that surrounds him. From the earliest extant tragedy (Aeschylus's *Persians*) to the end of the fifth century (Euripides' *Bacchae*) and perhaps beyond *(Rhesos)*, the messenger plays an important role in the self-reflection of the tragic texts: from humorous engagements with the convention to more elaborate forms of metatheater, the *angelia* finds itself the subject of a substantial amount of self-directed commentary staged by the plays. I hope that the following investigation will show that our attention to this conventional figure is not only warranted but already anticipated by the plays themselves.

What follows is not a comprehensive survey of all messenger-speeches in tragedy. Given that a large majority of plays contain at least one *angelia*, such a survey would be trying. And inasmuch as there would be more than a little repetition, it would also prove unnecessary. Rather, I have chosen plays that offer substantial and productive reflection on the role of the messenger, along with plays that make creative, if unconventional, use of this figure. As such, this study remains suggestive for approaching those plays not addressed here.

---

überspringt der attische Tragiker alle Grenzen, die ihm durch den Raum oder die Gegenstände seiner Handlung gesetzt sein könnten" (1971, 406).

# ONE

# Aeschylus's *Persians*
## *The Messenger and Epic Narrative*

> I am convinced there is nothing better than a conventional
> opening, an attack from which you can expect everything and
> nothing.
>
> > *Italo Calvino*, If on a Winter's Night a Traveler

Although far from satisfactory, the view of the messenger as a functional
device is not entirely without merit. Even if we insist that every narra-
tor is a focalizer and as such renders the narrative in question something
both more and less than a transparent representation, we can agree that
the tragic poets made practical use of the messenger along the lines in-
dicated by J. M. Bremer. In this capacity, the tragic messenger does not
appear ex nihilo: he stems, in fact, from a tradition that goes back at least
to Homer. Prior to the time of *Persians*, there is a traditional, or "liter-
ary," messenger who is defined in terms very similar to those that char-
acterize the tragic messenger as a (conventional and) functional figure.
This figure appears not only in Homer and the Homeric hymns, but also
in lyric poetry of the archaic and classical periods. Specifically, this lit-
erary messenger is swift, reliable, and always tells all.[1]

---

1. I discuss this literary messenger more thoroughly in chapter 2 below.

When (as often in the *Iliad*) Zeus tells Iris what to say, and shortly thereafter she repeats the message verbatim (excluding pronoun changes), the textual "redundancy" affirms the loyalty and reliability of the messenger. One critic has claimed that Iris's simple declaration "I am Zeus's messenger" constitutes a guarantee that her message repeats verbatim—with neither deletion nor addition—the words of Zeus.[2] And the textual repetition enables us to notice that nothing has been added or omitted.[3] So conventional is this reliable messenger that, as Françoise Létoublon argues further, the concept of the unreliable messenger occurs in Homer only by way of negation. In fact, the one moment in Homer of overt anxiety about a messenger's reliability—*Iliad* 15. 158–59, when Zeus warns Iris not to be a false messenger—has been read as evidence of Zeus's concern that Iris may weaken or even omit the harsh words he sends to Poseidon.[4] Zeus does in fact say:

βάσκ' ἴθι ᵀΙρι ταχεῖα, Ποσειδάωνι ἄνακτι
πάντα τάδ' ἀγγεῖλαι, μηδὲ ψευδάγγελος εἶναι.

Go, quick Iris, and *announce all these* things to Lord Poseidon and do not be a false messenger.

As this passage suggests, one of the marks of literary messengers is the claim or expectation that they will tell all.

Elsewhere in the *Iliad*, Zeus sends Dream as a messenger to Agamemnon, saying (2.8–10):

---

2. Létoublon (1987, 131) writes: "Les paroles d'Iris Διὸς δὲ τοι ἄγγελός εἰμι ([*Iliad* 24.]173) ont ainsi pour Priam la valeur d'une garantie (voir le *sceau* sur les messages écrits ultérieurs): 'Je répète textuellement un message dont je ne suis que le vecteur'."

3. By contrast, Odysseus's failure in *Iliad* 9 to deliver Agamemnon's entire message plays a pivotal role in that book and perhaps in the poem as a whole. See Lynn-George 1988, 83, 92 and 149.

4. See Luther 1935, 85. This passage is curiously omitted by Létoublon.

βάσκ' ἴθι οὖλε Ὄνειρε θοὰς ἐπὶ νῆας Ἀχαιῶν·
ἐλθὼν ἐς κλισίην Ἀγαμέμνονος Ἀτρεΐδαο
πάντα μάλ' ἀτρεκέως ἀγορευέμεν ὡς ἐπιτέλλω.

Go, deadly Dream, to the swift Achaean fleet, and when you get to
the tent of Agamemnon, Atreus's son, *tell him everything exactly* as I
bid you.

Here fidelity (ἀτρεκέως) is coupled with completeness to indicate char-
acteristic facets of the task of message giving.[5]

As a traditional figure, the literary messenger anticipates what we
find in tragedy. That this figure has a place in the genealogy of the tragic
messenger is indicated in part by the fact that in tragedy as well this sign
of completeness occurs frequently in conjunction with an *angelia*. Soph-
ocles' *Trachiniae* draws attention to completeness as a mark of reliabil-
ity. Lichas, having been challenged by the messenger, decides to reveal
the "true" story of Iole's identity to Deianeira. This story he character-
izes as being complete (472–74):

ἀλλ', ὦ φίλη δέσποιν', ἐπεί σε μανθάνω
θνητὴν φρονοῦσαν θνητὰ κοὐκ ἀγνώμονα,
πᾶν σοι φράσω τἀληθὲς οὐδὲ κρύψομαι.

Dear Mistress, since I realize that you, a mortal woman, are thinking
mortal thoughts and not senseless ones, *I will tell you the entire truth*
and I will hide nothing.

Lichas rounds off his account by repeating this claim 10 lines later (484),
saying: ἐπεί γε μὲν δὴ πάντ' ἐπίστασαι λόγον . . . ("since you know the
whole story . . . ").[6] Similarly, the messenger himself contrasts his own

5. ἀτρεκέως means literally "without twisting" (i.e., "precisely, accu-
rately").
6. This translation leaves out the three particles γε μὲν δή. Having just
confessed to Deianeira that he alone is responsible for misleading her,
Lichas contrasts his earlier duplicity with his current honesty by means of

"true" report with Lichas's lie in the same terms. Speaking of Iole, who she is, and how she has come to Deianeira's house, he says (338): τούτων ἔχω γὰρ πάντ' ἐπιστήμην ἐγώ ("for I have a complete understanding of these things").[7] Here and frequently elsewhere in tragedy, as in Homer, the "truth" from a messenger is marked as "the entire truth."[8]

This heritage and literary identity in part enable the tragic messenger to appear as a conventional figure who gives a reliable account of offstage events and who tells the entire story. As a medium of transmission endowed by tradition with a reliability unavailable to other *dramatis personae*, the messenger serves the tragic poet well: the poet's need to incorporate offstage events finds a tool in the messenger, whose persona is subordinated to the task he performs. And his status as such a figure charged with this task is marked by reference to his telling all. We will see that the *angelia* of Aeschylus's *Persians* is introduced by the invocation of this traditional quality as an attribute of the Persian runner who is the messenger. This case, however, presents a twist on the familiar pattern, one that points the way to uncovering what is at stake in the messenger's performance.

––––––

The year 1952 saw the publication of a papyrus establishing Aeschylus's *Persians* as the oldest surviving tragedy.[9] In addition to upsetting con-

––––––

this series of particles, which is "always definitely, and strongly, adversative" (Denniston 1954, 395).

7. Some have emended this line; others have expunged it. I give here the text of the manuscripts rather than that of Lloyd-Jones and Wilson who print τούτων—ἔχω γὰρ πάντ'—ἐπιστήμων ἐγώ. πάντα must be adverbial, if the text is sound. See Davies 1991 ad loc. A more literal translation: "I have understanding of these things in all aspects."

8. Elsewhere in tragedy: Aesch. *Ag.* 582; Soph. *Aj.* 734; *Ant.* 1193; *El.* 680; *Phil.* 603–4, 620; *Trach.* 349, 369, 453, 749 (Hyllus), 876; Eur. *HF* 799; *Phoen.* 1334; *IA* 1540. "Telling the whole story," is not, of course, confined to messengers; see Fraenkel 1950 *ad* 599.

9. By means of redating his *Suppliants. Oxyrhynchus Papyri* vol. 20, no. 2256, fr.3, is the relevant fragment.

ventional understandings of *Suppliants*, this new chronology placed perhaps twenty-five years between the date of Aeschylus's first dramatic competition and the performance of *Persians* in 472 B.C.E. This, our oldest, play was performed when Aeschylus was more than fifty years old.[10] Nonetheless, this play has on the whole conformed well to the expectations of critics who have often seen it as less complex and sophisticated than some of this author's subsequent works.[11] Thomas G. Rosenmeyer, for example, states the matter clearly: "The simplicity of *Persians* makes it, as always, a convenient laboratory for the study of Aeschylean techniques" (1982, 318). At the same time, the earliest of our tragedies occupies a place of privilege for any discussion of development or change within the genre. Consequently, the play bears testimony crucial not only for the study of Aeschylean technique but also for that of tragic practice more broadly.

And it is in this light that I suggest that we look at the lengthy messenger-speech in this play. In this "laboratory" we will find not only a "messenger-speech in its purest and at the same time most ambitious form" (Rosenmeyer 1982, 198); we will also find a remarkably sophisticated interest in the status of the tragic messenger. Structured around a virtuoso performance of an *angelia*, the play frames this performance with queries into its status that prove enlightening for the examination of tragic messenger-speeches elsewhere.

The play opens with the parodos (1–154), in which the chorus describe both the vast Persian expedition against Greece and their own fears about the safety of the expedition: here we are presented with an expansive view of the Persian army and their allies as well as those left behind and their anxieties about the outcome of the military expedition. Early on, the chorus hint at the impending disaster in speaking of their

10. For an account of Aeschylus's life and theatrical productions see Rosenmeyer 1982, 369–76.

11. When compared in particular to the Oresteia, the latest of Aeschylus's productions that we have, performed in 458.

"heart of ill-omen" (κακόμαντις . . . θυμός, 10–11) as they rehearse the dangers to the expedition (93–100, 115–20). This sense of anxiety and foreboding prepares for the arrival of the messenger, as the text underscores at 12–15:

πᾶσα γὰρ ἰσχὺς Ἀσιατογενὴς
οἴχωκε, νέον δ' ἄνδρα βαΰζει,
κοὔτε τις ἄγγελος οὔτε τις ἱππεὺς
ἄστυ τὸ Περσῶν ἀφικνεῖται·

For all the strength of Asia has gone, calling on the young man,
and neither messenger nor horseman has arrived in the city of
Persians.[12]

Not only, then, do the chorus seek relief from their anxiety in news about the Persian army; they explicitly declare that this anxiety arises in part from the absence of a messenger.

But if the chorus possess a "heart of ill-omen" (10–11), the Queen, who arrives onstage at 155, reports a dream and an omen that augment and extend the fears of the chorus. She has dreamed, she says, of Xerxes' failure to subdue two women—a Persian and a Greek (Doric)—when the Greek (evidently) broke free and smashed the yoke that joined them; she dreamed also of Xerxes subsequently tearing his robes. The broken yoke conveniently symbolizes the failed attempt to conquer the Greeks and "yoke" them to the Persian empire, as is confirmed, in part, by the appearance of Xerxes later in the play in tattered robes. Although the Persian defeat is determined from the start, the parodos and the encounter between chorus and Queen (155–245) both establish a strong sense of foreboding and portray all in Persia as apprehensively eager for news from the front. This news is provided by the messenger who enters at line 246.

*Queen's dream* ✱

---

12. I give here the text of Broadhead, who marks line 13 with obelisks. This line is notoriously difficult to translate; see Broadhead 1960, 249–50.

When the *koruphaios* (choral leader) introduces the Persian runner who will give the *angelia*, he invokes both the messenger's reliability and the fullness of his account (246–48):

ἀλλ' ἐμοὶ δοκεῖν τάχ' εἴσῃ πάντα ναμερτῆ λόγον·
τοῦδε γὰρ δράμημα φωτὸς Περσικὸν πρέπει μαθεῖν,
καὶ φέρει σαφές τι πρᾶγος ἐσθλὸν ἢ κακὸν κλύειν.

But I think you will soon have a complete and reliable report; this fellow seems to be Persian, judging from his gait, and he brings a clear account of something, whether good or bad.

Here the *koruphaios* conspicuously announces the messenger as one who corresponds closely to the literary messenger as described above.[13] This introduction situates the figure who enters (and the ensuing narrative he provides) within a framework that serves to construe the Persian runner not only as such a literary messenger but also as a conventional tragic messenger: the *logos* that the Persian runner will provide will adhere, says the chorus leader, to the form of a conventional *angelia*. This implicit announcement carries in large part the same import as the literal meaning of what the *koruphaios* says: the conventional messenger provides a complete and reliable report *(logos)*.

The messenger himself, however, does not entirely adhere to protocol. In spite of this introduction, he goes on to insist three times that in fact he does *not* tell the whole story.[14] In sharp contrast to the *koruphaios*'s introduction, the messenger not only denies that his report is complete; he also recasts the introduction itself. Nine lines after the *koruphaios* an-

13. The swiftness of the Persian runner here echoes the traditional swiftness of the literary messenger. Cf. *Il.* 5.353; 5.368; 18.2; 24.95; 24.188; Sappho 44.2 Voigt. Hes. *Th.* 265–69 makes Iris the sister of the Harpies, all characterized by their swiftness of flight. As often in tragedy, the messenger here in *Persians* arrives ahead of all others. Structurally the performance enacts this traditional quality.

14. 329–30, 429–30, and 513–14.

nounces the arrival of the messenger who will tell "the whole story" (*panta logon*), the messenger declares that although it is an awful task, he must tell "the whole suffering" (*pan pathos*) (253–54):

ὤμοι, κακὸν μὲν πρῶτον ἀγγέλλειν κακά,
ὅμως δ' ἀνάγκη πᾶν ἀναπτύξαι πάθος

How awful to be the first to report awful news! Still, I must unfold the whole *pathos*.

As I have said, the *koruphaios*'s introduction echoes a virtually formulaic expression of the messenger's conventional function. When the Persian runner proclaims, then, that he must unfold the entire *pathos*, the echo, now rephrased, is double. "To tell the whole story" becomes "to unfold the entire *pathos*," incorporating an important shift from *logos* to *pathos*. The messenger, whom the *koruphaios* expects to give a thorough account of what happened, announces that he will disclose the entire calamity. The calculation and dispassion of *logos* finds itself transformed into the misfortunes of the unlucky Persians. The unusual choice of words ("unfold"), together with the subjectivity of experience indicated by *pathos*, underscores the distance between the nearly formulaic introduction of the messenger and his own characterization of his task. The use of the singular (*pan pathos*), furthermore, rather than the plural (*panta pathē*), implies that he will recount the calamitous nature of what happened rather than the many calamities. Indeed the messenger's threefold insistence that he is in fact *not* telling all, makes clear that line 254 represents a significant alteration both of the *koruphaios*'s statement and of the conventional stance of the messenger.[15]

15. The Queen at 290–98 turns the messenger from his distracted state of lamentation (284–85) to his task of giving a report. She does so by quoting the messenger himself (293–95): ὅμως δ' ἀνάγκη πημονὰς βροτοῖς φέρειν / θεῶν διδόντων· πᾶν ἀναπτύξας πάθος / λέξον καταστάς ("Nevertheless, when the gods give trouble, mortals have no choice but to bear it. Stand still and tell me, as you unfold the whole *pathos*"). This further echo of an earlier echo maintains a fidelity absent in line 254: the Queen not only

This "rupture" between the traditional status of the literary messenger and that of the Persian runner here draws attention to the status of the latter. While Rosenmeyer is certainly right that he gives a "messenger-speech in its purest and at the same time most ambitious form" (1982, 198), the conventional machinery does not operate here without a hitch. To be sure, this provocative encounter of *logos* and *pathos* in no way jeopardizes the successful functioning of the *angelia* as a conventional element. Rather, this virtually paradigmatic messenger-speech appears framed by queries into its status. As such, the slippage here hints at the conventional framework of the messenger's functional status. While the messenger rhetorically posits a catastrophe so great that he cannot embrace the whole of it with his account, the text announces a messenger who will not rely on his literary inheritance to establish the authority of his report. The text therefore invites us to examine his narrative as such: without regard to the authorization of convention what does the narrative itself do to acquire or maintain its conventional authority? Is it possible to identify the practices and attributes that sustain the conventional status of the messenger?

Soon after entering and announcing in brief the calamity in Greece, the messenger makes a claim fundamental to his status as a reliable medium: he says that he himself saw what happened (266–67):

καὶ μὴν παρών γε κοὐ λόγους ἄλλων κλύων,
Πέρσαι, φράσαιμ' ἂν οἷ' ἐπορσύνθη κακά.

I was in fact there; I did not hear about it from others, Persians, and I can recount the awful events.

He bases his authority at the outset on a claim to presence at the events he is about to narrate. More specifically, he claims a presence that al-

---

preserves *pan pathos* and the verb of the messenger (ἀναπτύξας); she quotes him virtually verbatim, changing only an infinitive to a participle. This "fidelity" and its success in returning the messenger to his *angelia* recall and emphasize the earlier change from *logos* to *pathos*.

lowed him to *see* what happened, so that he did not need to rely on anyone to *tell* him. This is the standard (and understandable) basis of authority for messengers in tragedy. He knows because he has seen.[16]

Seymour Chatman has analyzed narrative in terms of point of view (1978, 151–58). Among the types of point of view he describes is what he calls "perceptual point of view." This term designates the physical location from which the events narrated were witnessed. As is often the case, the messenger's vision is the most important form of perception evident in his narrative. In part because this messenger claims legitimacy as a narrator on the basis of having seen what he is about to relate, I propose to examine his narrative for signs of his perceptual point of view. How does he situate himself with respect to what he tells? In looking for his point of view we should be able to discover how the messenger constructs a position for himself within the narrative.[17] This, I submit, will reveal that this tragic messenger—like those who come after him—has (or claims) abilities that distinguish him from others onstage.

After the foreboding of the parodos and the Queen's dream, the messenger arrives with a report that confirms the worst fears. In its length, his account of the Persian defeat reflects the scale of the battle: it creates "an overpowering vision of vast landscapes and events" (Herington 1986, 69). He describes, for example, the naval battle in terms that suggest the enormous scope both of the fight and of his visual field (409–20):

> ἦρξε δ' ἐμβολῆς Ἑλληνικὴ
> ναῦς, κἀποθραύει πάντα Φοινίσσης νεὼς
> κόρυμβ' ἐπ' ἄλλην δ' ἄλλος ηὔθυνεν δόρυ.
> τὰ πρῶτα μέν νυν ῥεῦμα Περσικοῦ στρατοῦ
> ἀντεῖχεν· ὡς δὲ πλῆθος ἐν στενῷ νεῶν

16. The same logic that lies behind the semantic value of οἶδα; see Nagy 1990b, 231.

17. I emphasize here that my interest is not that of a positivistic search for where the messenger "really" was at any given moment. Rather, I am interested in the nature of his self-representation.

ἤθροιστ', ἀρωγὴ δ' οὖτις ἀλλήλοις παρῆν,
αὐτοὶ δ' ὑπ' αὐτῶν ἐμβολαῖς χαλκοστόμοις
παίοντ', ἔθραυον πάντα κωπήρη στόλον,
Ἑλληνικαί τε νῆες οὐκ ἀφρασμόνως
κύκλῳ πέριξ ἔθεινον, ὑπτιοῦτο δὲ
σκάφη νεῶν, θάλασσα δ' οὐκέτ' ἦν ἰδεῖν
ναυαγίων πλήθουσα καὶ φόνου βροτῶν.

A Greek ship began the attack and thoroughly shattered a Phoenician vessel's stern. Each ship was steered straight at another. At first the Persian fleet held firm. But with the swarm of ships pressed into the strait, they could offer no help to one another. Striking each other with their bronze beaks, the ships smashed all of the rowing gear. In a circle around them the Greek ships smartly struck and sent the hulls of the ships upside down. The sea, full of shipwreck and mortal slaughter, was no longer to be seen.

At the same time, the broad sweep of his vision abuts a specificity of description signaling a proximity to events and a narrowness of scope characteristic of an entirely different point of view. He offers, for example, a vivid, close-up view of Matallos's end (314–16):

Χρυσεὺς Μάταλλος μυριόνταρχος θανὼν
πυρσὴν ζαπληθῆ δάσκιον γενειάδα
ἔτεγγ' ἀμείβων χρῶτα πορφυρᾷ βαφῇ.

As he died, Matallos of Chrysa, leader of thousands, submerged his flame-red, thickly full dark-shadowed beard, changing its color in the purple wash.

As the asyndetic adjectives pile up in such a way as to mimic the thickness of the beard they describe, the contrast between the implicit perceptual point of view here and that of the large-scale narrative sweep becomes stark. At the same time as we are invited to contemplate a catalogue of the dead we are treated to one full line conspicuously describing a beard. Amid a sea of corpses such descriptions stand out and indicate the twin perspectives of the messenger: he sees not only in broad strokes but also in fine detail. He places himself alternately at a distance from and very close to the scene.

In short, the perceptual point of view implicit in this narrative displays what amounts to omnipresence.[18] While critics have occasionally taken such omnipresence to be part of what defines the conventional messenger, there has been remarkably little discussion of how this shows up and what it might mean.[19] Aeschylus's play provides a rich "laboratory" for studying not only Aeschylean techniques, but also those of the tragic messenger in his conventional form. Among the elements that define this convention, I will argue, is in fact this omnipresence. But in order to understand how this messenger makes use of his implicit claim to omnipresence, we must examine his perceptual point of view more thoroughly.

In conjunction with the omnipresence implicitly claimed in his account of the battle, this messenger makes profitable use of self-effacement. Not only does his account minimize his own presence; often enough he seems to be missing altogether.[20] From line 353 to line 406

18. Cf. Chatman 1978, 212.

19. See Stevens 1971 *ad* 1100–57; Willink 1986 *ad* 1425. Although generally arguing that the (Euripidean) messenger "can only tell what he sees himself" (1991, 12), de Jong sees three instances where this "restriction of place" is overcome. One such case is Eur. *HF,* where she says of the messenger: "His omnipresence is conventional, the convention having been established in the *Iliad*" (1991, 12; cf. 20–24). It is surprising, however, that such a conventional element should be so rare. The claim that omnipresence is conventional may well be right, but if so, it requires demonstration. Perhaps more important, this omnipresence, along with such a continuity from epic to tragedy as posited by de Jong, contains significant implications for our understanding both of the messenger and of tragedy more broadly. As will become clear, I agree that this omnipresence is conventional and that it derives, at least in part, from epic narrative practice.

20. With respect to lines 353–432, where the messenger reports the sea battle at Salamis, de Jong comments that Aeschylus has overcome the restriction of place "by not giving the messenger-speech the form of a first-

we find only the third-person,[21] a construction crucial to his description
at 388–92 of the sound of the Greek chant echoing off the rock:

πρῶτον μὲν ἠχῇ κέλαδος Ἑλλήνων πάρα
μολπηδὸν εὐφήμησεν, ὄρθιον δ' ἅμα
ἀντηλάλαξε νησιώτιδος πέτρας
ἠχώ, φόβος δὲ πᾶσι βαρβάροις παρῆν
γνώμης ἀποσφαλεῖσιν.

At first from the Greeks there was a sound, a noise; they shouted
and sang auspiciously, and from the rocky island a piercing shout
echoed back: all of the barbarians, their hopes shattered, were over-
come with fear.

Although expressed impersonally, this statement tells of a particular
echo, while making no mention of the echo being heard. Here the mes-
senger (implicitly) claims to have been in an appropriate place to hear
the echo while representing the echo as something capable of existing
without regard to ears. We will, of course, infer from what he says next
that "all of the barbarians" heard the echo. That this group includes him
is yet another inference, which we may or may not make. The contra-
diction between the terrifying reality of the echo and the impersonality
of his report is exacerbated at 391–92 when he announces the conse-
quence of the alarming echo. What wavered between being an entirely
impersonal event and a specific sound (heard by the messenger) turns
into a sound heard by and terrifying to all the Persians. The messenger

---

person narrative" (1991, 13 n. 30), which for her means that he was not "a
participant in the events he is narrating" (2). On this definition she must
grant a silent eyewitness a privileged status. Whether, however, this expla-
nation suffices is unclear. This messenger himself, after all, makes a strong
claim to authority based on his presence at the events recounted. Does this
claim alone not insist that we place him in, or at least very near, the events
he relates?

21. With the exception of the Greeks' speech, which he quotes at 402–5.

alone appears immune, as the third-person construction allows him some room for safe exit.

The messenger's description of the slaughter that follows is striking in its reliance upon an impersonality that again elides him from the scene and shelters him from the danger (419–27):

θάλασσα δ' οὐκέτ' ἦν ἰδεῖν
ναυαγίων πλήθουσα καὶ φόνου βροτῶν·
ἀκταὶ δὲ νεκρῶν χοιράδες τ' ἐπλήθυον.
φυγῇ δ' ἀκόσμως πᾶσα ναῦς ἠρέσσετο,
ὅσαιπερ ἦσαν βαρβάρου στρατεύματος.
τοὶ δ' ὥστε θύννους ἤ τιν' ἰχθύων βόλον
ἀγαῖσι κωπῶν θραύμασίν τ' ἐρειπίων
ἔπαιον ἐρράχιζον, οἰμωγὴ δ' ὁμοῦ
κωκύμασιν κατεῖχε πελαγίαν ἅλα.

The sea, full of shipwreck and mortal slaughter, was no longer to be seen. The shores and rocky coast were also covered with corpses; every one of the barbarian ships, as many as were in the expedition, began to flee in chaos. Slicing to the bone, they hacked and whacked as though at tunas or a haul of fish, using broken oars and bits of wreckage—and all about groans and cries covered the sea.[22]

Amid the Persians being whacked and sliced like fish, somehow the messenger has been close enough to see it all in detail and yet escape. Lines 426–27 tell of groans and cries, but these seem to belong to no one in particular. His formulation is telling (οἰμωγὴ δ' ὁμοῦ κωκύμασιν κατεῖχε πελαγίαν ἅλα): the lamentation seems to exist on its own; no one appears to make the cries, and no one to hear them. The impersonal construction, coupled with a consistent use of the third-person,

22. The text is vague concerning the object of the striking and slicing. The imagery, however, leaves little doubt that it is the shipwrecked sailors who are being butchered. See Belloni 1988 *ad* 424–32.

presents the events as independent even of the observer. The messenger's self-effacement is nearly complete, as there is only a minimum of self-reference.[23]

As we listen to this narrative, then, we may easily lose sight of the narrator and perhaps even feel that we are listening to the story "tell itself."[24] So well does the messenger's narrative imply both omnipresence and nonpresence that one critic has called him "un spectateur idéal" (Cahen 1924, 305). And yet we must recall not only that this messenger is in fact one of the *dramatis personae*, but also that he himself has insisted that his account is that of an eyewitness. In confronting this dilemma, we might be inclined to assume that the messenger's location during the battle was the same as that of Xerxes—that he was an attendant of the king. Herodotus (8.88), for example, places Xerxes at a safe remove from

23. ἡμῶν at 502 is a noteworthy exception. See the next note.

24. Benveniste 1971, 208. From line 485 to the end of the messenger-speech, however, there are four occurrences of the first-person plural. While the first-person obviously draws the messenger into the scene he describes, it is possible to discern a function in some of these cases that helps explain their appearance. Three of these four (485, 488, 493) serve to move the messenger from one place to another. In the first case (485), he has just described the disorder of the fleet in flight. He then turns to the army in Boeotia and must explain that he was there to see what happened. This is the first major change of scene in his story, and he must account for it by moving himself along with the action. This διεκπερῶμεν does. The same can be said of ἡμᾶς at 488. The army on its way home passes through Achaea and Thessaly, and so must the messenger. Similarly, he must move himself along with the army as it arrives in Magnesia, Macedonia, and so on (493). These occurrences of the first-person, then, are necessary to validate the messenger's claim to autopsy. As I have suggested, the messenger's narrative strategy consists in the simultaneous claim to autopsy and the removal of himself from the events he narrates. It should not surprise us, then, if we find him doing both. But it is important to note that he speaks of himself (as part of a first-person plural) virtually only when he must. For a different explanation see Smethurst, 1989, 123.

the battle yet still with a clear view of events. The messenger in *Persians*, in fact, locates Xerxes on a hill nearby (466–67):

ἕδραν γὰρ εἶχε παντὸς εὐαγῆ στρατοῦ,
ὑψηλὸν ὄχθον ἄγχι πελαγίας ἁλός·

He had a seat in full view of the whole army, atop a high hill near the sea.

Such a vantage point, it might be thought, would afford both the views the messenger describes and the remoteness from the events implicit in his impersonal constructions. Indeed, a large part of the messenger's narrative does imply such a perceptual point of view: the large sweeping vision and grandiose quality of his account fit well with Xerxes' location. Two arguments, however, tell against this view. First, the messenger never locates himself anywhere, and certainly never explicitly with Xerxes. While there is in principle no problem in assuming him to have been with Xerxes, I would argue that his failure to locate himself is crucial: by passing over himself he allows his implicit claims of virtual omnipresence to pass unnoticed. That is, his silence in this regard is telling. Second, and more to the point, no specific location could, in fact, provide the views the messenger claims to have had. From atop the hill with Xerxes, Matallos's beard would surely be much less vivid, if visible at all.

Similarly, his claim to knowledge of events in the Greek camp suggests that this messenger cannot be precisely located, that he is, in short, Cahen's "spectateur idéal." He tells of the Greek preparations for nightfall (374–79):

οἱ δ' οὐκ ἀκόσμως, ἀλλὰ πειθάρχῳ φρενὶ
δεῖπνόν τ' ἐπορσύνοντο, ναυβάτης τ' ἀνὴρ
τροποῦτο κώπην σκαλμὸν ἀμφ' εὐήρετμον.
ἐπεὶ δὲ φέγγος ἡλίου κατέφθιτο
καὶ νὺξ ἐπήει, πᾶς ἀνὴρ κώπης ἄναξ
ἐς ναῦν ἐχώρει πᾶς θ' ὅπλων ἐπιστάτης.

Without disorder and obedient in mind, [the Greeks] prepared a meal, and each sailor fixed oar to row-ready oarlock. And when the day's light faded and night approached, every man, master of oar and in command of weapons, boarded ship.[25]

But if the messenger's knowledge of Greek dinner preparations betrays his claim to an ideal form of spectatorship, his characterization of these same Greeks as "obedient in mind" (πειθάρχῳ φρενὶ, lit.: "with a mind obedient to authority") reveals the extent of this claim. Not only, that is, does he implicitly claim to have seen on both large scale and small, both within the Persian camp and the Greek; he also claims (again implicitly) to know the φρήν of the Greeks.[26]

I began this examination of the Persian messenger by pointing out the attention the text draws to him and by considering the questions it raises concerning his status as a traditional figure. While jettisoning the privilege endowed by the explicit invocation of his conventional status, he acquires authority as a messenger by means of a claim to presence at the events he narrates. It has become clear, however, that we ourselves must confront a messenger who appears to employ two utterly different, and even contradictory, strategies: while claiming eyewitness status he largely removes himself from the narrative. His emphatic insistence that his own eyes saw what he tells encourages us to discover that he, a Persian runner, could have seen what he describes only through the eyes of "un spectateur idéal." Yet both his claim to eyewitness status and his

25. In taking the Greeks as the referent of οἱ δ' in line 374, I follow Hall 1996 *ad* 374–83; cf. Craig 1924, 100 (cited by Broadhead 1960, 120 n. 1). This, however, must remain in some doubt, and my comments on this passage, therefore, stand or fall along with this assumption. Bakewell (1998) argues against reading the text in this way.

26. Anticipating my remarks below is the comment of Broadhead on these lines: "The realistic details of this passage remind us of many an Homeric description" (1960 *ad* 374–76).

privileged position as such are crucial to his success. These twin strategies reveal, in fact, a tension fundamental not only to this *angelia*, but to those in tragedy more broadly: he is both one of the *dramatis personae* and a tool of the poet for incorporating the offstage world into the drama. As a character, of course, he can only speak of what has transpired elsewhere by claiming an authority consistent with the fiction: in *Persians*, as virtually always, this authority derives from his eyewitness status. As a tool of the poet, however, such an authority is inadequate. As a mere eyewitness whose narrative reflects the reality of his point of view and its consequent limitations, the messenger runs the risk of inviting doubt, and, perhaps more important, of lacking essential information. That is, as a character with a story he is subject to the same skepticism we direct toward the other *dramatis personae*. His self-effacement, however, defuses such skepticism by obscuring his status as a character. This messenger himself, however, shows the way toward understanding the tensions inherent in this position.

## NARRATIVE AND EPIC

Above I mentioned the threefold announcement by the messenger of his inability to tell the entire story, and I suggested that therein lies a query about the messenger's status. It is, in fact, one of the three disclaimers (429–30) that provides the most profound exposition and interrogation of the messenger's role. Although largely ignored,[27] these lines echo the narrator's invocation of the Muses in *Iliad* 2. I give the surrounding lines as well (484–90):

Ἔσπετε νῦν μοι Μοῦσαι Ὀλύμπια δώματ' ἔχουσαι·
ὑμεῖς γὰρ θεαί ἐστε πάρεστέ τε ἴστέ τε πάντα,
ἡμεῖς δὲ κλέος οἶον ἀκούομεν οὐδέ τι ἴδμεν·

27. Among the commentaries, only Belloni (1988) and Hall (1996) notice. See also Keller 1959, 11 n. 3, and Bundy 1972, 64.

οἵ τινες ἡγεμόνες Δαναῶν καὶ κοίρανοι ἦσαν·
πληθὺν δ' οὐκ ἂν ἐγὼ μυθήσομαι οὐδ' ὀνομήνω,
οὐδ' εἴ μοι δέκα μὲν γλῶσσαι, δέκα δὲ στόματ' εἶεν,
φωνὴ δ' ἄρρηκτος, χάλκεον δέ μοι ἦτορ ἐνείη.

Now tell me, Muses, you who live on Olympus—for you are god-desses, you are present and you know everything, while we hear only rumor, knowing nothing at all—who were the leaders and captains of the Danaans. The multitude I could never recount or name, not even if I had ten tongues, ten mouths, an unbreakable voice and a bronze heart inside.

Here are the messenger's lines (429–30):

κακῶν δὲ πλῆθος, οὐδ' ἂν εἰ δέκ' ἤματα
στοιχηγοροίην, οὐκ ἂν ἐκπλήσαιμί σοι.

The multitude of evils, not even if I went on for ten days, I could never recount for you in full.

The messenger's πλῆθος, οὐδ' ἂν[28] recalls Homer's πληθὺν δ' οὐκ ἂν, and his οὐδ' ἂν εἰ δέκ' clearly echoes Homer's οὐδ' εἴ μοι δέκα. Finally, the repetition of the negative οὐδ' ἂν εἰ δέκ' . . . οὐκ ἂν mimics Homer's οὐκ ἂν ἐγὼ . . . οὐδ' εἴ μοι δέκα. Aside from these clear verbal echoes, the contexts of the two passages are quite close and lend them-selves to comparison. The invocation of the Muses in *Iliad* 2 precedes the Catalogue of Ships, virtually a list of names nearly 400 lines in length. The messenger in *Persians* has just given a similar list (albeit

28. There is in fact a virtual plethora of forms of πλῆθος in this *angelia*: lines 272, 327, 334, 337, 342, 352, 413, 420, 421, 429, 430, 432, and 477. (On *plēthos* in the play as a whole see Michelini 1982, 86–98.) In addition to the effect of intensifying the sense of enormity of the battle itself, these multiple occurrences echo the *Iliad* passage cited precisely because this word is emphasized at *Il.* 2.488 both by its position (first in both sentence and line) and by the fact that a *plēthos* (in the form of the catalogue) truly does follow.

somewhat shorter) and is describing an enormous naval battle. The near citation is unmistakable.[29]

Greek tragedy, of course, makes ample use of the Homeric poems and contains many reminiscences of them.[30] Although each of these deserve careful consideration on their own terms, the echo of the *Iliad* 2 passage is worthy of more attention than merely chalking it up to Homer's influence on tragedy. It carries, in fact, a particularly strong charge inasmuch as the *Iliad* 2 passage stands out as both remarkable and unique in Homeric epic. These lines are not only among the rare moments of direct self-revelation on the part of the narrator, but they also represent a crucial act of self-definition. Here the narrative voice offers the most complete and compelling account of itself and its relation both to the Muses and to the poem as a whole. In recalling this passage, then, the messenger imports into his own performance the central reflection on the art of narrative to be found in the *Iliad*. In borrowing so conspicuously from the Iliadic narrator, the text suggests that the messenger's narrative resembles that of the epic bard. And this suggestion proves fruitful, because it provides a framework for understanding the narrative practice of the messenger more broadly.[31]

For the epic narrator, this act of self-definition, the invocation of the Muses, is also a moment of self-authorization. And the act of self-

29. Since Blomfield, critics have noted similarities between *Persians* 429–30 and *Odyssey* 3.114ff. and 11.328ff. Although he does not mention the *Iliad* 2 passage, Blomfield (1830 *ad* 429–30) comments: "Locus vero ex Homero adumbratus." Although the two *Odyssey* passages are parallel as expressions of what Curtius calls the "inexpressibility topos" (1953, 159), clear verbal echoes as well as similarities of context (catalogue) and subject matter (naval armada) produce an unavoidable echo of the *Iliad* 2 passage.

30. E.g., Garner 1990.

31. The act of "quoting" per se is no guarantee of a shared status, of course. We must in principle make room for irony and error. It will, I hope, become clear that this textual reminiscence of the Iliadic narrator provides a clue worth following.

authorization implies the need for such an act (i.e., an acknowledgment of the problematic nature of narrative authority). On this passage Andrew Ford comments: "The fiction of the Muses serves to distinguish heroic poetry from other oral traditions: it elevates such poetry above mere 'report' into contact, mediated to be sure, with an actual witness to the events" (1992, 61–62). As the messenger's appropriation of Homer's lines indicates, his position resembles that of the epic narrator: both need to authorize their narratives. By acknowledging the impossibility of the task for a mere mortal, the epic narrator offers his account as that of the Muses and implicitly impugns any other.[32] The Muses, because of their "presence," have seen and thus know and are able to tell of the events. The distinction between knowing/having seen, on the one hand, and hearing, on the other, establishes the privilege of the Muses, as is clearly marked by the opposition between Muses and mortals (ὑμεῖς γὰρ . . . ἡμεῖς δὲ) in lines 485–86.

This logic of authorization is, of course, identical with that used by the messenger of Aeschylus's *Persians* at line 266. In fact, the messenger uses the same verb as that which occurs at *Iliad* 2.485 (παρεῖναι), and the characterization of mortals in Homer as merely hearing rumor (κλέος οἶον ἀκούομεν) closely resembles the messenger's self-definition by negation (κοὐ λόγους ἄλλων κλύων). These logical and verbal parallels render the reminiscence not only more sure, but more complex as well.

In borrowing the language of the epic narrator, the messenger also lays claim to his narrative authority: as the epic narrator is differentiated from all others in the poem and speaks with an extradiegetic voice, so, too, does the text suggest that the messenger is an extradiegetic narrator. The implications of this Homeric echo are far-reaching, insofar as it suggests that the messenger, like the epic narrator, stands outside of his narrative. He no longer appears as merely one of the *dramatis per-*

---

32. See Ford 1992, 80–82, on the inexpressibility topos as a means used by other poets to distinguish their own poetry. Cf. Bundy 1972, 47, 64.

*sonae.*[33] His freedom of movement within the scenes he describes, like his invulnerability amid the carnage, derives from a self-effacement familiar from epic, where the narrator has access to a wide variety of perceptual points of view and yet nowhere appears in the fictional scene.

But, of course, unlike the epic narrator, the messenger claims to have seen the events himself. And as I have said, the logic of his authorization is the same as that of the Muses in *Iliad* 2. Insofar, then, as this borrowing suggests the epic narrator as an analogue of the messenger, the latter's claim to what the epic narrator most conspicuously lacks stands out: his presence at the events he reports and the direct knowledge of these events that this presence bestows are precisely what distinguishes the Muses from the epic narrator. The messenger also, it would seem, shares much with the Muses as represented in *Iliad* 2. The force of this Homeric echo, then, is double: the messenger's narrative practices resemble those of epic, while his claim to authority resembles that of the Muses.

It may seem that I am pressing the textual reminiscence too far, if it leads only to a contradiction that does little to help us understand the messenger. As the echo of *Iliad* 2, however, seems to move in two directions at once—toward both the epic narrator and the Muses—this double movement and the apparent contradiction it implies illuminate the messenger's predicament. It is possible to see in the double movement of the echo a reflection of the messenger's twin claims: (1) that, like the Muses, he was present at the events of the narrative, and (2) that, like the epic narrator, his voice is an extradiegetic one, free from the lim-

33. This echo is not, however, without danger. See Pucci 1980, 170–71, on the ambiguity inherent in the word *kleos*. Similar to the danger for the bard is the risk for the messenger: as he bases his authority on a claim to presence enunciated in precisely the terms used by Homer—namely, the opposition between presence and rumor—he opens the possibility that *his* narrative may appear to be mere hearsay. As Ford points out, "there is a gap between the multifariousness of experience and an account of it in speech; and this gap is repeatedly portrayed by Homer as a gap between the powers of sight and speech" (1992, 75).

itations on those within the narrative. As I have argued above, the messenger's claim to presence is crucial to his authority, and yet a close examination of his narrative reveals that he effaces himself from those events in such a way as to construct an ideal point of view. This point of view, as the echo suggests, strongly resembles that of the epic narrator. The messenger's claim, then, to resemble both Muses and epic narrator reflects his double strategy of asserting his presence while effacing himself. Although this strategy contains a fundamental contradiction, it reveals the unique predicament of the tragic messenger. He is caught between his claim to presence at the events he reports as a "real" member of the (fictional) world onstage and his need to absent himself from his narrative in order to create "the illusion of undistorted information" (Barlow 1971, 61).

The *Iliad* is of further help in understanding how the tragic texts come to terms with this predicament. Speaking of the *Iliad*, Keith Dickson suggests that the oral poet adopts a fundamentally similar double strategy, reflected in Kalkhas and Nestor. Kalkhas's speech is "timeless," "objective," inspired by a god, and is able to project forward in time (and in the narrative). Nestor, on the other hand, speaks from memory:

> Prophetic vision . . . represents a point of view that is basically "timeless" and *extratextual*, incorporating a strategy of control over the events it surveys that resembles the control exercised by a narrator over his tale. This atemporal focus is in turn mirrored in the detached role of Kalkhas among his social peers. The figure of Nestor, by contrast, is thoroughly embedded within Akhaian society as the spokesman of its traditions, and the specific kind of vision he enjoys is entirely conditioned by a historical perspective. (Dickson 1992, 345–46).

Dickson goes on to say that

> Kalkhas and Nestor exhibit different narrative strategies and delineate distinct narrative stances or *foci* in the text of the *Iliad*. It is tempting to entertain the possibility that together they trace the

contours of the position occupied by the oral poet himself, and in so doing manifest some of its inherent tensions. (349)

These two narrative strategies, I suggest, are precisely those of the messenger, and they generate tensions for him as well: he must establish his eyewitness status while claiming to speak with an extradiegetic voice. We might be tempted to think this a coincidence, were it not for the text's own suggestion that we read this *angelia* in light of the reflections on epic narrative found in *Iliad* 2.

––––––––

The suggestion that this *angelia* displays an affiliation with epic narrative may be accepted by some as but one example of a broader phenomenon, that of the tragic *angelia's* epic nature. It has long been recognized that messenger-speeches bear a resemblance to epic poetry, if there has not been agreement about what this means. Among even the earliest discussions of messengers the question of epicism is prominent.[34] The minimum similarity, of course, is the quality of lengthy narration.[35] More specific "epicisms" have found champions and critics, with the weight in recent times falling on the side of skepticism.[36] The most detailed and influential work on this question has been done by Leif Bergson in his 1953 and 1959 articles. In the latter, while acknowledging an epic quality ("Gut") in the tragic *angelia*, Bergson denies any intention on the part of the tragic poets to create a messenger specifically marked as epic. Rather, he says, the similarities are produced by practical constraints.[37]

34. See the introduction. See also Bergson 1959, 9; Lesky 1983, 158; Strohm 1959, 179.

35. Lengthy speech is not rare; lengthy narration is: see Michelini 1974.

36. A notable exception is Paduano, who takes the epic character of the messenger speech in *Persians* as a given and proceeds to elucidate the *non-*epic elements in this role (1978, 64–70). See also the remarks of Bassi 1899, 88–89; Rosenmeyer 1982, 197; and de Jong 1991, 12, all quoted above.

37. "Das homerische Gut in diesen Abschnitten [messenger-speeches] soll nicht geleugnet werden. Aber das Anbringen der Homerismen ist nicht

In Bergson's view the messenger and epic share a genre (i.e., narrative), and this explains the formal similarities: there is nothing of intention on the part of the poets involved.[38]

Bergson's argument consists principally of two assertions: first, that there is an appearance of epicism in messenger-speeches on account of the narration and epic diction; second, that the tragic poets had no intention of endowing their messengers with epic qualities and that such apparent qualities are entirely explicable on metrical/technical grounds or on the basis of content.[39] This holds also, argues Bergson elsewhere (1953), for the omission of the syllabic augment, a not infrequent occurrence in tragic *angeliai*.

Like G. Erdmann, Bergson argues for divorcing the messenger from epic, although he allows some overlap between the two. Without entering into a discussion of the argument in detail, we may take a cue from the Persian messenger and ask whether the conclusions Bergson draws from his analysis square with the results of the experiments carried out in the "laboratory" of *Persians*. That is, does Bergson's argument refute the messenger himself?

---

das Resultat eines Strebens nach homerischer Diktion, sondern ist vielmehr praktischen Bedürfnissen zu verdanken" (1959, 38). Erdmann (1964, 74) and Di Gregorio (1967, 11–15) concur.

38. "Diese Übereinstimmung ist aber auch unbeabsichtlich und beruht auf einer inneren Übereinstimmung der Dichtungsgattungen" (1959, 38). The same conclusion was reached by Henning, though with far less rigor of argumentation (1910, 42). The apparent similarities between the messenger-speech and epic poetry bring Erdmann to a discussion of the profound *differences* between the two (1964, 1–7, 86–90) and a firm denial of any epic quality of the messenger.

39. Bergson 1959, 38: "aus rein metrisch-technischen oder aus inhaltlichen Gründen." He cites three cases that cannot be explained on these grounds: (1) τοί at Aesch. *Pers.* 424; (2) two shortened aorists at Eur. *Hipp.* 1247 and *Phoen.* 1246; (3) a tendency toward loss of the article. The first two he ascribes to chance; the third he says is indicative not of epicism but of archaism.

We need not (seek to) answer the question concerning the origin of apparent epicisms to understand something of their effects. We may, that is, wonder whether the *appearance* of epicism in a messenger-speech might carry connotations that it would not elsewhere. That is, apparent epicisms—loss of syllabic augment, shortened aorists, loss of article, for example—when embedded in a lengthy narrative, may become for the audience confirmations of a more general sense of "epic narrative." The effect, finally, will be a complex one constituted by the broad generic qualities as well as the apparent epicisms that result from relatively narrow concerns. If in fact the tragic poets' intentions never encompassed an urge toward Homeric diction in messenger-speeches, it may be that the appearance of Homeric diction—in conjunction with the shared narrative strategies—renders that exhumed intention moot. In short, I am proposing not to set aside the results of Bergson's impressive studies. Rather, I think we need to reevaluate the effects of the epic "quality" of tragic *angeliai*, particularly in tandem with the range of narrative practices as exhibited in *Persians*. Taking a cue from the texts themselves, I will argue that tragedy makes use of a messenger whose privilege on-stage both resembles and depends upon the narrative practices perfected by epic.

---

It is true that other forms of (poetic) narrative might well elucidate some of the workings of the tragic *angelia*. That is, one might ask how the messenger's narrative differs from those of tragic choruses, or from those of nondramatic choruses, for example. Or, given the privilege of the messenger's narrative, one could ask how the authority of this conventional figure's report differs from the authority wielded by divine speech in tragedy. This latter is perhaps the most authoritative speech form in the genre.[40] This study restricts its analysis of (narrative) models to epic, not because other forms have nothing to teach. In fact, care-

40. For a study of divine and prophetic speech in Sophocles see Bushnell 1988.

ful study of choral narrative, for example, would certainly reveal that chorus and messenger share a number of traits with epic. We could find, for example, instances of self-effacement and implicit claims to comprehensive, detailed knowledge in Aeschylus's chorus of Argive elders (e.g., *Ag.* 104–59), or in Bacchylides' Theseus dithyramb (no. 17).[41] Comparative study of these forms of narrative might well be productive. Nonetheless, I maintain, epic proves to be the principal and most illuminating model—as *Persians* so clearly indicates, and as other invocations of the epic model attest. Indeed, as I will argue in the next chapter, Aristotle appears to have seen the tragic messenger as a kind of epic intrusion into tragedy.[42]

Aside from the testimony of *Persians*, and Aristotle (see below), however, there are reasons for addressing the messenger's epic borrowings apart from a more comprehensive study of other speech forms. Divine and prophetic speech, for example, surely wields an authority that the messenger can hardly match. Notwithstanding Euripides' repeated interrogations of divine privilege,[43] oracles and prophecy—not to mention the gods who themselves appear on the tragic stage—command an

41. Such narratives, however, do not rely upon implicit claims to privileged knowledge; rather, they imply a shared, perhaps even "inherited" knowledge. See below.

42. Similarly, a comparative study of historical narrative—as found in Herodotus and Thucydides, especially—and tragic *angeliai* might well shed light on both types of narrative. How the historians use, and avoid, the strategies outlined here is not without some relevance. One might, in fact, extend this kind of comparative analysis to include a wide range of speech types. The constraints are largely practical. Perhaps one point of entry here would be line 254—quoted above—where the Persian messenger uses a verb (ἀναπτύξαι) that is used elsewhere in reference to written works on rolls of papyrus. He says he must "unfold the whole *pathos*" (πᾶν ἀναπτύξαι πάθος). Herodotus, for example, speaks of unfolding, or unrolling, a papyrus: ἀναπτύξας τὸ βυβλίον (1.125). Does Aeschylus's text hint that the messenger's report constitutes a form of "writing"?

43. See, for example, Bushnell 1988, 108–27.

authority fundamental to the workings of the genre. (Indeed, one can readily understand Euripides' scrutiny of the gods as a response to their privileged status.) Tragedy often, in fact, rehearses the wide gulf that separates mortal and immortal, a distance measured in large part in terms of power. But divine authority in tragedy is a quantity rather different from that of the messenger-speech. Even the discursive authority of divine and prophetic speech is of another order. The authority of divine speech is principally a consequence of the broader power wielded by the gods. More specifically, divine speech often possesses a prophetic power, but rarely if ever does it possess narrative authority. That is, such speech is authoritative in tragedy principally on account of the speaker's identity as a god, not because of how it is spoken. Quite unlike the *angelia* that gains an important part of its power from the messenger's self-effacement, divine speech acquires its force from its divine source. Similarly, divine foreknowledge is vastly different from the messenger's implicit claim of epistemic privilege. While the latter is carefully and subtly produced in our texts without explicitly granting the messenger special powers or abilities, divine foreknowledge is again a consequence of immortal privilege. Whereas the tragic texts forge from otherwise mundane material the peculiar privilege of the messenger, divine speech derives its power from an altogether different source.

Choruses, both tragic and nondramatic, might seem a more likely analogue for the messenger. Not only do they often incorporate narrative into their performances; unlike gods and prophets, choruses also acquire little, if any, authority from their identity. They, like the messenger, in fact, are nameless. These similarities are enticing, and, as I have said, likely to be a productive avenue of inquiry. At the same time, however, it is clear that choral narrative is a more distant relative of the tragic *angelia* than is the narrative of epic. On formal grounds, the narrative of the messenger shares little with choral narrative, whether tragic or not. Unlike the messenger, choruses sing their narratives to musical accompaniment while dancing. The messenger's (overwhelmingly) spoken iambic lines—together with the great many such lines that make up the tragic texts—make use of the meter closest to spoken language (according to Aristotle, *Poetics* 1449a). In this they differ markedly from the likewise overwhelming majority of (sung) choral passages. Similarly, the multiple voices of the chorus contrast sharply with the single voice of the messenger. These formal differences certainly leave room for other shared traits, as I have indicated; but they also suggest that both Aristotle and *Persians* are right to look to epic as the principal model for the messenger.

Perhaps more important, the unified voice of the chorus signals its distance from the messenger. In a recent study of nondramatic poetry, Eva Stehle speaks of choral poetry as "community poetry." Such poetry, she argues, "usually expresses the viewpoint of a particular community" (1997, 18), with the chorus speaking "both for and to the audience; they serve as both reflection of and model for the communal opinion" (38).[44] Stehle argues further that the unified voice of the chorus enables this function, since the many voices "all speaking the same words would provide an image of communal harmony" (69). In support of this claim she cites a Simonides fragment (519 fr. 35.8–10 PMG):

καὶ σέ, ἄναξ ἑκαβ[
 ̣].ετα ἱέμενοι ἐνοπὰν ἀγανοῖσιν [
] εὔφαμον ἀπὸ φρενὸς ὁμορρόθο[υ

Also you, Lord Apollo [ ] (we) sending forth an auspicious cry with gentle [ ] from a mind that moves in unison.[45]

These lines, Stehle argues, express "what choral dancing ideally implied: unity of thought" (69).

44. Although Stehle addresses only nondramatic poetry, her remarks quoted here, I submit, apply to tragic choruses as well. (Cf. Barlow [1971, 25], who speaks of the chorus's "focusing perspective.") In fact, given that nondramatic choral poetry is the earlier form, and that, as Herington (1985) has shown, tragedy borrows freely from its predecessors, it is to be expected that fundamental properties of this earlier choral poetry will have survived into tragedy.

45. I here borrow the translation of Stehle.

Against this model of choral poetry, Stehle contrasts what she calls "bardic" or "hexameter" poetry. This latter includes, of course, epic. Unlike choral poetry with its "mind that moves in unison," bardic poetry on Stehle's account is fundamentally agonistic:

> Bards . . . do not speak for a community and do not speak to it from within. Instead, their songs are brought to an audience from without. . . . Consequently a bard's self-presentation must differ from that of a performer of community poetry. He does not seek to present an exemplary status in social terms. . . . He presents himself only as a speaker, but a speaker with special knowledge of a comprehensive "truth," about which he must persuade the audience. (1997, 173–74)

Stehle here draws upon the work of Richard Martin, who has argued that Homeric epic is performed "in a context where authority is always up for grabs." This poetry, writes Martin, is "inherently agonistic," and the poet is "a poet against others, out to obliterate their performances by speaking in more detail, about more topics" (1989, 238).

As such, the epic bard proves to have much more in common with the tragic messenger than does the chorus: both seek authority in an agonistic context. (As I have argued, both rely on many of the same strategies for acquiring this authority. Furthermore, if the bard brings poetry "from without," so does the messenger bring a report from offstage. If a bard's agonistic efforts are displayed in the accumulation of detail, the messenger-speech typically presents a level of detail reminiscent of epic. In both cases, this surplus of detail may itself be persuasive.)[46] Thus even in a fundamentally agonistic context, the tragic chorus's song can often be viewed as presenting "a hypothesis about meaning rather than a final assertion of the play's meaning. It can be regarded as a kind of thought-experiment, exploring and trying to understand the meaning of

46. Cf. Barthes's "reality effect" (1968).

otherwise unintelligible suffering" (Segal 1996, 20). Its song, that is, may be viewed not as an attempt to persuade, but rather as an offering to the audience as it struggles with the meaning of the play. In short, the chorus does not necessarily participate on an equal footing in the rhetorical contest that otherwise largely defines the play. Rush Rehm, in fact, distinguishes between "the lyric of the chorus and the rhetoric of the actors" (1996, 45).[47] Insofar as the tragic messenger produces a narrative that abuts a swarm of competing modes of speech, his (implicit) claims to authority mark his narrative as engaging agonistically in the drama in a way that the tragic chorus may not. In this way, then, the tragic chorus resembles the nondramatic chorus in Stehle's analysis, as it performs a kind of "community poetry."[48]

One sign that the tragic chorus does offer such a "community" point of view is the fact that choruses very frequently recount events without claiming eyewitness status. In fact, they often speak of events in the distant past. The chorus of Theban women in Aeschylus's *Septem*, for example, rehearse in brief the story of Oedipus, introducing the story as "ancient" (παλαιγενῆ, 743). Similarly, the chorus of Phoenician women, in Euripides' play of that name, tell of Cadmus's arrival in Thebes long

47. This does not mean that the choral songs do not define one of many modes of speech on the tragic stage. If we view the chorus as less agonistic than other members of the *dramatis personae*, the complexity of speech forms onstage is not compromised. Indeed, one might well conclude that a choral "hypothesis about meaning" avoids the agonistic "rhetoric" of the other actors, while still "competing" insofar as it offers an alternative to what surrounds it. Even if in some sense this view simplifies things for the chorus itself, it does not necessarily do the same for the spectator.

48. Michael Silk comments that the chorus "is a carrier of responses and ideas. It has no privileged knowledge; perhaps it has no knowledge, in the strict sense, at all. What it has is a privileged claim to be heard and a privileged capacity to universalize the specifics of the action" (1998, 21–22). Cf. Gould 1996, 222–24.

ago (638–75). In all such cases, of course, the chorus can only know and tell what they do because they have *heard* it from another source. Sometimes the fact that the chorus did not witness what they relate is emphatically announced. This same Euripidean chorus, for example, tell us that before coming to Thebes they *heard* about the race that sprouted from the dragon's teeth there (ἀϰοὰν ἐδάην, 819). As though to mark their distance from the messenger on this score, the chorus in Aeschylus's *Persians* repeat the grim news they have heard from him, acknowledging that their report derives from his (εἰσαϰούομεν, 565). In Sophocles' *Trachiniae* the eponymous chorus claim to retell the struggle for Deianeira between Herakles and the river Achelous "as a spectator would."[49] Thus do they signal both that their own knowledge is a form of shared knowledge based on what others have seen—and told them—and that it is the eyewitness who can provide the most authoritative account. Such moments are familiar in tragic choral narrative. Even when choruses do offer narratives based upon a claim to eyewitness status—whether explicit or implicit—they claim no privileged knowledge. They make no attempt to distinguish their narratives as reliable, as does the messenger in Aeschylus's *Persians*, for example. This lack of attention to such matters reflects, I suggest, the status claimed for these narratives: the product not of a privileged point of view, but of a view shared by all. These narratives, that is, rely upon a form of shared knowledge, a form of "community" knowledge, just as their group performance in unison implies.

As I have said, however, both choral narrative and divine speech may well bear valuable testimony for understanding the tragic messenger-speech. My choice here to limit the scope of the analysis stems principally from practical concerns. Due to the richness of the tragic messenger's epic inheritance, I have chosen to address this particular

---

49. At line 526. I borrow the translation of Easterling 1982 ad loc. This line is recognized by all to be corrupt. Like Easterling, I adopt Zielinki's emendation. See Davies 1991 ad loc.

form of generic affiliation, and to leave to another time the question of other generic parallels in tragic *angeliai*. This choice results in part as well from the conviction that an understanding of the messenger's epic borrowing can provide some guideposts for subsequent analysis of the traits shared by the messenger's narrative and other forms of speech.

# TWO

# The Literary Messenger, the Tragic Messenger

οὐκ ἐμοῦ ἀλλὰ τοῦ λόγου ἀκούσαντας ὁμολογεῖν σοφόν ἐστιν
ἓν πάντα εἶναι.

Listening not to me but to the logos, it is wise to agree that all
is one.

*Heracleitus fr. 50 D-K*

In the previous chapter I suggested that Aeschylus's *Persians* makes reference to an established literary figure who predates the tragic messenger. This literary messenger appears already in Homer and is characterized by swiftness and reliability. More specifically, the messenger's reliability appears not only as the accuracy (ἀτρεκέως, at *Il.* 2.10, for example) but also as the fullness of her/his report: a messenger who leaves nothing out performs the assigned role well. Such a figure lies behind tragedy's use of its messenger, offering a ready-made model that supports the tragic messenger's conventional claims. But there is more in the tradition of the literary messenger that provides a foundation for the success of the conventional tragic figure.

## THE LITERARY MESSENGER

In Homer, both messenger (ἄγγελος) and herald (κῆρυξ) share the quality of speaking for another. Both perform the function of mediator, moving between the sender and the recipient of a pronouncement. Iris carries the word of Zeus and stands as guarantor of its authenticity, while Talthybios does the same for Agamemnon. In both cases the mouthpiece sustains the (political) will of the king: Zeus's proclamations emanate via Iris and, through her speed and reliability, support a political order in the (world of the) poem; similarly Talthybios delivers Agamemnon's word and thus extends the king's political authority through the Greek camp.

The two terms have distinct, although compatible, meanings. Unlike the term ἄγγελος, κῆρυξ attaches only to mortals. Iris in the *Iliad* and Hermes in the *Odyssey*, for example, are messengers, but they never receive the title κῆρυξ. This distinction indicates one of the essential characteristics of a herald: that of performing a ritual function within a religious context.[1] But if in some respects herald and messenger perform different functions, they also share certain qualities and find their roles overlapping. On several occasions the herald is called ἄγγελος (*Od.* 16.468–69; *Il.* 1.334) or charged with delivering an *angelia* (*Od.* 16.328–29). A brief look at the herald and what distinguishes him, then, will provide some clues about the literary messenger as well.

The name of the herald (κῆρυξ) is cognate with a Sanskrit word for "bard" ("karu"; Chantraine 1970 s.v. κῆρυξ). It has, in fact, been argued that herald and bard derive from a common (pre-Homeric) ancestor who performed the functions of both figures. The herald, that is, appears to derive from a figure associated with the performance of song.[2] The suggestion provided by etymology that the herald and bard have much in common is in fact confirmed in other ways.

---

1. See, for example, *Il.* 3.245–74; 9.171–76; 19.196–97, 250–51.
2. Brown 1969, 30–32; see also Mondi 1978, 148.

From Hesiod's *Theogony* we know that the identification of political authority and eloquence was traditional (81–84):

ὅντινα τιμήσουσι Διὸς κοῦραι μεγάλοιο
γεινόμενόν τε ἴδωσι διοτρεφέων βασιλήων,
τῷ μὲν ἐπὶ γλώσσῃ γλυκερὴν χείουσιν ἐέρσην,
τοῦ δ' ἔπε' ἐκ στόματος ῥεῖ μείλιχα·

Whomever among the divine kings the daughters of great Zeus [i.e., the Muses] honor and look upon, on his tongue they pour sweet dew, and from his mouth flow words like honey.

This passage attributes the king's authority to his eloquence, remarking on the sweetness of his speech. While the poem here speaks of the voices of the kings, it is worth recalling that the king often speaks via the herald. The herald performs his function only if what he says is indistinguishable from what the king says. In short, the words *(epea)* of the king are often those of the herald as well.

Hesiod goes on to say that in this regard bards are like kings (94–97):

ἐκ γάρ τοι Μουσέων καὶ ἑκηβόλου Ἀπόλλωνος
ἄνδρες ἀοιδοὶ ἔασιν ἐπὶ χθόνα καὶ κιθαρισταί,
ἐκ δὲ Διὸς βασιλῆες· ὁ δ' ὄλβιος, ὅντινα Μοῦσαι
φίλωνται· γλυκερή οἱ ἀπὸ στόματος ῥέει αὐδή.

From the Muses and Apollo the Far-Shooter do men on earth become bards and kithara-players, and kings are from Zeus. Whomever the Muses love, he is fortunate: a sweet voice flows from his mouth.

If Hesiod tells us clearly that bards and kings alike possess an eloquence from the Muses,[3] the herald as spokesman for the king and "sibling" of the bard surely represents the king's authority by means of a similar elo-

---

3. Thalmann 1984, 139ff., provides an excellent discussion of this issue.

quence, as his kinship with the bard is suggested already by the etymology of the word κῆρυξ.[4]

In addition to the broad similarities between herald and bard—such as being δημιουργοί and carrying a staff—specific and fundamental connections between these two appear in the Homeric poems. The phrase θεοῖς / θεῷ ἐναλίγκιος αὐδήν ("like the gods/god in voice") occurs three times in Homer, with reference either to a bard or to a herald.[5] In each case the person in question is likened to a god with respect to the voice. Further, aside from kings, only these two are designated as godly or divine *(theios)* on the basis of their social standing.[6] Thus do the Homeric poems distinguish these two figures from other mortals, and in so doing approximate them to the gods.

A more subtle and complex parallel between these two figures arises in book 22 of the *Odyssey*, where the herald Medon and the bard Phemios together are saved in a single act.[7] Telemachus intervenes on behalf of the two, asking his father Odysseus to spare them in his retaliation against the suitors. The text emphasizes the likeness of their positions in several ways. Phemios supplicates Odysseus and is described as rushing forward and grabbing the knees of Odysseus (προσαΐξας λάβε γούνων, 342). Medon supplicates Telemachus and is described with the same phrase

---

4. Jesper Svenbro has argued persuasively for seeing the poetry of the Homeric bard as reflecting a political order symbolically controlled by the Muses (1976, 16). If the herald delivers the message of the king, and thus represents the king's political will, the bard delivers the "message" of the Muses. That is, both bard and herald function as emissaries of a "political order," and both employ the charm of eloquence in performing their task.

5. See Clay 1974. At *Od.* 1.371 the phrase describes Phemius; at *Od.* 9.4, Demodocus; at *Il.* 19.250, Talthybius.

6. Mondi (1978, 148) cites Plato's discussion of Hermes as interpreter and messenger (*Cra.* 407e–408b): the patron of heralds (and messengers) is distinguished by a linguistic talent.

7. See Pucci 1987, 228–35.

(365). In both cases, immediately after this phrase follows the line καί μιν λισσόμενος ἔπεα πτερόεντα προσηύδα ("and supplicating him spoke winged words"). Not only are they both δημιουργοί whose lives are in jeopardy for having served the suitors, but their strategies for survival are nearly identical both in posture and in word.

The herald, then, shares a history and certain traits with the bard. He also, as we have seen, shares with the messenger the ability to deliver messages. These relationships, I suggest, indicate that all three of these figures are distinguished by a privileged voice. This privilege, further-more, is based upon a claim to transparency: just as the function of mes-senger is appropriately performed by transmitting accurately and com-pletely the entrusted message, so the bard performs his function well if the song he sings is that of the Muses, rather than his own. In short, all of these figures speak with an authority that derives from their claim to be transmitting the words of another. The bard is a vehicle of the Muses; the herald represents the will of the king; and the messenger delivers words entrusted to him by another (of greater authority).

The *Iliad* records the Muses' demand that the bard be a "transparent" or anonymous performer. Book 2 tells in brief the story of Thamyris, whom the Muses deprived of song after he boasted that he could defeat even the Muses in a singing competition (597–600):

στεῦτο γὰρ εὐχόμενος νικησέμεν, εἴ περ ἂν αὐταὶ
Μοῦσαι ἀείδοιεν, κοῦραι Διὸς αἰγιόχοιο·
αἱ δὲ χολωσάμεναι πηρὸν θέσαν, αὐτὰρ ἀοιδὴν
θεσπεσίην ἀφέλοντο καὶ ἐκλέλαθον κιθαριστύν·

For he claimed in a boast that he would triumph, even if the Muses themselves, the daughters of aegis-bearing Zeus, should sing. An-gered, they maimed him, took away his divine song, and made him forget how to play the kithara.

This brief account reveals that if a bard claims a song as his own, he vi-olates the requirements of the tradition: the song belongs not to him, but rather to the Muses. Jesper Svenbro argues that Thamyris in book 2 of the *Iliad* exemplifies this principle, claiming that it is precisely Thamyris's boast to surpass the Muses that leads to his loss of voice. When the bard claims the song as his own, says Svenbro, he is deprived of song altogether.[8]

The example of Thamyris acquires a particular poignancy occurring where it does. It arises from the mention of Dorion in the Catalogue of Ships, the recital of which is preceded and made possible by the invocation of the Muses. In this invocation, discussed above in chapter 1, the bard announces his inability to sing without the aid of the Muses, as he reminds us that it is they who speak, not he. Thamyris, then, violates the principle so well articulated and performed by the *Iliad*'s narrator.

George Walsh argues that the poetics of Homeric epic demonstrate much the same thing. Because in Homer there is no distinction between the verbal skill of the bard and the truthfulness of his song, the question of a bard's particular ability does not arise. Referring to Alkinoos's likening of Odysseus to a bard at *Odyssey* 11.363–68, Walsh remarks of the bard that his

> words have beauty *(morphē)* only when they are also accurate . . . so that truthfulness or the story itself rather than the singer seems responsible for his verbal skill. The story comes ready-made for singing, its verity assured because it cannot be contrived by a human being who assembles words according to his own uncertain imperatives.[9]

Insofar, then, as herald, bard, and messenger as poetic constructs share the distinction of voice and the skill of self-effacement, all three transmit words of far greater authority than what they themselves are capable

8. "Lorsque l'aède Thamyris se vante de surpasser les Muses, elles se vengent en le privant de sa voix. Au moment même où l'aède revendique son chant comme privé, il est privé du chant" (1976, 24–25).

9. Walsh 1984, 30–31. Cf. Clay 1983, 10: "The poet mediates between Olympus and his audience. In calling on the Muse and transmitting her song, the poet presents himself as a mere instrument, a vehicle of the goddess, submerging his own voice to the song of the Muse."

of producing. And if this is a valuable scheme in epic, it remains so for subsequent poetry as well.

Numerous passages reveal that within the poetic tradition the messenger and herald were often interchangeable and that both of them served as metaphor for the poet.[10] It is possible, then, to identify a continuity that serves to underpin the claims of the tragic messenger: the literary messenger appears to be deputized by the poet himself.

While in Homer there is certainly a distinction between ἄγγελος and κῆρυξ, we have seen that Homer often ignores this distinction. Later poetry presents a similar picture. Sappho fragment 44 Voigt preserves the Homeric practice of dubbing Idaios ἄγγελος (2–3):

κᾶρυξ ἦλθε θε[     ]ελε[. . .] . θεις
Ἴδαος ταδεκα . . . φ[. .] . ις τάχυς ἄγγελος

the herald came . . . Idaios . . . the swift messenger

Pindar likewise equates herald and messenger at *Pythian* 1.32, where the herald (κάρυξ) is said to announce (ἀγγέλλων) the victory at Delphi. At *Olympian* 8. 81–83 Pindar apparently invents the personified Ἀγγελία and provides her with a partial genealogy:

Ἑρμᾶ δὲ θυγατρὸς ἀκούσαις Ἰφίων
Ἀγγελίας, ἐνέποι κεν Καλλιμάχῳ λιπαρὸν
κόσμον Ὀλυμπίᾳ.

Iphion, hearing of it from Hermes' daughter Angelia, could tell Callimachus about the shining glory at Olympia.

Hermes, the divine messenger of the *Odyssey* and *Iliad* 24, is fittingly the father of Ἀγγελία. He is also, of course, the patron of heralds, suggesting the ease of interchange between these two figures.[11]

10. Nünlist 1998, 69–80, provides a list of such passages.
11. See Nünlist 1998, 68. As noted by Mondi 1978, 1, this practice continues in Herodotus and tragedy as well. See, for example, Aesch. *Supp.* 931; Soph. *OC* 1511; *Trach.* 348. Cf. Hipponax fr. 54 West.

Similarly, both herald and messenger appear as figures for the poet. Plutarch (*Sol.* 8.1) reports that in the wake of its lengthy dispute with Megara over the island of Salamis (ca. 600 B.C.E.), Athens passed a law banning public speech advocating the city's claim to the island (μήτε γράψαι τινὰ μήτ' εἰπεῖν). In response, Solon pretended to be out of his mind, put on a little felt hat, and mounted the herald's stone. He then recited the poem beginning (fr. 1 West):

αὐτὸς κῆρυξ ἦλθον ἀφ' ἱμερτῆς Σαλαμῖνος,
κόσμον ἐπέων ᾠδὴν ἀντ' ἀγορῆς θέμενος.[12]

I have come in person as a herald from lovely Salamis, composing song, an adornment of words, instead of speech.[13]

Solon speaks of his public performance as the act of a herald, while emphasizing that his pronouncement is a song. We cannot, of course, know the reaction of those who heard these lines, but Plutarch expresses no surprise at this combination. The original identity of the two roles, on the other hand, suggests something of the logic behind this formulation. In fact, Plutarch's introduction of this couplet mimics Solon's language, naming the spot where Solon stood as the herald's stand:

ἀναβὰς ἐπὶ τὸν τοῦ κήρυκος λίθον, ἐν ᾠδῇ διεξῆλθε τὴν ἐλεγείαν

Mounting the herald's stone, he sang the elegy.

Pindar, too, speaks of himself as a herald when he says he has come to tell of the games: κάρυξ ἑτοῖμος ἔβαν (*Nem.* 4.74).[14]

12. West suspects ᾠδὴν.
13. I borrow this translation from Douglas Gerber (1999, 111).
14. See also fr. 61.18–20 (Bowra = 70b.23–25 Snell-Maehler). The overlap between herald and poet is, in fact, an important source for Pindaric poetry, inasmuch as the epinician performs, in part, a function comparable to that of the herald at the games: both announce the victor, his father, and city (Nash 1990, 7). On Pindar's creative use of his own status as "herald" see

More frequent than either of these equations or metaphors, though, is the appearance of the messenger as a figure for the poet and the message as a figure for the poem. Theognis makes a simple equation between servant and messenger of the Muses as he defines the task of the poet (769–72):

χρὴ Μουσῶν θεράποντα καὶ ἄγγελον, εἴ τι περισσὸν
  εἰδείη, σοφίης μὴ φθονερὸν τελέθειν,
ἀλλὰ τὰ μὲν μῶσθαι, τὰ δὲ δεικνύναι, ἄλλα δὲ ποιεῖν·
  τί σφιν χρήσηται μοῦνος ἐπιστάμενος;

The servant and messenger of the Muses, if he knows anything important, must not be stingy with his wisdom; rather, [he should] seek after some things, reveal others, and compose yet others. What good is it to him if only he knows?[15]

The epic system of the Muse speaking through the poet clearly lies behind this formulation: as servant of the Muses, the poet does not speak for himself.

Pindar, too, frequently poses as messenger. In a poem marked by a concern with the function of poetry (*Nem.* 6),[16] he sings his poem as an ἄγγελος (57–59):

ἑκόντι δ᾿ ἐγὼ νώ-
  τῳ μεθέπων δίδυμον ἄχθος

---

Nash 1990, 45–63. Cf. Bacchyl. *Ep.* 13.230–31: τερψιεπεῖς νιν ἀοιδαὶ/ παντὶ καρύξοντι λα[ῶ]ι.

15. Line 771 is variously interpreted. Carrière (1948) translates: "Qu'il les cherche à la fois et les enseigne aux hommes, et les confie encore à l'art." Gerber (1999) translates: "Meditate on (seek out?) some things, display some things, and compose other things." Van Groningen reads the infinitives as marking generic distinctions (1957, 107–9). For Lanata, ἄλλα distinguishes ποιεῖν as creative poetic activity (1963, 66–67). Cf. Ford 1985, 92–93.

16. Lines 26–30, 45–50, 53–54. Not an uncommon concern, of course, for Pindar.

ἄγγελος ἔβαν,
   πέμπτον ἐπὶ εἴκοσι τοῦτο γαρύων
εὖχος ἀγώνων ἄπο.[17]

I have come as a messenger, gladly taking a double burden on my
back, singing of this 25th victory at the games.

Here again, as in the Solon fragment above, the poet's self-description
as ἄγγελος occurs at a moment of reflection on his role as poet.

If the messenger serves as a metaphor for the poet, the message (ἀγ-
γελία) serves similarly as metaphor for the poem. Pindar *Olympian* 9.21–
26 defines itself as such:

ἐγὼ δέ τοι φίλαν πόλιν
μαλεραῖς ἐπιφλέγων ἀοιδαῖς,
καὶ ἀγάνορος ἵππου
θᾶσσον καὶ ναὸς ὑποπτέρου παντᾷ
ἀγγελίαν πέμψω ταύταν.

Setting this dear city afire with my blazing song, I will send this
message in all directions faster than a headstrong horse or a
winged ship.

The demonstrative pronoun (ταύταν) makes explicit what elsewhere re-
mains rather implicit.[18] Perhaps the most intriguing of these cases is
*Olympian* 4, where the poet poses as a witness to the events that are the
ostensible subject of his song (1–5):

17. On this passage see Nagy 1990b, 15–16. See also Simonides 542.26
PMG; Pind. *Ol.* 6.87ff.; 7.21; *Pyth.* 9.2; *Nem.* 5.3. Pindar's δίδυμον ἄχθος
perhaps parallels the double strategy of the epic poet as suggested by Dick-
son 1992: inasmuch as a poet works in a tradition and yet speaks anew there
is perhaps inevitably a δίδυμον ἄχθος particularly evident in passages of self-
definition.

18. See also *Ol.* 14.21; *Pyth.* 2.4, 4.278. Cf. Bacchyl. *Ep.* 2.1. On "mes-
sages" in Pindar see Segal 1998.

Ἐλατὴρ ὑπέρτατε βροντᾶς ἀκαμαντόποδος
    Ζεῦ· τεαὶ γὰρ Ὧραι
ὑπὸ ποικιλοφόρμιγγος ἀοιδᾶς ἑλισσόμεναί μ' ἔπεμψαν
ὑψηλοτάτων μάρτυρ' ἀέθλων·

Mighty driver of tireless-footed thunder, Zeus: yours are the seasons, spinning to the dappled song of the lyre, which have sent me as witness to the greatest of competitions.

If this seems to suggest the messenger, the following lines confirm the association (6–7):

ξείνων δ' εὖ πρασσόντων
ἔσαναν αὐτίκ' ἀγγελίαν ποτὶ γλυκεῖαν ἐσλοί·

The noble fawn over the sweet news *[angelia]* of friends doing well.

Of course the relationship between the ἀγγελία and the poem remains implicit, but the equation is clear. Further on we hear an echo of the claim familiar from messengers elsewhere (21–22): οὐ ψεύδεϊ τέγξω / λόγον ("I will not blemish my report with falsehood"). Here the metaphor virtually governs the composition: as ἀγγελία, the poem must issue from the mouth of an eyewitness who promises fidelity. For Pindar here, the claim to eyewitness status serves the function of authorizing his account, even if a literal reading is unnecessary.[19]

If the members of the triad of herald, poet, and messenger appear to transform into one another at will in the poetic tradition, Sappho fragment 44 Voigt may succinctly tell us as much. Lines 2–4 introduce Idaios:

κᾱρυξ ἦλθε θε[    ]ελε[. . .] . θεις
Ἴδαος ταδεκα . . . φ[. .] . ις τάχυς ἄγγελος
‹                                             ›
τάς τ' ἄλλας Ἀσίας . [.]δε.αν κλέος ἄφθιτον·

---

19. Cf. Gildersleeve 1965 ad loc.

the herald came . . . Idaios . . . the swift messenger . . . and of the rest of Asia . . . undying fame.

Although the text is fragmentary, it appears likely that Idaios, the herald, not only receives the title τάχυς ἄγγελος, as noted above, but also speaks the κλέος ἄφθιτον of Hector. And even though his role in the poem makes perfect sense when viewed as that of herald/messenger, the phrase κλέος ἄφθιτον is highly marked in any context, but especially so in a poem that draws so clearly on traditional epic material. This phrase is marked, of course, as poetic speech or song: that which preserves fame.[20]

Finally, a densely metaphorical passage in Pindar's *Olympian 6* endows the performer of the poem with qualities perhaps more readily understood as belonging to the poet. Toward its end, the poem addresses Aeneas, the leader of the chorus (87–91):

ὄτρυνον νῦν ἑταίρους,
Αἰνέα, πρῶτον μὲν ῞Ηραν Παρθενίαν κελαδῆσαι,
γνῶναί τ' ἔπειτ', ἀρχαῖον ὄνειδος ἀλαθέσιν
λόγοις εἰ φεύγομεν, Βοιωτίαν ὗν.
    ἐσσὶ γὰρ ἄγγελος ὀρθός,
ἠϋκόμων σκυτάλα Μοισᾶν, γλυκὺς κρα-
    τὴρ ἀγαφθέγκτων ἀοιδᾶν·

Arouse your companions now, Aeneas, first, to sing of Hera Parthenia, and then to know whether by means of our true account we have escaped the old reproach "Boeotian sow"; since you are a reliable messenger, message staff *[skytala]* of the Muses, sweet mixing-bowl of deep-sounding song.[21]

---

20. Nagy 1979, 15–17. On the "reciprocal relationship between the man whose accomplishments or qualities are celebrated by *kleos aphthiton* and the man who sings that *kleos*" (Nagy 1990b, 226) and what this may suggest about Idaios see Nagy 1990b, 187–88.

21. The term *skytala* designates the staff the Spartans used to send messages. A strip of leather or parchment was wrapped around a stick and then

Having seen that Pindar employs the metaphor of messenger and message for poet and poem respectively, here we find that he displaces this metaphor onto the performer. The chorus leader is a messenger—of the poet, presumably—in that he will perform the poem. His status as "reliable" (ὀρθός; literally: "straight") guarantees that the performance remains true to the poet's instruction.[22] Thus are the qualities of the literary messenger transferred (by the poem) to the leader of the chorus. In amplifying this theme, the poem explains Aeneas's reliability as that of a *skytala*: this messenger performs his role as accurately as a coded system of writing that relies upon inanimate objects to transmit the message. Little, if any, room for discrepancy remains.

But the metaphor of the message staff specifies that the staff belongs to, or comes from, the Muses. The messenger is the metaphor of choice here for the performer of song, as it is for the poet. As in the Platonic account of poetic inspiration (*Ion* 533d–535a), the poem here passes from the Muses through the poet and to the performer(s). If Aeneas is the *skytala*, Pindar is the author of the words that it transmits. But insofar as the Muses stand behind both text and performance, Pindar and Aeneas alike are vehicles of their song. In short, the reliability of Aeneas as performer depends upon the reliability of Pindar as author: the poem constructs both as "messengers" of the Muses.[23]

From Homer, then, into the fifth century the literary messenger appears as a figure for reliable and complete transmission of language or song. Both as character and metaphor, the messenger assures the reliability and authority of the "message." As such, his voice is uniquely

---

inscribed. Removed from the stick and delivered to the recipient, it was then mounted on a stick of the same size, allowing it to be read.

22. In fact, the self-reflective incorporation of this injunction into the poem itself performs the reliability of the "messenger" as the audience witnesses the poet's act of deputizing Aeneas.

23. The Muses, of course, are not always unproblematically reliable. See, for example, Hes. *Th.* 27–28.

marked as a "transparent" medium offering virtual immediacy: in his voice one hears that of the source of the "message," whether king, Muse, or poet.

## ANCIENT LITERARY CRITICISM

The use of messenger and message as metaphors for poet and poem, respectively, reappears in somewhat altered form in ancient literary criticism. In distinguishing drama from narrative, both Plato and Aristotle employ the term *apangelia* (ἀπαγγελία) to designate the latter.[24] An *apangelia*, then, is spoken not by a character within the fiction, but rather by the poet (or narrator): it designates an extradiegetic voice. While etymology alone does not demonstrate that this word was used intentionally to call to mind the messenger, it is suggestive, for messenger-speeches, too, are designated by this term.[25] The use of *apangelia* to distinguish narrative from drama, I suggest, points to the unique status of the messenger on the tragic stage. I turn to Aristotle and Philodemus, whose discussions of narrative and tragedy help to confirm this suggestion.

In the *Poetics* Aristotle defines tragedy by contrasting it with narrative (1449b24–28):

ἔστιν οὖν τραγῳδία μίμησις πράξεως . . . δρώντων καὶ οὐ δι' ἀπαγγελίας.

Tragedy, then, is the representation [*mimesis*] of an action . . . [presented by] people acting rather than through narration.

---

24. Pl. *Resp.* 394b-c; Arist. *Poet.* 1449b24–27. Plato, in fact, speaks of the ἀπαγγελία of the poet himself (ἀπαγγελίας αὐτοῦ τοῦ ποιητοῦ). Cf. *Poet.* 1448a21, where ἀπαγγέλλειν is used of the poet. (At *Resp.* 396c7 Plato uses this term to designate the narrative of an actor.) Arist. *Poet.* 1449b11 distinguishes *epic* from *tragedy* in calling the former ἀπαγγελία. On Aristotle's ambiguous usage of these terms see Halliwell 1986, 128–29.

25. Aristotle speaks of (tragic) messengers as τῶν ἀπαγγελλόντων at *Rh.* 1417b9.

"At first sight this would seem to imply that messenger-speeches . . . are not at home in drama. This conclusion is, however, unwarranted, since . . . Aristotle means the assuming of the role of narrator *by the poet*" (de Jong 1991, 117). Although Aristotle clearly seeks to distinguish between extradiegetic narrative and the performance of fictitious characters, the implication remains that the *angelia* itself—both etymologically and referentially contained in Aristotle's *apangelia*—in some measure escapes the confines of the stage. Or more simply, it is perhaps no coincidence that the term used to distinguish narrative from tragedy is nearly identical to that which designates the messenger-speech, and can, in fact, refer to an *angelia*. While there can be no doubt that the messenger's act of narrating constitutes part of the *mimesis*, as is implied in Aristotle's definition, the terminology itself suggests that the *angelia* may be more than this.

In a polemic against Aristotle, Philodemus's *On Poems* 4 confirms that this terminology itself is significant.[26] Responding to Aristotle's lost dialogue *On Poets*, Philodemus maintains that the narrative of the tragic messenger does not represent the adoption of an epic element by the genre of tragedy. It appears that Aristotle had argued that narrative intruded into tragedy only in the form of messenger-speeches and that this constituted an epic element in tragedy. I give the text of Philodemus in question (col. V):

> . . . αὐτὸς ἐν ἄλ[λ . . . . ἀμειβόμεν[ος] . . . πράττει, ἂν κἀν τοῖ[ς]
> ἔπε[σι] τα κἀν ταῖς τραγῳ‹ι›δίαις. ὥστε οὐ τῆς μὲν τραγῳ‹ι›δ[ί]ας
> τό τε ἀπαγγέλλειν μ[όνον] ἀγγέλοις, καὶ τὸ πρακ[τι]κ[ὸ]ν ἐν τοῖς
> ἄλλοις, ἐν δ[ὲ τοῖς] ἔπε[σ]ι τὸ μόν[ο]ν [ἀ]παγγέλλειν, ἀλλ' ὅμοιον
> ἐ]φ' ὧ‹ι› καὶ δαψιλέστερον, τὸ ἀπαγγέλλειν.

26. In what follows I rely upon both argument and text of Janko 1991. It is well to remember that the text of Philodemus is in a bad state and restorations are often questionable. It may be some consolation, however, to note that in the parts most central to my argument the texts of Janko and of Sbordone (1969) agree.

. . . as he himself [says?] elsewhere, changing . . . [how?] does he act, if "the things present in tragedies are also present in epics"? Consequently, it is not the case that "tragedy has narrative [only] in messenger-speeches, and the dramatic in its other parts, but in epics there is narrative only"; but the narrative is alike <in both>, with the proviso that it is more ample <in epic>.[27]

It is important to note that, as in the passage from Aristotle's *Rhetoric* quoted above, the messenger-speech here is a form of *apangelia*. More important, however, is what Philodemus's argument suggests about that of Aristotle. Philodemus here responds to an attempt to distinguish the genres of epic and tragedy by opposing narrative and dramatic modes. Aristotle evidently had insisted that the *apangelia* was an element fundamentally foreign to tragedy, appearing only in the form of an *angelia*. Judging from the argument of Philodemus, it appears that for Aristotle such a narrative was an epic element.[28] Philodemus, however, argues that such a distinction is unwarranted. He goes as far as to say—again disputing Aristotle—that narrative *(apangelia)* must be considered part of drama (col. V): ἐ[πιθ]ετέογ τὴν ἀπαγγ[ελί]αν ὡς μόριον τῆς δ[ρα]στι-κῆς. Against Aristotle, Philodemus argues that the messenger-speech—as an instance of narrative—deserves to be considered part of the genre rather than an import from elsewhere.

If Francesco Sbordone and Richard Janko are right in identifying Aristotle as the author of the text against which Philodemus argues, it may not be unwarranted to reconsider Aristotle's *Poetics* 1449b24–28 (quoted above), where tragedy is defined in opposition to *apangelia*. Janko (1991) has shown that the arguments against which Philodemus positions himself are in many particulars consistent with or even identical to arguments in the *Poetics*. It would, then, be a small step to consider the comments

27. Trans. Janko (1991, 14).

28. See the comments of Sbordone (1969, 354–56). Aristotle's project of establishing generic distinctions was in part the object of Philodemus's criticism. See Janko 1991, 24, and Greenberg 1990, 129.

apropos of the *apangelia* and tragedy in the extant work to conform with what appeared in *On Poets*. And if that is the case, we may be entitled to consider Aristotle's distinction between tragedy and narrative (*apangelia*) in the *Poetics* to have some application to the messenger-speech. In short, if Aristotle in *On Poets* sought to identify the messenger-speech as an intrusion of epic narrative into tragedy, his brief comments in the *Poetics* may well do much the same. Aristotle surely implies, if he does not make explicit, that the tragic *angelia* leads a peculiar life onstage.[29]

This peculiarity, I would like to suggest, derives from the tragic messenger's possession of the qualities that define the literary messenger. If Aristotle and Plato use the term *apangelia* to designate the narrative of the poet/narrator as well as to distinguish between epic and drama, the discourse of ancient literary criticism on this point recapitulates much of what the poetic tradition enacts. The suggestion that the *angelia* is a form of *apangelia* restates one of the principal roles of the messenger in the poetic tradition: as metaphor for the poet, the messenger constitutes an extradiegetic voice. And insofar as the messenger of tragedy is constructed on the model of his literary predecessor, the use of this metaphor suggests that the remarks of Aristotle (and Plato) about the *apangelia* apply with some force to the tragic messenger as well.

Aristotle's apparent identification of the *angelia* as an epic intrusion into tragedy not only underscores the near identity of *apangelia* and *angelia* at the level of poetic function: both constitute the exercise of (or claim to) an extradiegetic voice; it also formulates in more abstract terms what Aeschylus's *Persians* reveals about the tragic messenger: he acquires his privileged status by adopting the narrative practices of epic. In this way, the tragic messenger proves to descend from the literary messen-

---

29. One need not, of course, agree with Aristotle. Philodemus, after all, did not. The argument here is simply that the terminology generally, and Aristotle in particular, suggests that the messenger is "at home" in tragedy only by special arrangement.

ger, as he speaks an *angelia* that claims to be the ἀπαγγελία αὐτοῦ τοῦ ποιητοῦ ("the narrative of the poet himself").

In positing a messenger with an extradiegetic voice, both Aristotle and the poetic tradition encourage us to consider the tragic messenger as a figure with (a claim to) special privilege. As I have argued, however, such a privilege would contradict fundamental premises and interests of the tragic genre. And as Irene de Jong (1991) has shown, this privilege is at best flawed, for the messenger is merely another member of the fictional world onstage. As *dramatis persona* and as eyewitness to the events he reports, the messenger must submit to the constraints imposed by the stage. Or even his narrative constitutes a form of action. As inheritor of the literary messenger's privilege and as extradiegetic narrator, however, the messenger claims to escape those constraints. This double status, then, defines a central aspect of the conventional messenger, as he speaks with a voice that must negotiate the tensions that result from his ambiguous position. His narrative not only forms part of Aristotle's *mimesis;* it also claims—and to an appreciable degree functions as though possessing—an extradiegetic status.

Before moving on to an examination of some plays that offer extended commentary on the tragic messenger and the tensions inherent in his special status, I will make a brief survey of some techniques employed by tragic messengers in making this claim of privilege. My aim here is not to offer a comprehensive account of all *angeliai.* Rather, my interest is only to establish that the practices on view in Aeschylus's *Persians* are widespread, and that the tragic *angelia* typically seeks a status comparable to that of the *apangelia* as described above.

---

> In painting, the artist sometimes depicts himself (usually at the edge of the picture). The self-portrait. The artist depicts himself as an ordinary person and not as an artist, not as the creator of the picture.[30]

30. Bakhtin 1986, 149.

Central to the messenger's task of self-authorization is his claim of having been an eyewitness. His use of the first-person figures prominently in this task: he has to explain his position or vantage point vis-à-vis the action he reports. The messenger in Sophocles' *Antigone*, for example, begins his narrative by establishing his eyewitness status (1196–98):

ἐγὼ δὲ σῷ ποδαγὸς ἑσπόμην πόσει
πεδίον ἐπ' ἄκρον, ἔνθ' ἔκειτο νηλεὲς
κυνοσπάρακτον σῶμα Πολυνείκους ἔτι·

I followed your husband as an attendant to the edge of the field where the unpitied body of Polyneices, mangled by dogs, was still lying.

Similarly, in *Ajax*, in response to the *koruphaios* asking how and what he knows about Kalkhas's prophecy, the messenger places himself in the midst of the events he goes on to narrate (748):

τοσοῦτον οἶδα καὶ παρὼν ἐτύγχανον·

I know this much, as I happened to be present.

This sort of initial self-placement at the scene is very common in Euripidean messenger-speeches as well.[31] For example, at *Bacchae* 677–80 the messenger tells us what he was doing and where he was:

ἀγελαῖα μὲν βοσκήματ' ἄρτι πρὸς λέπας
μόσχων ὑπεξήκριζον, ἡνίχ' ἥλιος
ἀκτῖνας ἐξίησι θερμαίνων χθόνα.
ὁρῶ δὲ θιάσους τρεῖς γυναικείων χορῶν.

The grazing herds had just started to climb toward the hill country [at the time] when the sun sends its rays to warm the earth. I saw three bands of women dancing.

Similarly at 1043–45:

---

31. De Jong 1991, 4–5. Most often a plural is used.

ἐπεὶ θεράπνας τῆσδε Θηβαίας χθονὸς
λιπόντες ἐξέβημεν Ἀσωποῦ ῥοάς,
λέπας Κιθαιρώνειον εἰσεβάλλομεν.

When we had left behind the dwellings of the Theban country-
side and the waters of Asopus, we entered the rocky scrub of Mt.
Cithaeron.

In Euripides' *Suppliants* the messenger claims an excellent view (650–52):

λαμπρὰ μὲν ἀκτὶς ἡλίου, κανὼν σαφής,
ἔβαλλε γαῖαν· ἀμφὶ δ' Ἠλέκτρας πύλας
ἔστην θεατὴς πύργον εὐαγῆ λαβών.

The shining light of the sun, clear beam, struck the ground; I stood
as a spectator near the Electran gate, occupying a tower with a
clear view.

Similarly, the messenger in Euripides' *Electra* describes the location of
the events he reports (774–76):

ἐπεὶ μελάθρων τῶνδ' ἀπήραμεν πόδα,
ἐσβάντες ᾖμεν δίκροτον εἰς ἁμαξιτὸν
ἔνθ' ἦν ὁ καινὸς τῶν Μυκηναίων ἄναξ.

When we left the house, we came to a road for two wagons, and
there was the new lord of Mycenae.

While these uses of the first-person clearly place the messenger within
the frame of his story, they do no more than that. That is, although he
prepares his audience(s) for his story, he almost always makes himself no
more than a bystander.

In those cases where the messenger explicitly places himself at the
scene via the first-person, he tends to "fade into the background" as his
story progresses.[32] In his closing statement he often reminds us of his
role as narrator by using the first-person singular and perhaps by mak-

32. De Jong 1991, 5.

ing a judgment on the situation he has just described.[33] While there can be no doubt that in almost all cases the messenger takes care to legitimate his report by establishing his credentials as an eyewitness, the narrative that follows is a more complicated matter. Here it is possible to discern and analyze the tensions generated by the conflict between the messenger's role as an individual eyewitness and as narrator with a claim to extradiegetic status. I will begin by looking at the problem of physically locating the messenger in the events he describes.

## SOPHOCLES' *TRACHINIAE*

The nurse in Sophocles' *Trachiniae* arrives onstage from the house to report the death of Deianeira. The chorus finally understand that Deianeira has died by the sword, and then ask the Nurse if she saw the outrage (888):

> ἐπεῖδες, ὦ ματαία, τάνδ' ὕβριν;[34]

> Did you, in fact, see the gruesome deed?

The Nurse replies (889):

> ἐπεῖδον, ὡς δὴ πλησία παραστάτις.

> I saw it, as I was standing right next to her

Her response repeats the verb, emphasizing her eyewitness status as it doubly invokes the familiar claim of presence and proximity with πλησία and παραστάτις. The Nurse repeats her claim to autopsy and proximity, distinguishing herself from the chorus, who were not there and did not see (896–97):

> μᾶλλον δ' εἰ παροῦσα πλησία
> ἔλευσσες οἷ' ἔδρασε, κάρτ' ἂν ᾤκτισας.

---

33. See Friis Johansen 1959.

34. I depart from Lloyd-Jones and Wilson here in keeping the text of the manuscripts. See Easterling 1982 ad loc.

If you had been nearby and had seen what she did, you would have felt great pity.

Although always to some extent a cornerstone of the messenger's raison d'être, the claim to autopsy forms a refrain for the Nurse uncommon even among *angeliai*.[35] Between lines 899 and 946 she refers explicitly to her own vision four times (ὁρῶ, 912; λαθραῖον ὄμμ' ἐπεσκιασμένη / φρούρουν, 914–15; ὁρῶ δὲ τὴν γυναῖκα, 915; ὁρῶμεν, 930). This emphatic attention to her own vision acquires greater potency from the broader thematic importance of vision in her narrative. The Nurse represents the actions of Deianeira leading up to her death specifically as things seen, and she goes to some trouble to establish her claim of eyewitness status. Such a claim, however, is not a small one, as Deianeira moves about the house trying to escape notice (903, 907–9):

κρύψασ' ἑαυτὴν ἔνθα μή τις εἰσίδοι . . .
ἄλλη δὲ κἄλλη δωμάτων στρωφωμένη,
εἴ του φίλων βλέψειεν οἰκετῶν δέμας,
ἔκλαιεν ἡ δύστηνος εἰσορωμένη.

Hiding herself where no one would see her, . . . she wandered from one part of the house to another, and if she saw one of her servants, the pitiful woman would gaze at her and cry.

The Nurse here speaks not only about Deianeira, when she reports that she tried to hide, passing from room to room; she speaks also about herself. In addition to the repetitions mentioned above, Deianeira's own reluctance to be seen focuses our attention on the fact that the Nurse did manage to watch it all. Deianeira's pursuit of secrecy, we find, has been surpassed by that of the Nurse. Additionally, the Nurse begins two lines (914, 927) with the first-person singular pronoun (κἀγώ), marking her presence even more sharply. Furthermore, the Nurse's emphasis on her

---

35. The Nurse here employs the term used by the messenger in the *Persians* and of the Muses in the *Iliad* (παρεῖναι), as discussed above.

own vision is mirrored by Deianeira's desire to avoid being seen. That is, aside from dramatizing the accomplishment of the Nurse in bringing back her report, Deianeira's secrecy charges the phenomenon of vision even more.[36]

The Nurse begins her narrative with an account of what Deianeira saw(900–902):

ἐπεὶ παρῆλθε δωμάτων εἴσω μόνη
καὶ παῖδ' ἐν αὐλαῖς εἶδε κοῖλα δέμνια
στορνύνθ', ὅπως ἄψορρον ἀντῴη πατρί . . .

When she went alone into the house and saw her son spreading the hollow bedding so that he could go back to meet his father . . .

Deianeira's catching sight of Hyllus preparing the litter for Herakles initiates the narrative and seems to set the rest of the events in motion. Here the role of sight is underscored. The Nurse invokes her own vision to authorize her report as she identifies that of Deianeira as integral to the events that follow. Similarly, the servants in the house (φίλων οἰκετῶν, 908) are largely defined with respect to vision. Three times within seven lines the Nurse speaks of them seeing or being seen (μή τις εἰσίδοι, 903; βλέψειεν, 908; εἰσορωμένη, 909). This repetition crowds the passage with verbs of seeing as it incorporates the others into the narrative by defining them as visible or seeing subjects. They neither act nor feel: they are but eyes trying to catch a glimpse of Deianeira, or objects of her pathetic gaze.[37]

---

36. The participle εἰσορωμένη in line 909 aptly suggests this. Usually read as active in sense (Easterling 1982 *ad* 908, for example), it can also, of course, be read as passive: Deianeira's anxiety revolves around what she sees, as well as being seen.

37. It must be acknowledged that in representing the servants in this way the Nurse also creates an intensity of pathos perhaps not otherwise attainable. The image of Deianeira hunted by everyone's eyes, or feeling so hunted, surely suggests a pathetic scene.

Amid the repeated claims of autopsy by the Nurse, Deianeira's efforts to elude the gaze of others, and the definition of the servants in terms of vision, one person alone manages to see while remaining unseen: the Nurse. I have said that Deianeira's effort to hide calls attention to the Nurse's success in seeing what she reports. Similarly, the failure of Deianeira to elude the gaze of the Nurse emphasizes the Nurse's own ability to escape notice during her autopsy. In a narrative so overtly concerned with vision, this feat on the part of the Nurse deserves notice. I say the Nurse manages to escape notice. Clearly this is true of 912–26, where she acknowledges as much (912–16):

ἐπεὶ δὲ τῶνδ' ἔληξεν, ἐξαίφνης σφ' ὁρῶ
τὸν Ἡράκλειον θάλαμον εἰσορμωμένην.
κἀγὼ λαθραῖον ὄμμ' ἐπεσκιασμένη
φρούρουν· ὁρῶ δὲ τὴν γυναῖκα δεμνίοις
τοῖς Ἡρακλείοις στρωτὰ βάλλουσαν φάρη.

Then she stopped, and suddenly I saw her rushing into Herakles' bedroom. Secretly from the shadows I watched. I saw the woman arrange the bedding strewn on Herakles' bed.

But is it equally true that she goes unseen in 900–911? Although I do not think it possible to answer this question definitively, it remains a question worth asking. As she begins her account, she says that she saw what Deianeira saw (900–906):

ἐπεὶ παρῆλθε δωμάτων εἴσω μόνη
καὶ παῖδ' ἐν αὐλαῖς εἶδε κοῖλα δέμνια
στορνύνθ', ὅπως ἄψορρον ἀντῴη πατρί,
κρύψασ' ἑαυτὴν ἔνθα μή τις εἰσίδοι,
βρυχᾶτο μὲν βωμοῖσι προσπίπτουσ' ὅτι
γένοιντ' ἐρῆμοι, κλαῖε δ' ὀργάνων ὅτου
ψαύσειεν οἷς ἐχρῆτο δειλαία πάρος·

When she went alone into the house and saw her son spreading the hollow bedding so that he could go back to meet his father, hiding herself where no one would see her, she moaned, falling at the altars, that they would be deserted, and she cried whenever she touched some object that she, pitiful woman, used to use.

Whether line 903 (κρύψασ' ἑαυτὴν ἔνθα μή τις εἰσίδοι) moves Deianeira from where she sees Hyllus or not,[38] she clearly hides herself at some point after she has seen her son. From her hiding place she moans, presumably thinking herself hidden. P. E. Easterling comments: "She evidently sees and is seen by the servants."[39] The only evidence for this conclusion is the existence of the *angelia* itself. That is, the Nurse at any rate saw her. But what of the other servants? They are certainly included in μή τις εἰσίδοι. But we hear no more of them until 908, at which point Deianeira is on the move again. I think we can agree with Easterling on this point only if we assume that the Nurse's vantage point is the same as that of the other slaves. But does this conflation make sense in light of the Nurse's narrative as a whole?

When she does mention the servants overtly, she speaks of them in such a way as to dissociate herself from them: at 908 she speaks of Deianeira seeing one of the servants. This does not, of course, necessarily exclude the Nurse herself, but it would be stretching the Greek here to understand the Nurse to be speaking in this way of a group she belongs to. Furthermore, at 912–26 she clearly distinguishes herself from the others, and we learn that she alone saw what she there describes. Even if we must hesitate to say that the Nurse escaped Deianeira's notice throughout the entire episode, it is clear that she represents her point of view as unique and distinguished by elusiveness. Lines 914–15 epitomize the character of her self-representation:

38. Easterling (1982 ad loc.) takes it this way. Although this makes good sense, especially since there is no indication that Hyllus hears her when she moans at 904, it is not the only possible reading. The focus of the narrative might gain in intensity by ignoring the effect of the moan on Hyllus. In fact, one might reasonably expect that Hyllus would have heard such a sound— βρυχᾶτο—even from another part of the house.

39. Easterling 1982 *ad* 903.

κἀγὼ λαθραῖον ὄμμ' ἐπεσκιασμένη
φρούρουν· ὁρῶ δὲ τὴν γυναῖκα . . .

Secretly from the shadows I watched. I saw the woman . . .

She alone saw what happened. She alone was not seen.

## ALCESTIS

The servant in Euripides' *Alcestis* delivers an *angelia* (152–98) notable for its lack of first-person pronouns.[40] Because she is an *exangelos* (a messenger who emerges from the house to report events there), her claim to eyewitness status requires little if any justification. If we have no doubt that she saw (and heard) what she reports, we nonetheless are never reminded that the narrative we hear represents her experience. Unlike the messengers of *Persians* and *Trachiniae*, here the servant is entirely absent.[41]

The servant begins her narrative in a manner quite similar to that of the Nurse in *Trachiniae*. At 158–59 the action begins with Alcestis perceiving the arrival of the day of her death:

40. De Jong 1991, 7.

41. De Jong comments that "the messenger should be understood as included in the third-person plural of 192 . . . which is not difficult after her introduction in 136–7 as ἀλλ' ἥδ' ὀπαδῶν ἐκ δόμων τις ἔρχεται δακρυρροοῦσα" (1991, 7). She is undoubtedly right that a positivistic search for this servant (messenger) will place her among the other servants. My interest, however, is in the rhetorical effect of her use of the third-person, that of noticeably removing the messenger from the narrative. Citing Erdmann (1964, 90 n. 2), de Jong remarks: "The self-effacement of this Messenger seems intended not to give the story 'den Anschein größeren Objektivität', but to concentrate as much as possible on the figure of Alcestis" (1991, 7). Aside from the question of intention, the effect of this self-effacement clearly encompasses what both de Jong and Erdmann see. For my purposes, Erdmann's remark is more illuminating: the apparent absence of the messenger confers a greater authority on her narrative, inasmuch as it creates the "illusion of greater objectivity."

ἐπεὶ γὰρ ἤσθεθ' ἡμέραν τὴν κυρίαν
ἥκουσαν . . .

For when she realized that the day of reckoning was at hand . . .

Whereas in *Trachiniae* the strategy of self-effacement gives way to repeated claims of autopsy, here in *Alcestis* the initial stance of the servant vis-à-vis her narrative remains unchanged: she is not in it. We can only infer, for example, that she followed Alcestis through the house: Alcestis bathes (159–60); takes clothing "from inner chambers or closets";[42] moves to the altar of Hestia (162–69); visits all of the altars (πάντας) in the house, ritually breaking off shoots of myrtle at each (170–74); withdraws to the bedroom (175–85); and begins to leave the bedroom and then returns (185–88).

The servant's implicit claim to autopsy is made more strictly necessary by her two direct quotations of Alcestis. At 163–69 Alcestis prays at the altar of Hestia, and at 177–82 she bids farewell to her marriage bed. With these two passages of direct speech we realize that the servant was not merely watching from a fixed spot, noting to which parts of the house Alcestis went. She must have been close by in order to hear the words clearly.[43] Furthermore, she describes in some detail what Alcestis did at the altars (172) and in the bedroom (183ff). If we ask, we must conclude that this servant followed Alcestis on her wanderings through the house.

When she does finally mention the group to which she presumably belongs, she speaks of them inclusively as a group (192–95):

πάντες δ' ἔκλαιον οἰκέται κατὰ στέγας
δέσποιναν οἰκτίροντες· ἡ δὲ δεξιὰν

---

42. Dale 1954 *ad* 160.

43. In principle it is not, of course, impossible either that the house was small enough to allow the servant to hear everything from some specific place or that Alcestis spoke very loudly. Perhaps line 170—πάντας δὲ βωμούς, οἳ κατ' Ἀδμήτου δόμους—is most telling that the house is not small.

προύτειν' ἑκάστῳ κοὔτις ἦν οὕτω κακὸς
ὃν οὐ προσεῖπε καὶ προσερρήθη πάλιν.

All of the servants through the house cried, pitying their mistress.
She reached out her right hand to each of them, and no one was too
lowly for her to speak to and listen to in turn.

This group in some sense surely includes her. But the use of the third-person here endows this messenger with a presence that leaves little trace. Although the extent of self-effacement here represents something of an extreme case, it exhibits features present in other *angeliai* as well.

## PHOENISSAE

Two of the four messenger-speeches in Euripides' *Phoenissae* (1219–58 and 1356–1424) share with that of the servant in *Alcestis* the complete absence of the first-person.[44] The final *angelia* (1427–79) introduces a first-person only after 35 lines, at 1461. After reporting Eteocles' proposal of the single combat of the two brothers and Polyneices' approval, the messenger recounts the response of the two armies (1238–39):

πάντες δ' ἐπερρόθησαν Ἀργεῖοι τάδε
Κάδμου τε λαὸς ὡς δίκαι' ἡγούμενοι.

All of the Argives and Cadmeans roared back in approval, thinking his proposal just.

In conjunction with the inclusive phrasing (πάντες . . . Ἀργεῖοι . . . Κάδμου τε λαὸς), his use of the third-person silently removes him as an

---

44. ὤφελον at 1222 clearly inserts the messenger's opinion, however. Obviously the absence of explicit references to himself in his narrative does not remove signs of the messenger altogether. On these passages from Eur. *Phoen.* see Mastronarde (1994 *ad* 1217–63), who identifies cases of "epic reminiscence."

actor from the scene. This is again a presence that leaves few traces, aside from the narrative itself.

A few lines later preparations for the fighting begin (1248–53):

παρεξιόντες δ' ἄλλος ἄλλοθεν φίλων
λόγοις ἐθάρσυνόν τε κἀξηύδων τάδε·
Πολύνεικες, ἐν σοὶ Ζηνὸς ὀρθῶσαι βρέτας
τρόπαιον Ἄργει τ' εὐκλεᾶ δοῦναι λόγον·
Ἐτεοκλέα δ' αὖ· Νῦν πόλεως ὑπερμαχεῖς,
νῦν καλλίνικος γενόμενος σκήπτρων κρατεῖς.

Approaching them from various spots, their allies encouraged them with words, saying the following: "Polyneices, it is for you to set up a statue of triumph for Zeus and to bring fame to Argos." And then to Eteocles: "Now you are fighting for the city; now with a victory you will control the scepter."

Here the *philoi* of Polyneices and Eteocles are similarly "others" (ἄλλος ἄλλοθεν).[45] The third-person here is intensified by the vague generalization that grants speech to numerous anonymous people.[46]

After being fitted with their armor, Polyneices and Eteocles approach each other between the armies. Polyneices utters a prayer to Hera, asking that he be allowed to kill his brother. The messenger then tells us of the reaction among the armies (1370–71):

πολλοῖς δ' ἐπῄει δάκρυα τῆς τύχης ὅση
κἄβλεψαν ἀλλήλοισι διαδόντες κόρας.[47]

Many shed tears at the magnitude of the events, casting glances at one another.

45. One might reasonably expect that the messenger is not counted among the φίλοι but for Jocasta's greeting to him at 1072: ὦ φίλτατ'.
46. Cf. de Jong 1987.
47. In keeping τύχης of the manuscripts, I follow Mastronarde 1994 rather than Diggle, who prints Hermann's εὐχῆς.

Again, the pathos of the moment is reflected only in others: the messenger appears to be immune.

The messenger further removes himself from the events and from the narrative at 1371 where he describes the looks exchanged by those in tears. Here, in addition to the acting subjects being in the third-person, the messenger constructs a perceptual point of view that verges on the ideal. He not only remained immune to what many (πολλοῖς) found grievous, but he was able to observe the tearful glances of the others. His description of their looks, furthermore, contains a degree of detail that suggests the ideality of his viewpoint. The specificity of the periphrasis (διαδόντες κόρας) freezes the action temporarily and allows us to look—along with him—into the eyes of the "many" as they look at one another.[48]

Another passage generates its pathetic effect by exploiting the immediacy of vision. Shortly after the start of their combat the two brothers crouch behind their shields for protection. Each then tries to get a glimpse of the other (1384–89):

εἰ δ' ὄμμ' ὑπερσχὸν ἴτυος ἅτερος μάθοι,
λόγχην ἐνώμα, στόματι προφθῆναι θέλων.
ἀλλ' εὖ προσῆγον ἀσπίδων κεγχρώμασιν
ὀφθαλμόν, ἀργὸν ὥστε γίγνεσθαι δόρυ.

48. Parallel passages provide a clue to deciphering this expression. Similar phrasing occurs twice in *Or.*: δόχμιά νυν κόρας διάφερ' ὀμμάτων at 1261 and ἑλίσσετέ νυν βλέφαρον, / κόρας διάδοτε πάντα διὰ βοστρύχων at 1266–67. Willink (1986 *ad* 1261–62) comments: "The whole chorus . . . is to direct one eye to the left, the other to the right (as it were)". Although the text at 1266–67 is in some doubt, attention is called not only to the pupils of the eyes but also to the eyelids. That is, the phrase here does not mean simply "look." The emphasis on the features of the eyes suggests a degree of care and concentration beyond a simple command to "look." A similar expression occurs at *Bacch.* 1087. Cf. Roux 1970 *ad* 1086–87.

πλείων δὲ τοῖς ὁρῶσιν ἐστάλασσ' ἱδρὼς
ἢ τοῖσι δρῶσι διὰ φίλων ὀρρωδίαν.

If either one of them saw the other's eye beyond the edge of the
shield, he launched his spear, hoping to hit him straightaway with its
sharp point. But they skillfully peered through the shields' eyelet
holes, so that the spear would fall in vain. Those watching sweated
more than the actors out of fear for their friends.[49]

Although one might want to locate the messenger among the onlookers,
there are no signs that sweat dripped from the messenger, as it did from
the others watching, or that he was subject to the fear they felt. Just as at
1370, his ability to perceive and to describe these relatively subtle effects
of apprehension and anxiety implies that he himself was largely unaf-
fected. His presence at the scene is unlike that of the others described,
as the use of the third-person affirms.[50]

Erich Henning remarks that in messenger-speeches the poet often
describes not actually what happened, but rather the effect of events on
those who witnessed them. Apropos of *Phoenissae* 1388–89 he claims
that the messenger describes the scene in such a way as to make us un-
derstand that all present were moved (1910, 32–33). His formulation is
particularly telling inasmuch as it is so inclusive. Surely Henning is right
that as a result of such a narrative we (are to) understand that everyone
present was affected.[51] The messenger's implicit self-portrayal, there-
fore, constitutes a striking anomaly.

49. Here again I use the text of Mastronarde (1994), although he denies
that there could be such holes in the shield (ad loc.). Perhaps we should
translate "They peered skillfully over the shields' grainy edges."

50. Mastronarde (1994 *ad* 1388–89) speaks of "the epic use of an imag-
inary spectator's reaction" and refers to Eur. *Supp.* 684–87a, 719–20b, with
the note of Collard.

51. As *comparanda*, he cites *Med.* 1167–80; *Hipp.* 1173–77, 1204–05,
1216–17; *HF* 952; *Supp.* 718–19; *Ion* 1205–6; *IT* 1339–44; *Hel.* 1549–51,
1589–91.

## HERAKLES

The messenger in Euripides' *Herakles* arrives onstage to report the deaths of Herakles' children. He recounts the sacrificial ritual within the palace, amid which Herakles comes to a sudden stop as his madness sets in. Herakles then, we are told, announces his intention to go to Mycenae to kill Eurystheus, whereupon he imagines that he mounts his chariot. This clearly bizarre turn of events elicits a double reaction from the attendants (950–52):

> διπλοῦς δ' ὀπαδοῖς ἦν γέλως φόβος θ' ὁμοῦ,
> καί τις τόδ' εἶπεν, ἄλλος εἰς ἄλλον δρακών·
> παίζει πρὸς ἡμᾶς δεσπότης ἢ μαίνεται;[52]

> At the same moment, laughter and fear came over the servants, and as they looked at one another someone said, "Is our master playing with us or is he mad?"

Richard Kannicht groups this passage with *Andromache* 1104 and *Helen* 1589 as deriving from the Homeric phrase ὧδε δέ τις εἴπεσκεν ἰδὼν εἰς πλησίον ἄλλον ("Thus did someone speak looking at his neighbor").[53] This particular formulation introducing what is called a "*tis*-speech" appears four times in Homer,[54] while a closely related formulaic sentence

---

52. This form of expression, the *tis*-speech, appears, of course, in Homer, and this is one of several examples in Euripides. See Kannicht 1969 *ad* 1589; Bond 1988 *ad* 950–52; de Jong 1987 and 1991, 14 n. 13. The same kind of "confusion" of singular and plural is common in Homer as well: e.g., *Il.* 2.271ff., 3.297ff. De Jong argues that in the *Iliad* these *tis*-speeches "are really spoken as such by an anonymous character. . . . The iterative verbform in the introductory formula and the plural in the capping formula are only meant as an indication for the narratee that the one speech quoted in the text must be taken as representative for a whole body of speeches with similar content" (1987, 82).

53. Kannicht 1969 *ad* 1589.

54. At *Il.* 2.271 = 4.81 = 22.372 = *Od.* 8.328.

—ὧδε δέ τις εἴπεσκεν Ἀχαιῶν τε Τρώων τε· ("Thus did [one of] the Achaeans and Trojans speak")—appears twice.[55] *Herakles* 951 is indeed similar to the Homeric examples but differs in an important way from the other Euripidean citations. The Homeric passages present the quotation as spoken both by an individual and by a group. Neither the *Andromache* nor the *Helen* passage shares this characteristic: although we do not know who in particular spoke the lines quoted in these two plays, we do know that a single person uttered the words. This, of course, cannot be said of the Homeric passages nor of that from *Herakles*. And the comparison of the latter passage with those from Homer is instructive.

Reading the Homeric examples in such a way as to eliminate confusion, de Jong argues that "there are no indications *within* the *tis*-speeches themselves that point to a compiling activity by the primary narrator." She goes on to conclude that "the one speech quoted in the text must be taken as representative for a whole body of speeches with similar content" (1987, 82). Whether we conclude that such *tis*-speeches in Homer represent a compiling activity or not, we can agree with de Jong that these speeches offer "a glimpse of the mind of the masses, which are normally bound to silence in epic" (82).

Thus understood, such speeches imply a certain form of self-portrayal by the narrator: he implicitly presents himself as the arbiter of what constitutes a representative speech. He implicitly claims either that he heard many statements and chose from among them one that could fairly stand in for all the others, or that he heard many statements and that he has ordered elements from any number of them into a coherent, representative example. In either case, he claims a familiarity with the group as a whole and with the individual members of the group. And this familiarity is such that it enables him to select (or to compose) a "representative" speech.[56]

---

55. At *Il.* 3.297 = 4.85.

56. See Richardson 1990, 79–82, and 224 n. 28, where he argues against de Jong, suggesting instead that the *tis*-speech represents the invention of the narrator.

For Homer this presents no problem. From the beginning of each of the two epics the narrator presents himself as endowed with such abilities, aided by the Muse in telling a story of another time and place. The structure of the fiction provides him with timeless access to other places and other minds. He defines himself and his role in the poem in such a way as to authorize his omniscience and omnipresence. It therefore causes no surprise at all if we find him claiming to know what each one of a group said, assuming even that they spoke randomly, often at the same time, and with varying degrees of loudness—all things quite likely. It is, in fact, the task of such a narrator to synthesize, or at least to order, such a plethora of voices into a comprehensible narrative.

For the messenger, on the other hand, things are different. He does not have timeless access to other places and other minds. Consequently, the implicit claim that he heard the many voices and either chose one as representative or compiled a representative speech raises the simple question, How? Far from uttering one of the many statements that line 952 represents, he was busy listening to and evaluating all of those statements. Far from feeling the confusion that lies behind line 952, he moved among the attendants as the Homeric narrator moves among the soldiers before Troy.

If any doubt about this matter remains, one need only remember that line 951, as all commentators point out, closely echoes Homer. Similar lines are in fact not infrequent in Homer, making the echo only more forceful. In appropriating a line of the Homeric narrator, the messenger implicitly claims a comparable authority. Wilamowitz understood this Homeric borrowing to accomplish precisely this.[57] Simply put, this messenger claims the status of an extradiegetic narrator, modeled on the Homeric example.[58]

57. "Der Dichter gesteht durch diese Paraphrase des homerischen ὧδε δέ τις εἴπεσκεν ἰδὼν εἰς πλησίον ἄλλον, daß er eine epische Erzählung liefert" (1895 *ad* 951).

58. Two Euripidean passages parody the convention of the messenger endowed with a status comparable to that of the Homeric narrator. The

The tragic *angelia* has been likened to film.[59] The apparent intention behind this analogy is the characterization of the messenger as a passive recording device, a kind of "camera" that reliably tells exactly and only what it has seen. The *angelia*, of course, produces rather than records the events it narrates, and this narrative, like that of the camera, has been shown to be highly "edited" and rhetorical.[60] Nonetheless, the camera and the tragic messenger do find analogues in one another, at least in "classical narrative film."[61] Both play important roles in the production and editing of their "narratives," and yet both seek to efface this role. The self-effacement of the messenger is comparable to

> the imperative that the camera deny its own existence as much as possible, fostering the illusion that what is shown has an autonomous existence, independent of any technological interference or any coercive gaze.[62]

This need, says Kaja Silverman, gives rise to the practice of shot/reverse-shot that produces the effect that "the gaze which directs our look seems to belong to a fictional character rather than the camera."[63] Both mes-

---

messenger in *Helen* pushes this conventional authorization to the breaking point, as he recounts his miraculous escape from the slaughter carried out by Menelaos on the ship; see especially 1613–18, with the comments of Kannicht (1969 ad loc.). The *Orestes* is the most famous Euripidean parody of the *angelia*; see especially 1425 where the ideality of this messenger's point of view is mocked.

59. Groeneboom 1930 *ad* 249–52 and Howald cited by Di Gregorio 1967, 19.

60. Principally de Jong 1991. Cf. Roisman 1990.

61. Browne 1986, 102.

62. Silverman 1983, 201–2. Of course this "imperative" may be (intentionally) violated, especially in cinema that does not belong to the "classical narrative" type.

63. "The shot/reverse-shot formation is a cinematic set in which the second shot shows the field from which the first shot is assumed to have

senger and camera attempt to obscure their own productive roles. The practice of attributing a perception to a character within the fictional world is one tool that supports this project.

In describing the sacrifice in Euripides' *Electra*, the messenger reports that Orestes responds to a challenge from Aigisthos to "prove true the rumor about the Thessalians" (818) that reflects the Thessalian boast of their ability to butcher bulls and tame horses. Orestes proceeds to cut up the calf (819–26), whereupon Aigisthos takes up the innards in his hands and examines them. At this point the wide-angle view of the narrative gives way to a close-up, and we see what Aigisthos sees (826–29):

> ἱερὰ δ' ἐς χεῖρας λαβὼν
> Αἴγισθος ἤθρει. καὶ λοβὸς μὲν οὐ προσῆν
> σπλάγχνοις, πύλαι δὲ καὶ δοχαὶ χολῆς πέλας
> κακὰς ἔφαινον τῷ σκοποῦντι προσβολάς.

> Taking the innards into his hands, Aigisthos stared at them. The liver lacked a lobe, and the double openings near the gallbladder revealed to him as he looked [that] a hostile attack [was coming].

Whatever the proper interpretation of these lines,[64] the detail of the view they offer stands out. Although it is certainly possible that the messenger, a servant of Orestes, was positioned close enough to the sacrifice to see the portal vein and gallbladder,[65] the messenger avoids this ques-

---

been taken" (Silverman 1983, 201). As Silverman points out in a note on the following page, this order may be reversed. That is, the first shot may show "the field from which" the following shot "is assumed to have been taken." This is the order in the examples that follow.

64. See Denniston 1939 ad loc.

65. The first 16 lines of the messenger's narrative (774–90) make frequent use of the first-person. He locates himself, along with Orestes and Pylades, in the watery meadow (777) and then moves himself, along with the others, to Aigisthos's house or cottage (if one keeps 790). Once the movement has stopped, however, wherever the group may be (see Denniston 1939 *ad* 791ff.), the first-persons vanish along with the messenger (aside from his

tion by introducing this detailed view as the object of Aigisthos's gaze: we see, for the moment, with Aigisthos's eyes. The syntactical ambiguity of the participle in the dative case (τῷ σκοποῦντι) underscores this: as complement of the verb (ἔφαινον), the participle may indicate anyone who looked at the innards; construed as the object of the coming hostile attack (κακὰς προσβολάς), it clearly defines Aigisthos as author of the gaze. The importance of this shot/reverse-shot presentation lies in its subtle manipulation of the apparent relationship between the messenger and his narrative: the particular condition of the innards and what they signify appear not as the object of the messenger's perception, but rather as the objects of Aigisthos's perception. Here a character entirely within the frame of the narrative poses as guarantor of the offered perception, thus inscribing not only the perceived object but also the perception of that object entirely within the narrative frame. As a result, the narrator, that is, the messenger, appears to vanish in much the same way as the camera removes the traces of its own existence in the shot/reverse-shot sequence.

———

A similar sequence occurs in Euripides' *Herakles*. The narrative tells of a sacrifice of purification that Herakles oversees. Present are Amphitryo, Megara, and a group of children (presumably including the children of Herakles).[66] While performing the preparatory ritual Herakles is struck by madness and falls suddenly silent (928–30). As Herakles' silence persists, the gaze of the narrator gives way to that of Herakles' sons. They train their eyes on their father, establishing a frame for and silently authorizing the image that follows (930–34):

———

presence as marked by σε at 808 and σῷ κασιγνήτῳ at 814, for example). The slaves of Aigisthos prepare the sacrifice (798ff.) and are then pushed away by Orestes as he enlists Pylades as his assistant (821–22). These lines give the impression of thoroughly accounting for those present. In fact, we see that there is one notable omission.

66. Reading τέκνων at 925 with Canter et al.

καὶ χρονίζοντος πατρὸς
παῖδες προσέσχον ὄμμ'· ὁ δ' οὐκέθ' αὑτὸς ἦν,
ἀλλ' ἐν στροφαῖσιν ὀμμάτων ἐφθαρμένος
ῥίζας τ' ἐν ὄσσοις αἱματῶπας ἐκβαλὼν
ἀφρὸν κατέσταζ' εὐτρίχος γενειάδος.

As their father paused, the children directed their gaze at him; he was no longer himself, but rather with spinning eyes he was wasting away, and with bulging bloodshot eyes he oozed foam down his hairy chin.

This first manifestation of Herakles' madness, though not yet explicitly identified as such, appears to arise entirely within the scene independently of the narrative voice. As a result, the gruesome quality of the scene is offered as what the children saw, rather than as the product of the messenger's narrative skill.

———

Finally, I turn to Euripides' *Medea*. Following a familiar pattern, the messenger here makes relatively frequent use of the first-person (1136–44), after which the first-person disappears entirely until his concluding reflection (1222–30). The scene depicting Glauke's reception of Jason and his children and her subsequent donning of the poisoned robe is structured by many references to her vision. The first four lines of this narrative mention her sight or her eyes three times (1144–49):

δέσποινα δ' ἦν νῦν ἀντὶ σοῦ θαυμάζομεν,
πρὶν μὲν τέκνων σῶν εἰσιδεῖν ξυνωρίδα,
πρόθυμον εἶχ' ὀφθαλμὸν εἰς Ἰάσονα·
ἔπειτα μέντοι προυκαλύψατ' ὄμματα
λευκήν τ' ἀπέστρεψ' ἔμπαλιν παρηίδα,
παίδων μυσαχθεῖσ' εἰσόδους·

The woman whom we now call Mistress, instead of you, before she saw your two sons, looked with eager eye toward Jason. She then covered her eyes and turned her white cheek away, loathing the children's arrival.

After Jason's attempt to soothe her (1151–55), we learn that it was not his eloquence that changed her mind, but rather the robe that she saw (1156–57):

ἡ δ' ὡς ἐσεῖδε κόσμον, οὐκ ἠνέσχετο,
ἀλλ' ἤνεσ' ἀνδρὶ πάντα.

When she saw the robe, she could not hold herself back; she agreed with her husband about everything.

She then wraps herself in the new robe and adorns herself with the golden crown. Her fascination with what she sees and with how she appears reaches a peak when she gazes at herself in the mirror (1161–66):

λαμπρῷ κατόπτρῳ σχηματίζεται κόμην,
ἄψυχον εἰκὼ προσγελῶσα σώματος.
κἄπειτ' ἀναστᾶσ' ἐκ θρόνων διέρχεται
στέγας, ἁβρὸν βαίνουσα παλλεύκῳ ποδί,
δώροις ὑπερχαίρουσα, πολλὰ πολλάκις
τένοντ' ἐς ὀρθὸν ὄμμασι σκοπουμένη.

She arranges her hair in the bright mirror, smiling at the lifeless image of her body. Then rising from her chair, she walks through the house, stepping gingerly with her gleaming white feet, taking great delight in the gifts, and very frequently she gazes with her eyes at her foot stretched out straight.

Here the pleonasm πολλὰ πολλάκις finds an echo in ὄμμασι σκοπουμένη, and the double redundancy mimics the constancy of her vision.

Nowhere in this passage do we encounter a substantial description of what Glauke sees.[67] And yet the many directions and objects of her gaze provide a sketch of the scene in outline form, so to speak. The sheer

---

67. She sees : ξυνωρίδα, 1145; Ἰάσονα, 1146; κόσμον, 1156; κόμην, 1161; ἄψυχον εἰκὼ, 1162; τένοντα ὀρθὸν, 1166.

number of references to Glauke as seeing subject suggests that she is the one beholding much of what constitutes the scene.[68]

If thus far (1166) the point of view of the messenger makes ample room for that of Glauke, at 1167 the eye of the absent eyewitness defining the ideal perceptual point of view reasserts its primacy. The messenger tells us that what followed was terrifying (δεινόν) to behold. As we have seen elsewhere, the subject of the terrifying perception remains unnamed. He tells us that Glauke's skin changed color and that she fell trembling into a chair (1168–70). Thereupon, an old woman-servant, thinking a god had intervened, uttered a cry of joy (1173–75)

πρίν γ' ὁρᾷ διὰ στόμα
χωροῦντα λευκὸν ἀφρόν, ὀμμάτων τ' ἄπο
κόρας στρέφουσαν, αἷμά τ' οὐκ ἐνὸν χροΐ·

before she saw the white foam pour from the mouth, the pupils spinning out of the eyes and the absence of blood in her skin.

Here the perception marking the old woman's cry as inappropriate belongs to the old woman herself: the details of Glauke's symptoms appear as objects of the old woman's gaze. This sequence, too, constitutes the equivalent of the shot/reverse-shot in cinema.

As in the case of *Herakles*, the presence of eyewitnesses to the horror allows us, as we hear about the ghastly events, to imagine the emotional reaction of the eyewitnesses.[69] The presence of someone looking at what we hear about encourages us to visualize what we hear and to identify

68. Page summarizes Glauke's condition: "She cannot bear to *see* the children who remind her that Jason has long been married to another woman . . . she cannot take her *eyes* off her wonderful Jason . . . she is quick-tempered . . . but gives in the moment she *sees* the new dress and the crown . . . she tries them on at once, arranges her hair, and smiles at herself in the *mirror*, almost before her visitors have gone. Then she walks daintily up and down and turns to *see* how the dress hangs at the back" (1938 *ad* 1156, emphasis added).

69. Cf. Henning 1910, 32–33.

with the viewing eyewitness. Nonetheless, although the messenger was just such an eyewitness, he does not offer himself as such. Instead, he effaces his own presence as he attributes the disturbing view to another. This practice seeks to draw us into the subjectivity of someone other than the narrator and in the process to obscure the fact that this very "subjectivity" is his own creation. If the presence of this (other) eyewitness renders the horror more dramatic and somehow more "real," it also demonstrates the refusal of the messenger as narrator to play the role of eyewitness. The gaze of these others, then, marks the (apparent) absence of the messenger's gaze.[70]

Employing such practices as these, the tragic messenger borrows from epic narrative in his attempt to claim the privileged status of the literary messenger. Tragic *angeliai* frequently frustrate the attempt to locate the narrator at the scene; they often endow the narrator with virtual disembodiment that allows for free, safe, and invisible movement within the scene reported; and they employ strategies that serve to establish perceptions either as autonomous or as belonging to figures other than the narrator. Narratives engaging in these practices contain an implicit claim to extradiegetic status. As such, tragic messenger-speeches claim that as *angeliai*, they are *apangeliai* as well.

———

Before turning to the examination of several plays in greater detail, it is worth pausing briefly to consider which figures in the tragic texts are in fact messengers. While many tragic messengers bear names in our manuscripts that explicitly identify them as such (ἄγγελος or ἐξάγγελος), a good number of figures who perform roles often indistinguishable from these named figures are not so named. This latter group ranges from the herald (κῆρυξ) in Aeschylus's *Agamemnon* to the servant in Euripides' *Ion* and Talthybios in his *Hecuba*, for example. As this last example sug-

———

70. Metz, speaking of the effect of the "spectator" within the film, remarks that "as we see through him we see ourselves not seeing him" (1982, 46).

gests, named characters who appear elsewhere in myth, and who may even have other roles within the drama, can perform as messengers. Hyllus in Sophocles' *Trachiniae* (749–806)[71] is among the most striking cases of those who are far from being limited to the role of messenger and yet produce reports of off-stage events virtually indistinguishable from those of figures explicitly identified as messengers.[72] Similarly, there are characters in tragedy who perform in a manner akin to that of *angeloi*, who have otherwise small roles, and who yet frustrate any attempt to classify them with figures explicitly identified as messengers, or with those generally understood to belong to such a class. This (small) group includes the guard in Sophocles' *Antigone* and the Phrygian in Euripides' *Orestes*. These two figures are comic, and this shared trait holds a clue to understanding their anomalous status as messengers, for part of the comedy in both cases is parody of the conventional messenger.[73]

It is not hard to see that any system of classification that could comprehend all of these figures in a single category would tell us little. But the challenge need not be that of deciding who is and who is not a messenger. Such a project, I submit, would amount to a matter of definition. A more productive approach, I suggest, is to recognize that all tragic messengers, near messengers, and pseudomessengers have been produced more or less in accordance with, or at variance with, a conventional, "ideal" type.[74] As such, these "real" tragic figures represent the texts' ongoing engagement with an idealized conventional form.

71. Including an omitted augment in the manuscripts at 767.

72. One might also place in this category Oedipus of Soph. *OT* 774–833, or perhaps even Clytemnestra of Aesch. *Ag.* 281–350.

73. See, for example, *Ant.* 223–30 with the remarks of Seidensticker 1982, 78–80, and Griffith 1999 ad loc.; *Or.* 1425 with the comment of Willink 1986 ad loc. In some respects the charioteer of *Rhesos* may be grouped with these two figures. See below, chapter 5.

74. "Pseudomessenger" here refers to the Paidagogos in Sophocles' *Electra*. Some may choose to include other characters in this category.

Far from being a static and inconsequential functional device, the messenger proves in each case to be the result of a complex negotiation of conventional form. In short, our own difficulty in answering the question of who is a messenger reflects how this very question lives on in our texts. As I will argue below, the texts effectively restate this question even as they offer possible answers to it. As they negotiate the conventional form, tragic texts not only demonstrate the range of this figure's utility, but they also illuminate, interrogate, and mock the very workings of the theatrical convention at issue. In the chapters that follow I will argue that each of the texts in question performs precisely these kinds of negotiations.

Consequently, I would rephrase the question, "Who is a messenger?" and ask, "How does [the character in question] embody, alter, or reject the traits of the conventional figure?" Although I would maintain in principle that no "pure" messenger exists—that is, that all of the messengers in our texts constitute to a greater or lesser degree a rewriting of a preexisting conventional form—as a practical matter it will be useful to think of the messenger in Aeschylus's *Persians* as a close approximation of this "ideal" type.[75] T. G. Rosenmeyer, for example, has called the narrative of this character a "messenger-speech in its purest and at the same time most ambitious form" (1982, 198). In short, although every tragic messenger-speech affords adequate opportunity to question the convention, the Persian runner's report can serve as a practical point of reference for the analysis of *angeliai* elsewhere. In this way, we can gain more by asking how Hyllus in Sophocles' *Trachiniae*, for example, constitutes a commentary on the conventional figure—or, indeed, how an understanding of the conventional figure as outlined in this study sheds light on the role of Hyllus—than by asking whether or not this Sopho-

75. See above, chapter 1, where I argue that even this, our earliest, text displays a (perhaps) surprising interest in the functioning of this conventional figure.

clean character is a messenger.[76] In the pages that follow I will take up several of the more provocative and enlightening engagements with this conventional form, arguing both that the individual messengers in question illuminate the workings of the convention and that an appreciation of what this convention entails discloses much that has gone unnoticed about these messengers and about the plays they inhabit.

There is, however, one common aspect of the identities of tragic messengers that deserves notice. Although, again, to some extent dependent upon whom one includes in the "canon" of messengers, these figures in tragedy typically occupy positions of social marginality. Often servants, and virtually always subordinate to the protagonists of the play, messengers rarely have any claim to a life onstage — or offstage — beyond that of delivering their report.[77] This status is reflected in their typical anonymity. As will be readily recognized, such a status facilitates their functioning in the manner discussed throughout this chapter. This anonymity and marginality serve to disassociate messenger-speeches from those who speak them by flattening and depersonalizing the thin identity these messengers typically have. This marginality, then, proves to be of strategic value to the tragic texts in their deployment of this conventional figure.

The marginal status of messengers is in fact underscored by the virtual disembodiment that often characterizes their narratives. While, as I have argued, this freedom from the constraints of the body grants tragic messengers an important epistemic privilege, such "freedom" also signals the striking position of these figures within the fifth-century gender system. In particular, the disembodiment so crucial to their narrative success situates them at a clear distance from the standard of masculinity that

---

76. It is, nonetheless, reasonable to ask which figures in the tragic texts might with profit be considered as engaging with this conventional form. See the appendix for my working list of messengers.

77. Cf. de Jong 1991, 67.

assigns great value to the (strong) body.[78] The messenger's own body is implicitly—and explicitly on occasion[79]—a hindrance, inasmuch as his success *as a messenger* depends upon his acquiring the invulnerability granted by freedom from bodily constraints. In this sense, at least, the messenger typically presents some feminine characteristics. And this feminization corresponds to, as it compounds, his already marginal status.[80] The tragic texts make use of the messenger's gendering in a variety of ways, ranging from the rare appearances of female messengers to two highly feminized (and comic) figures.[81] Most often, however, tragic messengers occupy something of a middle ground in the gender system, and this position contributes to their marginal status.

At the same time, the peculiar privilege of the tragic *angelia* must be understood as at least in part the product of this marginality. In constructing a voice that substantially evades the partiality that defines most

78. See, for example, Halperin 1990, 88–112, esp. 96–99. Cf. Stewart 1997, 86–107, esp. 93–96.

79. See below, chapter 5.

80. It is important to note that "feminine" here refers to the distance from the masculine standard, for femininity in the fifth century also implied a bodily standard. The messenger's virtual disembodiment, then, corresponds to neither standard but nonetheless marks his compromised gender status. Apropos of ancient Greek culture in general, Karen Bassi has recently argued that there is a "gender-specific opposition between nonmediated and mediated speech" (1998, 44), the latter being a feminized form. In her analysis, the messenger, like the tragic actor, is a vehicle of mediated speech and therefore a feminized figure. She discusses the epic messenger as an analogue of the dramatic actor, paying little attention to the tragic messenger. Insofar, however, as the tragic messenger is constituted on the basis of the epic messenger, her remarks would apply as well to the tragic figure. Furthermore, her analysis of theatrical performance is "predicated on the possibility for a kind of disembodied speech" (90), indicating that it would apply *a fortiori* to the messenger.

81. Female messengers appear in Soph. *Trach.* and in Eur. *Alc.*; the comic figures in question are the Phrygian in Eur. *Or.* and the charioteer in *Rhes.*

other tragic voices, our texts rely significantly upon the messenger's status as a peripheral figure. It is important to note, however, that the discursive privilege attaches not to the messenger, but to his report. Although the *angelia* typically acquires an authority that exceeds that of the speech forms surrounding it, the messenger himself, in his capacity as a character in the drama, does not acquire a comparable authority. As I have argued above, the authority of a disembodied voice has been well mapped by epic, and in this sense the messenger's marginalization supports much the same project as does his epic affiliation.

While these brief remarks are far from a comprehensive account of the messenger's social positioning, they serve to indicate one direction for further study. It might well be fruitful to ask, for example, how gendered aspects of the tragic messenger's identity alter our understanding of tragedy's insistent attention to gender more broadly. Or, how the intersection of gender and discursive privilege in tragic *angeliai* illuminate the genre's interest in language, rhetoric, and communication.[82] My hope is that the present study will stimulate new work on these and related questions. Not only does the tragic messenger remain a relatively unknown quantity; the testimony he bears about tragedy's attention to generic, epistemic, and discursive issues invites new questions about a range of topics such as those suggested here.

82. On speech and gender in Athenian drama more broadly see McClure 1999, esp. 32–69.

# THREE

# Euripides' *Bacchae*

## *The Spectator in the Text*

Visibility is a trap.

*Michel Foucault*, Discipline and Punish

If tragic messengers make claims such as those I have identified, not all critics are seduced by them. In a study examining the various reports from Mt. Cithaeron in Euripides' *Bacchae*, Richard Buxton argues against reading the narratives of Euripidean messengers as impartial or transparent accounts of the events they describe. In concluding his careful analysis of the messengers in this play Buxton claims that "these narrators too stand firmly *within* the drama" (1991, 46).[1] From articulating what distinguishes the narratives of these figures, Buxton proceeds to include the messengers with the other *dramatis personae* in a single category of those

I borrow the felicitous phrase "the spectator in the text" from Browne 1986.

1. Emphasis in the original. Buxton's focus is on the two messengers, but he includes the "narratives" of Dionysos (23–42), Pentheus (215–25), and the servant (434–50) in his discussion. See also Bierl 1991, 193. When I speak of "messengers" here I mean the herdsman who enters at 660 and the servant who enters at 1024.

"within the drama." The narratives of the messengers, like everything else said onstage, Buxton argues, are imbued with their own distinctive emotion and rhetoric: "In no two cases is the relationship between content and narrator identical" (40). His argument directs itself precisely against the not uncommon tendency silently to grant a distinct and privileged status to the narratives of tragic messengers.[2]

Complementing the work of de Jong (1991), Buxton rejects the use of the term "messenger" in the singular as injuriously general and neglectful of "the subtle divergences between the reports" (1991, 46). I will argue that Buxton's formulation, although laudable for the attention it pays to rhetorical variation in the narratives it studies, simplifies the status of the messengers in Euripides' play. Rather than being "firmly *within* the drama," the messengers occupy a place on the stage very different from that of the other *dramatis personae*. A reading founded on meta-theatrical studies of the play will show that an important part of *Bacchae*'s self-conscious interest is directed at the status of the messengers, particularly with respect to how they define and are defined by Pentheus. The play produces messengers substantially "outside" the drama—virtual "spectators-in-the-text"—and in so doing expands our notion of what is possible on the tragic stage while clarifying the status of the spectator within the play's metatheater. Although by means of a starkly different route, this metatheater reveals a messenger very much akin to the one we find in Aeschylus's *Persians*. These two plays together are central texts for the understanding of the tragic messenger, as they map out and comment on this conventional figure's privileged status.

The metatheatricality of the play has found extensive critical exposi-

2. Buxton (1991, 46 n. 14) cites Barlow 1971 as an example of this tendency. He, like de Jong (1991, 63–64), ignores the qualification Barlow offers in acknowledging that the status of the messenger is complex and that the poet seeks to establish an unproblematic figure in the messenger against the constraints of the tragic stage. See the introduction above, and Heath 1987, 44.

tion in recent years.[3] The studies of Charles Segal (1982, 215–71) and Helene Foley (1985, 205–58) remain central to any discussion of the play as metatheater, while that of Anton Bierl (1991, 186–217) pushes the fundamental insights of Segal and Foley close to their limits.[4] All of these studies depart in principle from the fact that Dionysos is both the god of theater and the focus of the play: with this as a foundation, the text amply suggests that we read it as a prolonged reflection on theater itself.

Both Segal and Foley astutely discuss the play-within-the-play, Dionysos as director and Pentheus as unwitting protagonist. Segal remarks: "As an actor among actors, Dionysus stands on the same level as the other characters in the orchestra. But he is also director, dressing and instructing his 'actors' for the role they will have to play" (1982, 225). Pentheus's pilgrimage to Mt. Cithaeron to watch the Maenads and the *sparagmos* that forms the climax of the play become under Dionysos's direction a performance akin to tragedy in the theater of Dionysos at Athens. Indeed, the play-within-the-play coincides largely with the play we call *Bacchae*.

As Segal and Foley have shown, Pentheus's status as would-be spectator is central to the play's metatheatricality: much of the elaborate "drama" organized by Dionysos turns on Pentheus's desire to watch the Maenads in the mountains while remaining unseen himself. He wants to be a spectator (θεατής, 829), like the audience in the theater. And like the spectator in the theater, he is tempted by the offer Dionysos makes to see the "performance" on the mountain. In fact, the persistent thematic importance of vision underlies much of the metatheater of the play: the prospect of seeing the Bacchants marks a turning point for Pentheus. Dionysos asks him at 811:

3. There has been some objection to the term "metatheater" and to the validity of its use as an interpretive tool. For a good summary of views and a reply to these objections see Segal 1997, 369–78. For a concise and lucid exposition of what metatheater is see Falkner 1998, 29–33.

4. See also Goldhill 1986, 259–64, 267–86.

βούλῃ σφ' ἐν ὄρεσι συγκαθημένας ἰδεῖν;

Do you want to see them sitting together in the mountains?

And if Dionysos's taunt at 829 suggests the parallel with the audience, it does so in terms of vision:

οὐκέτι θεατὴς μαινάδων πρόθυμος εἶ;

Are you no longer eager to be a spectator of Maenads?

(Indeed, the word *theatēs* defines the audience in terms of vision.) Similarly, Pentheus himself, so the messenger tells us, emphasizes his obsession with seeing the Maenads (1058–62):

Πενθεὺς δ' ὁ τλήμων θῆλυν οὐχ ὁρῶν ὄχλον
ἔλεξε τοιάδ'· Ὦ ξέν', οὗ μὲν ἕσταμεν,
οὐκ ἐξικνοῦμαι μαινάδων ὅσσοις νόθων·
ὄχθων δ' ἔπ', ἀμβὰς ἐς ἐλάτην ὑψαύχενα,
ἴδοιμ' ἂν ὀρθῶς μαινάδων αἰσχρουργίαν.[5]

Pentheus, the wretch, not seeing the group of women, said such things as these: "Stranger, from where we stand I cannot reach the impostor Maenads with my eyes. But if I climb the tall fir on the hill, I could see the Maenads' disgraceful behavior clearly."

The text emphasizes Pentheus's desire to pass through town unobserved and to watch the Bacchants without being detected. To this end Dionysos garbs him with a full Dionysian costume, including wig, peplos, and thyrsus (831–35).[6] Once on the mountain, of course, Pentheus proposes, in the passage cited above, to mount the fir tree. From above he should not only have a good view but also remain undetected, as the vertical movement implies a withdrawal from the horizontal field of action. Indeed this is what Pentheus himself anticipates: ἐλάταις δ' ἐμὸν κρύψω δέ-

5. I follow here the text of Dodds 1960.
6. See Foley 1985, 224.

μας ("I will conceal my body among the fir trees," 954). To which Dionysos pleonastically responds (955–56):

κρύψῃ σὺ κρύψιν ἥν σε κρυφθῆναι χρεών,
ἐλθόντα δόλιον μαινάδων κατάσκοπον.

You will hide yourself in a hidden manner as you should be hidden
by secretly going to spy on the Maenads.

Here Dionysos repeats the word "spy" (κατάσκοπον) from line 916, where he applies this term to Pentheus for the first time. The god offers not only a view, but a secretive one: Pentheus imagines being an invisible spectator.

His hopes are dashed, or rather, inverted, as he becomes instead the unseeing spectacle, as the messenger reports (1075):

ὤφθη δὲ μᾶλλον ἢ κατεῖδε μαινάδας.

He was seen more than he saw the Maenads.

On both counts of vision and visibility the events on the mountain reverse the plan of his desire.[7]

## THE SERVANT

As Pentheus fails to become a spectator, however, Dionysos is not the only one who "remains a spectator" (Foley 1985, 212). As invisible to critics as Pentheus wants to be to the Maenads, the messenger is the true spectator of Dionysos's drama on the mountain. He sees the entirety of what transpires, including Pentheus's transformation from spectator to spectacle. He alone remains unseen.[8]

---

7. Foley comments: "Pentheus, representing his city, goes to the mountain intending to be a spectator. Instead, his sight changes, and he becomes a spectacle and participant" (1985, 212).

8. Dionysos as the stranger, of course, vanishes; but this avenue is not open to mere mortals. Or he goes unseen only by disappearing, while the messenger remains at the scene and still goes unnoticed.

The text, however, prepares us to overlook the messenger as the successful spectator. The elaborate dressing scene preliminary to the trip to the mountain emphatically distinguishes Pentheus the protagonist from the messenger. When Pentheus says at 961–62:

κόμιζε διὰ μέσης με Θηβαίας χθονός·
μόνος γὰρ αὐτῶν εἰμ' ἀνὴρ τολμῶν τόδε.

Take me through the middle of the Theban land; for I am the only man among them daring to do this.

we may readily acquiesce in his claim to uniqueness. And Dionysos's response at 963 with its emphatic repetition of μόνος, initial and final, again encourages us to view Pentheus's position as unique:

μόνος σὺ πόλεως τῆσδ' ὑπερκάμνεις, μόνος·

Alone you struggle for this city, alone.

By the same token, the incomparability of Pentheus's role as spectator-become-spectacle constitutes the ambiguity both of the dressing scene and of lines 961–63: the dressing of Pentheus, while ostensibly (in Pentheus's eyes) designed to allow him to pass unobserved, really, of course, marks Pentheus as the protagonist of the play-within-the-play. As he thinks he is disguising himself so as to become an unseen spectator, he places himself in the center of Dionysos's play. These two scenes, then, clearly work to distinguish Pentheus as unique in his role as would-be spectator. He is unique, however, not in being a spectator, but rather in failing to become one.

The messenger himself reveals the significance of his own role. As he begins his narrative in the first-person plural, he enumerates the members of the embassy (1043–47):

ἐπεὶ θεράπνας τῆσδε Θηβαίας χθονὸς
λιπόντες ἐξέβημεν Ἀσωποῦ ῥοάς,
λέπας Κιθαιρώνειον εἰσεβάλλομεν

Πενθεύς τε κἀγώ (δεσπότῃ γὰϱ εἱπόμην)
ξένος θ' ὃς ἡμῖν πομπὸς ἦν θεωϱίας.

When we had left behind the dwellings of the Theban countryside
and the waters of Asopus, we entered the rocky scrub of Mt. Cithae-
ron, Pentheus and I—since I was following my master—and the
stranger who was our guide in the embassy for viewing the spectacle.

There were three, he says: Pentheus, the stranger, and himself. These
lines not only establish his claim to presence at the scene; they also place
him *alone* as the eyewitness on the mountain. Whereas the messenger's
use of the term *theōria* at line 1047 underscores Pentheus's desire (and
subsequent failure) to become a spectator, to watch unseen, it simulta-
neously signals the eventual success of the messenger on this score.

The messenger goes on to emphasize that the strategy of seeing un-
seen included him (1048–50):

πϱῶτον μὲν οὖν ποιηϱὸν ἵζομεν νάπος,
τά τ' ἐκ ποδῶν σιγηλὰ καὶ γλώσσης ἄπο
σῴζοντες, ὡς ὁϱῶμεν οὐχ ὁϱώμενοι.

First we sat down on a grassy glen and kept silent, not a word on our
tongues, so that we might see without being seen.

He alone accompanied Pentheus and the stranger, and he (too) watched
secretly.

Perhaps most telling is Agave's instruction to the women while
Pentheus is up in the tree (1106–9):

Φέϱε, πεϱιστᾶσαι κύκλῳ
πτόϱθου λάβεσθε, μαινάδες, τὸν ἀμβάτην
θῆϱ' ὡς ἕλωμεν μηδ' ἀπαγγείλῃ θεοῦ
χοϱοὺς κϱυφαίους.

Come on, grab a branch, Maenads, and form a circle so we can catch
the climbing beast, lest he report [ἀπαγγείλῃ] the secret dances of
the god.

In terms that invoke the role of the messenger, Agave here articulates the motivation for the hunt that will bring Pentheus's end : the final act of the drama organized by Dionysos is announced by Agave as she warns that Pentheus may do what the messenger—who relates all this, of course— does. Until this moment Pentheus and the messenger lead parallel lives.

Although interested neither in parallels between Pentheus and the messenger nor in the play's metatheater, E. R. Dodds sees "several apparent reminiscences" of the *Iliad* in the messenger's account of Pentheus's death (1960 *ad* 1061). And these "reminiscences" underscore the metatheatrical presentation of Pentheus as a would-be spectator and as a would-be messenger. The Iliadic passage describes the arrival of Hera and Hypnos on Mt. Ida as they begin to carry out Hera's plan to seduce Zeus and to put him to sleep so as to distract him from the battle, thereby enabling Poseidon to come to the aid of the Greeks. To this end, Hera enlists the aid of Hypnos (along with that of Aphrodite). The lines from *Iliad* 14 referred to by Dodds describe Hypnos as he spies on Zeus, and they occur in a passage as much structured by the theme of vision perhaps as is *Bacchae* itself.

Hera asks Hypnos to put Zeus to sleep, drawing attention to his eyes as the object of her concern: κοίμησόν μοι Ζηνὸς ὑπ' ὀφρύσιν ὄσσε φαεινώ ("Put to sleep Zeus's eyes shining under his brow," 14.236). Hypnos does not agree immediately, negotiating the terms of his involvement. Hera then agrees to give him Pasithea (one of the Graces) in marriage, and he abandons his initial reluctance to scheme against Zeus. After their bartering, the two arrive among the forests of Mt. Ida, where Hypnos remains behind before Zeus can see him: ἔνθ' Ὕπνος μὲν ἔμεινε πάρος Διὸς ὄσσε ἰδέσθαι ("Hypnos stayed there before Zeus's eyes could see him," 14.286). Then follow the lines cited by Dodds (14.287–89), which tell of Hypnos mounting the fir tree:

εἰς ἐλάτην ἀναβὰς περιμήκετον, ἣ τότ' ἐν Ἴδῃ
μακροτάτη πεφυυῖα δι' ἠέρος αἰθέρ' ἵκανεν·
ἔνθ' ἧστ' ὄζοισιν πεπυκασμένος εἰλατίνοισιν

[Hypnos] mounting the high fir, which, being the tallest one then on Mt. Ida, reached the upper air. There he sat, hidden by the thick fir branches.

From this vantage point Hypnos is not only invisible to Zeus, but he is well-positioned to watch the ensuing seduction and slumber of Zeus. The thematic centrality of vision in this entire episode is made yet clearer by what follows. Zeus sees Hera approaching, and this act of seeing alone accomplishes the seduction (293–94):

> ἴδε δὲ νεφεληγερέτα Ζεύς.
> ὡς δ' ἴδεν, ὥς μιν ἔρως πυκινὰς φρένας ἀμφεκάλυψεν.

> Cloud-Gathering Zeus saw her. And when he saw her, *eros* enveloped his mind.

When Zeus soon after asks Hera to delay her (pretended) visit to Okeanos and Tethys and to make love to him, she demurs on the grounds that they would be seen (331–35):

> εἰ νῦν ἐν φιλότητι λιλαίεαι εὐνηθῆναι
> Ἴδης ἐν κορυφῇσι, τὰ δὲ προπέφανται ἅπαντα·
> πῶς κ' ἔοι εἴ τις νῶϊ θεῶν αἰειγενετάων
> εὕδοντ' ἀθρήσειε, θεοῖσι δὲ πᾶσι μετελθὼν
> πεφράδοι;

> If you want to go to bed now and make love here on top of Ida, everything will be open to view. How would it be if one of the eternal gods should see us sleeping together and tell it to all the gods?

Zeus then attempts to reassure her, saying that no one can see them, not even Helios who has the sharpest vision of all (342–45):

> Ἥρη, μήτε θεῶν τό γε δείδιθι μήτε τιν' ἀνδρῶν
> ὄψεσθαι· τοῖόν τοι ἐγὼ νέφος ἀμφικαλύψω
> χρύσεον· οὐδ' ἂν νῶϊ διαδράκοι Ἠέλιός περ,
> οὗ τε καὶ ὀξύτατον πέλεται φάος εἰσοράασθαι.

Hera, have no fear that any of the gods or mortals will see us; I will cover us with such a golden cloud. Even Helios will be unable to see us through it, he whose brightness is the sharpest vision of all.

Hypnos, of course, is the one who does witness Zeus's slumber from high up in the fir tree. His ascent of the tree is recalled, suggests Dodds, by the messenger's account of Pentheus mounting the fir tree (1059–65, 1068–74):

> ὦ ξέν', οὗ μὲν ἕσταμεν,
> οὐκ ἐξικνοῦμαι μαινάδων ὄσσοις νόθων·
> ὄχθων δ' ἔπ', ἀμβὰς ἐς ἐλάτην ὑψαύχενα,
> ἴδοιμ' ἂν ὀρθῶς μαινάδων αἰσχρουργίαν.
> τοὐντεῦθεν ἤδη τοῦ ξένου θαυμάσθ' ὁρῶ·
> λαβὼν γὰρ ἐλάτης οὐράνιον ἄκρον κλάδον
> κατῆγεν ἦγεν ἦγεν ἐς μέλαν πέδον [. . .]
> ὡς κλῶν' ὄρειον ὁ ξένος χεροῖν ἄγων
> ἔκαμπτεν ἐς γῆν, ἔργματ' οὐχὶ θνητὰ δρῶν.
> Πενθέα δ' ἱδρύσας ἐλατίνων ὄζων ἔπι,
> ὀρθὸν μεθίει διὰ χερῶν βλάστημ' ἄνω
> ἀτρέμα, φυλάσσων μὴ ἀναχαιτίσειέ νιν,
> ὀρθὴ δ' ἐς ὀρθὸν αἰθέρ' ἐστηρίζετο
> ἔχουσα νώτοις δεσπότην ἐφήμενον·

"Stranger, from where we stand I cannot reach the impostor Maenads with my eyes. But if I climb the tall fir on the hill, I could see the Maenads' disgraceful behavior clearly." And then I see the stranger's miracle: grabbing a branch at the peak of a towering fir, he bent it down, down, down to the black earth [ . . . ] with his hands the stranger bent the mountain tree to the ground, an act beyond mere mortals, and putting Pentheus atop the fir, he smoothly released the tree straight up, taking care lest the tree throw him off; it rose straight toward the sky with master sitting at the top.

Dodds compares the Iliadic

> εἰς ἐλάτην ἀναβάς (14.287)

with

ἀμβὰς ἐς ἐλάτην (1061)

and

ἔνθ' ἦστ' ὄζοισιν πεπυκασμένος εἰλατίνοισιν (14.289)

with

Πενθέα δ' ἱδρύσας ἐλατίνων ὄζων ἔπι (1070)

and

δι' ἠέρος αἰθέρ' ἵκανεν (14.288)

with

ὀρθὴ δ' ἐς ὀρθὸν αἰθέρ' ἐστηρίζετο (1073).[9]

Just what Dodds intends by stating that these lines of Euripides' play contain "reminiscences" of the *Iliad* scene is unclear, and I see no need to press the question. Whether the *Iliad* passage was a source consciously used by Euripides or not, it stands as a suggestive parallel. The coincidence of Hypnos's invisibility and his privileged position as spectator surely encourages reading the messenger's account as (in part) a reworking of the Iliadic passage. But the invisible eyewitness in the *Iliad* here has even more to offer as a model for Pentheus and his efforts to become a spectator.

In her mock resistance Hera suggests that the danger in being seen is that the voyeur might tell the rest of the gods (θεοῖσι δὲ πᾶσι μετελθὼν / πεφράδοι, 334–35). This, of course, does not happen, because the two are shrouded in a golden cloud. But this successful screening is only a trick: Zeus's satisfaction with the invisible lovemaking and the slumber that ensues stand as the visible objects of Hypnos's gaze. Hera's decep-

9. Dodds 1960 *ad* 1070 and 1073.

tion of Zeus is just that of Pentheus: in thinking himself hidden he becomes most visible and most vulnerable.

As Zeus falls asleep, Hypnos departs to tell Poseidon (354–55):

βῆ δὲ θέειν ἐπὶ νῆας Ἀχαιῶν νήδυμος Ὕπνος
ἀγγελίην ἐρέων γαιηόχῳ ἐννοσιγαίῳ·

Sweet Sleep sped to the ships of the Achaians with a message [ἀγγελίην] for the one who holds and shakes the earth.

Hypnos becomes the messenger. Here, as in *Bacchae*, we find that it is the invisible spectator who is able to tell the story. Just as Agave alerts us to the coincidence of invisible spectatorship and messenger status, so does Hera, together with the chain of events of book 14, equate the two. As parallel to, if not source of, the messenger's account, the *Iliad* passage stands as an illuminating commentary on the metatheatrical status of Pentheus as would-be spectator and the success of the messenger on this score.

That the role of spectator aimed at by Pentheus entails or creates the possibility of reporting—as Agave makes explicit—is alluded to already in the messenger's opening words. At line 1047 (cited above) he calls the journey to Mt. Cithaeron a θεωρία. Beyond the mundane meaning of "viewing," this term often carries connotations of both responsibility and authority. Those sent in an official capacity by the city—to athletic games or to the oracle at Delphi—embark upon a θεωρία. It is the charge of such persons to report accurately what they "see." Theognis invokes this burden of accuracy (805–10):

τόρνου καὶ στάθμης καὶ γνώμονος ἄνδρα θεωρὸν
  εὐθύτερον χρὴ ‹ἔ›μεν Κύρνε φυλασσόμενον,
ᾧτινί κεν Πυθῶνι θεοῦ χρήσασ' ἱέρεια
  ὀμφὴν σημήνῃ πίονος ἐξ ἀδύτου·
οὔτε τι γὰρ προσθεὶς οὐδέν κ' ἔτι φάρμακον εὕροις,
  οὐδ' ἀφελὼν πρὸς θεῶν ἀμπλακίην προφύγοις.[10]

10. I give the text of West 1989.

A *theōros* must be straighter than a straightedge or a plumb line,
Cyrnus, more reliable than a compass and very careful—he to
whom the priestess of the god at Pytho gives an oracular sign from
the sumptuous shrine; for you won't find a solution by adding any-
thing and you won't avoid offending the gods by omitting anything
either.

However we read the relationship between *theōros* and poet in Theog-
nis,[11] the emphasis this passage places on the reliability of the one un-
dertaking a *theōria* is striking: nothing must be added to his report, and
nothing taken away. With the institution of *theōria* demanding such a
*theōros* (or at least the pretense of one), the messenger as he embarks
on his narrative quietly clothes himself with the mantle of one granted
a privileged, authoritative voice. He (along with Pentheus) goes not
merely to watch; he goes with the task of watching with special care. His
invocation of the *theōria* implies that his is no idle mission; it is as though
organized by the polis itself.[12]

If the messenger succeeds where Pentheus fails, in that he brings a re-
port from the mountain to the city, he also, and as a precondition to be
sure, succeeds in passing unseen through the city as well as on the moun-
tain itself. Not only do we know from the fact of his survival and pres-
ence onstage toward the end of the drama that he was invisible to Agave
and the other women, but the text reveals something more at work than
Agave's limited vision. In his *angelia* the messenger consistently remains

11. Nagy reads this passage as a moment of self-authorization on the
part of Theognis: "Just as the priestess . . . *semainei* 'indicates' the message
of the god, so also the poet speaks authoritatively, as if a lawgiver" (1990b,
165). See also Nagy 1985, 37, on the poet as *theōros*.

12. Massenzio (1969, 85–89) examines the failings of Pentheus's vi-
sion—he who would be a *theōros*. De Jong comments: "On the level of ex-
ternal communication (between Euripides and the spectators), the words
[πομπὸς θεωρίας] indicate a ritual procession, with Pentheus the victim
about to be sacrificed" (1991, 36). For a recent, far-reaching discussion of
the institution of *theōria* see Nightingale 2001, esp. 29–33.

disengaged from the events. Only once after he situates himself at the scene does he overtly refer to himself.[13] But his invisibility as eyewitness is marked by more than mere rhetorical self-effacement. Having established that he was one of three in the party, he tells first of Pentheus mounting the fir tree (1064–74) and then (1077) of the stranger disappearing. The moment Dionysos dematerializes is the same moment Pentheus becomes visible atop the tree (1076–77):

ὅσον γὰϱ οὔπω δῆλος ἦν θάσσων ἄνω,
καὶ τὸν ξένον μὲν οὐκέτ' εἰσοϱᾶν παϱῆν.

He was just becoming visible sitting on high when the stranger was no longer to be seen.[14]

Just as Pentheus achieves the position that he hopes will fulfill his wish, he becomes fatally visible to all. And at this same moment Dionysos vanishes from sight. This miraculous moment marks Pentheus as the center of the spectacle and engages both the visible Pentheus and the invisible Dionysos in a reciprocal relation that seems complete in its embrace: the seen and the unseen simultaneously define one another. But in this moment, as the text works to establish this view of Dionysos and Pentheus as broad and comprehensive, the third member of the party performs a different kind of disappearing act. He alone is unaccounted for, beheld by none even as an absence. And his invisibility on the mountain finds a parallel in the theater: not only does the messenger elude the women; he escapes the attention of many critics as well. Indeed, the success of his performance is indicated by the fact that even critics addressing the play's metatheatricality have not appreciated his status as invisible eyewitness on Mt. Cithaeron.

13. ὁϱῶ at line 1063. Of course he speaks in the first-person again in concluding, at 1148–52. De Jong (1992, 578) takes ὁϱῶ at 1063 as one of many signs of this messenger's focalization, in support of her claim that "le messager, comme tous les narrateurs, ne peut pas échapper à sa focalisation" (576).

14. My translation here follows Dodds (1960 ad loc.).

A substantial amount of criticism of the play maintains that Pentheus's (failure in his) mission to Mt. Cithaeron and his death at the hands of the Maenads bear witness to his alienation from and opposition to the society of Dionysiac worshippers, as well as testifying to his disturbed psychological state. Segal (1982, 263), for example, attributes Pentheus's failure to neurosis:

> He [Pentheus] would be a spectator, *theatēs* (829), but not as a member of an audience in a *theatron*. Instead, he is a voyeur, isolated in his private neurotic world. . . . He is shut out of the participatory community established by true theater or true belief in Dionysus.[15]

But in a drama so concerned with drama, this explanation may seem incomplete. While it surely speaks to his position with respect to the society of Dionysiac worshippers construed in its broadest sense and to his state of mind, Pentheus's failure is also metatheatrical in that it demonstrates the condition of and the constraints upon the *dramatis personae*. Pentheus desires to become a spectator of the metatheatrical drama on the mountain, and for him to do so would mean ceasing to be an actor while gaining the ability to "authorize a view" (Browne 1986, 109). But it is precisely this that he fails to do. The thrust of the metatheatrical commentary here suggests that he simply cannot leave behind—even temporarily—his position as a figure constituted and determined by his status as actor in the drama; he can only remain "within the drama," his perceptions, understanding, and speech all bounded by the greater and more comprehensive view of the real spectators, the invisible audience in the theater. As Bierl comments concerning the moment that graphically marks the reversal of Pentheus's status, turning spectator into ac-

---

15. Foley reads Pentheus's demise as following on his status as "an enemy to festival" and his "attempt to exclude festival and its benefits from his recently formed and crudely hierarchical city" (1985, 231 and 241). On Pentheus's psychological state see, for example, Seidensticker 1972; Sale 1972; LaRue 1968.

tor: "The fall [from atop the fir tree] symbolizes the fact that Pentheus is thrown down to the level of the stage where he must 'perform a role.'"[16] It is the privilege of the anonymous and unseen audience to watch, contemplate, and judge the *dramatis personae*, who are confined to their status as actors onstage. The failure of Pentheus to become a spectator metatheatrically enacts and reaffirms this fundamental distinction.[17]

If it seems tautologous to argue that the tragic protagonist cannot abandon his position as actor to become a spectator, the significance of this claim lies in what it says about the status of the messenger. That is, if Pentheus's failure to become a spectator seems predetermined in metatheatrical terms, the success of the messenger might seem to be ruled out on the same grounds. In fact, as we have seen, the messenger does succeed and in so doing threatens to expand our notion of what is possible on the tragic stage: contrary to Buxton's claim, this messenger occupies a position substantially "outside" the drama in that he achieves spectator status and remains invisible to the Maenads. (His success on these counts, furthermore, has achieved a similar "invisibility" in criticism.) Indeed, the play-within-the-play reveals that Pentheus's desire to watch unseen is not entirely off-limits to some of the *dramatis personae*. And the case of the first messenger, the herdsman who reports the activities of the Maenads on Mt. Cithaeron, reveals that the servant is not the only

16. "Der Sturz symbolisiert die Tatsache, dass Pentheus auf die Ebene der Bühne geworfen wird, wo er 'mitspielen' muss" (1991, 213).

17. As he is about to meet his end Pentheus tries yet again to escape the confines of his status by removing his mitra (1115–16): in metatheatrical terms he attempts to remove his costume (Segal 1982, 228). Foley points out that Pentheus's opposition to festival "is expressed primarily as a failure of sight, or a failure to benefit from *theōria*" (1985, 241). *Theōria*, as we have seen, implies a privileged kind of viewing, such as that of the audience in the theater. Vernant (1988b, 43) describes the relation of the audience to the inhabitants of the fictional world in complementary terms. On Vernant's formulation, however, see now Gould 1996, 218–21, and Goldhill 1996, 244–46.

messenger endowed with this privilege of spectatorship that is marked by a virtual invisibility and disembodiment.

## THE HERDSMAN

The herdsman arrives to tell of the marvels performed by the Bacchants, and although he does not tell us explicitly where he was, we may infer that he was with the cattle he mentions at 677–78. Such a position seems evident a bit later when he and his fellow herdsmen hide (722–23). Indirectly, then, we get an idea of where he was as he saw the events that make up his story.

This position remains virtually unchanged until 734 where we find him (with the other herdsmen) fleeing the attacking women. Although we do not hear where they go, Dodds (1960 *ad* 751–52) reasonably takes them to flee toward Thebes.[18] After describing the *sparagmos* at lines 735–47, the herdsman proceeds to tell of the "flight" of the women (748–54):

> χωροῦσι δ' ὥστ' ὄρνιθες ἀρθεῖσαι δρόμῳ
> πεδίων ὑποτάσεις, αἳ παρ' Ἀσωποῦ ῥοαῖς
> εὔκαρπον ἐκβάλλουσι Θηβαίοις στάχυν,
> Ὑσιάς τ' Ἐρυθράς θ', αἳ Κιθαιρῶνος λέπας
> νέρθεν κατῳκήκασιν, ὥστε πολέμιοι
> ἐπεσπεσοῦσαι πάντ' ἄνω τε καὶ κάτω
> διέφερον·

> Like birds aloft, they sped across the understretch of plain that bears
> an abundant Theban crop by the river Asopus. And like enemies
> in battle, they fell upon Hysia and Erythra in the lowlands of Mt.
> Cithaeron and turned them all upside down.

Even if we take into account Dodds's note (1960 *ad* 751–52) that the herdsmen "would pass them [the towns of Hysia and Erythra] in their flight," it would be easy to show that the herdsman could not possibly

18. Seaford concurs (1996 *ad* 748–52).

have witnessed all that he describes. He says, after all, that the women flew "like birds."[19] Not only does he not say he accompanied them—which is standard for a messenger to do when a change of location occurs—but the context makes clear that even if he had tried, he would not have succeeded: the special power of Dionysos was obviously the enabling force for the women.[20]

His account of the women's return to the spot where his narrative begins is equally implausible, for he says not only that they returned there, but that they went to the springs and washed themselves (765–68):

πάλιν δ' ἐχώρουν ὅθεν ἐκίνησαν πόδα
κρήνας ἐπ' αὐτὰς ἃς ἀνῆκ' αὐταῖς θεός,
νίψαντο δ' αἷμα, σταγόνα δ' ἐκ παρηίδων
γλώσσῃ δράκοντες ἐξεφαίδρυνον χροός.

They turned back whence they had come, to the very springs the
god had made flow for them. They washed off the blood, and snakes
licked away the drippings from their cheeks.

If, as Dodds suggests, the herdsman fled to Thebes immediately after his attempted ambush of Agave, he would not have been once again on the mountain to witness this.

It would be easy to show that this messenger's narrative clearly exceeds what he could realistically know.[21] But my interest is not to prove

19. Roux (1970 ad loc.) remarks: "Il ne s'agit pas ici d'une simple figure de style, mais d'un nouveau miracle."

20. Verrall (1910, 86) takes a different view, rejecting the herdsman's report as unbelievable: "The man does not know what he saw, and is not making any attempt to consult his memory and reproduce the record." Oranje, however, dismisses Verrall's argument, claiming that by means of "the messenger speech the spectator comes face to face with events in the play which are enacted off-stage. The level of reality cannot be tampered with" (1984, 74 n. 183).

21. Dodds (1960 *ad* 765–68) remarks: "The Herdsman is allowed to round off his narrative by describing what he cannot well have seen." And

the messenger a liar. This would tell us little, if anything. The importance of the remarks above lies in what they tell us about the messenger's self-representation. Here we see him appropriating a freedom of movement within the scene he describes that is clearly the province of one not confined by the limits placed on a "real" eyewitness: indeed, as his comparison of the women's flight to that of birds recalls certain Homeric similes, so his freedom from the realistic constraints of the scene he describes and his virtually disembodied presence at that scene recall the narrative practice of the epic bard. He claims a place within his narrative that at once allows him to see and prevents us from seeing him.

The absence of any indication of his whereabouts after line 734 (where he and the other herdsmen are pursued by the women) aids his project greatly. He tells us only that he went away from the spot of the ambush, without indicating a direction. Agave, it seems, has chased the messenger not only out of his ambush, but out of the narrative altogether. For the remainder of the narrative there are no first-persons, and indications of what he saw are either implicit or indicated by oblique or impersonal means. At 737–38, for example, he tells Pentheus:

καὶ τὴν μὲν ἂν προσεῖδες εὔθηλον πόριν
μυκωμένην ἔχουσαν ἐν χεροῖν δίχα.[22]

And you would have beheld her holding the well-teated, mooing heifer torn apart in her hands.

At 760 he employs an impersonal expression:

οὗπερ τὸ δεινὸν ἦν θέαμ' ἰδεῖν, ἄναξ.

Then there was a terrifying sight to behold, sir.

---

surely he is right to add that this "is not unusual, and does not authorize us to regard him as a liar."

22. Similarly at 740, εἶδες δ' ἂν. I depart here from Diggle in retaining ἔχουσαν of the manuscripts.

These subtle forms of self-excision aid in his performance of his own miracle of locomotion as he tracks with his narrative the miraculous deeds of the Bacchants.[23]

These references to impersonal vision (760) and to what "you" would have seen (737–38, 740) serve another function as well. This detachment from his own point of view of what the messenger claims to have seen seeks to normalize his privileged status. "You, too," he tells Pentheus, "would have seen all this." But as will become clear, Pentheus would not (and in the end did not). Pentheus, most of all, would not have seen. At 1060 he says:

οὐκ ἐξικνοῦμαι μαινάδων ὅσσοις νόθων·

I am not able to reach the impostor Maenads with my eyes.

This invocation of Pentheus's potential (safe) witnessing of what the herdsman saw—the very witnessing that becomes the object of Pentheus's desire, central to the metatheatrical manipulations of Dionysos—makes clear the privilege inherent in the messenger's vision and in his status as spectator.

The narrative of the herdsman, however, also offers a stiff challenge to my claims about the play's messengers. He tells us that as he and his comrades watched the miraculous activities of the Maenads, they hid in ambush and attempted to catch Agave. In sharp contrast to the invisible spectator, this messenger heads directly for the center of the action as he leaps at Pentheus's mother (728–30). Although this scene appears to confirm Buxton's claim that the messengers, too, "stand firmly within the drama," it illustrates that the messenger in fact does not successfully attain the role of actor at which he aims.

For the first 39 lines of his narrative (prior to line 714) we hear of only one herdsman, namely, the messenger. He uses the singular when he

23. This is not to deny that these lines may serve other purposes as well. For example, it is clear that the herdsman's use of the second-person encourages and augments Pentheus's desire to see the women himself.

says, for example, that he saw (ὁρῶ, 680) three groups of Bacchants. After describing in detail the remarkable doings of the women on the mountain, he turns to speaking of himself and those with him. Suddenly we find that he was not alone (714–16):

> ξυνήλθομεν δὲ βουκόλοι καὶ ποιμένες
> κοινῶν λόγων δώσοντες ἀλλήλοις ἔριν
> ὡς δεινὰ δρῶσι θαυμάτων τ' ἐπάξια.[24]

We cowherds and shepherds assembled to compete with each other in tales of their terrifying and amazing deeds.

At the moment when we first hear of their discussion and attempted ambush of the Bacchants, these intrusive elements—which call attention to the *action* of the messenger rather than to his *vision*—seek to deflect our attention from its focus on the messenger onto the group as a whole. The quoted speech at 718–21 directs our attention to the herdsmen and away from the women, but as it does so it somewhat obscures the messenger himself by offering us the words of another member of the group. We hear one of the herdsmen speak, but the narrator himself remains "silent": it is the urbane herdsman who speaks (717–18):

> καί τις πλάνης κατ' ἄστυ καὶ τρίβων λόγων
> ἔλεξεν εἰς ἅπαντας.

And someone who wanders through town and has a way with words spoke to everyone.

The group, swayed by the slick talker, decide to hunt (*thērasōmetha*, 719) the women, and they therefore lie in ambush.

As Jeanne Roux (1970 *ad* 719) remarks, the shepherd here employs some of the vocabulary used earlier by Pentheus (his θηρασώμεθα echoes Pentheus's θηράσομαι at 228, for example), and this new hunt presages to some extent the fate that awaits Pentheus.[25] Similarly, the shepherds

24. Diggle brackets line 716.
25. See also Buxton 1991, 42–43.

mimic the act of observation on the part of the spectator in their self-concealment (722–23):

> θάμνων δ' ἐλλοχίζομεν φόβαις
> κρύψαντες αὑτούς·

We hid in the foliage of the bushes, concealing ourselves.

But the hiding and mere observation do not last. As the women begin their ritual shaking of the thyrsoi and chanting (723–27), Agave comes near the herdsman, and he springs forth. As he does so he calls attention to the fact that he acts alone (κἀγὼ, 729). Here for the first time since the initial ὁρῶ of line 680—and also for the last time in the narrative proper—he uses the first-person singular (728–30):

> κυρεῖ δ' Ἀγαυὴ πλησίον θρῴσκουσ' ἐμοῦ,
> κἀγὼ 'ξεπήδησ' ὡς συναρπάσαι θέλων,
> λόχμην κενώσας ἔνθ' ἐκρύπτομεν δέμας.

Agave came leaping near me, and I, wanting to grab her, sprang
forth from the thicket where we were hiding.

As he leaps out of the bushes, he ceases to be a mere witness and underscores this in distinguishing himself again from the group of herdsmen. As he leaves behind the literal cover of the ambush he abandons the status achieved by the messenger who reports the death of Pentheus: his attempt to catch Agave marks his attempt to become an actor in his narrative and the focus of our attention. The impact of this move toward involvement in the action is augmented by the fact that this messenger's leap takes him from his place of hiding, where he is virtually invisible.

The herdsman's role as near protagonist (of his narrative), however, is short-lived and finds a telling end. At this charged moment, with the messenger suspended in midair, his account turns to Agave (731–33):

> ἡ δ' ἀνεβόησεν· ῏Ω δρομάδες ἐμαὶ κύνες,
> θηρώμεθ' ἀνδρῶν τῶνδ' ὕπ'· ἀλλ' ἕπεσθέ μοι,
> ἕπεσθε θύρσοις διὰ χερῶν ὡπλισμέναι.

And she howled: "My running dogs, we are being hunted by these men. But follow me, follow, armed with your thyrsoi."

The herdsman remains aloft "wanting to grab" (συναρπάσαι θέλων) Agave. Precisely at the moment when he attempts to realize his desire to take part in the action he finds himself oddly frozen in midair. This leap that never reaches its target, I suggest, succinctly expresses the status of this (and the later) messenger as a figure endowed with a virtual disembodiment that both makes possible the narrative feats I have described and also denies him the ability to partake in the action he reports. Indeed, one might with profit compare the Homeric account of Achilles' frustrated attempt to embrace the likeness of Patroklos in his sleep (*Il.* 23.99–101) or that of Odysseus's similarly frustrated efforts to embrace the shade of his mother (*Od.* 11.203–8). Just as these two reach toward a realm that is off-limits to them, the herdsman attempts to leap from his position as spectator into the realm of action.[26] As the text shows that this leap does not succeed, it suggests in fact that it cannot succeed: not only does the herdsman, as messenger, have access to the kind of privileged spectatorship that Pentheus desires, but this privilege marks him as a figure confined to the role of eyewitness.

What next transpired we do not hear. This remarkable effort of the herdsman gives way to a colorless "we escaped" immediately following Agave's remark (734–35):

ἡμεῖς μὲν οὖν φεύγοντες ἐξηλύξαμεν
βακχῶν σπαραγμόν.

We fled and escaped the bacchic *sparagmos*.

Given that the Bacchants possess remarkable powers, it may well not have been a trivial affair for the herdsmen to escape. We need not question the

---

26. Cf. Antikleia's explanation of the gap between the living and dead at 11.218 ("This is the way it is for mortals," αὕτη δίκη ἐστὶ βροτῶν), underlining the impropriety, and impossibility, of bridging this gap.

plausibility of their escape to notice that after so carefully setting the stage for his attack and insinuating himself into the center of his story, the herdsman suddenly ceases to be an actor in his narrative. The sudden and dramatic appearance of the messenger as actor in the story—κἀγὼ 'ξεπή-δησ'—calling attention as it does to his role in the narrative, vanishes as quickly as it comes about. Having drawn our gaze upon the herdsman as would-be actor in his story, the text leaves us to ponder the absence of any interaction between herdsman and Maenads. And this absence repeats and extends the effect of the herdsman's leap: he fails to occupy the position of actor and instead resumes his role as eyewitness (and narrator).

That the two messengers together share the privilege of spectatorship and occupy a realm that is off-limits to Pentheus is made even clearer by the journey of Pentheus from Thebes to Mt. Cithaeron, for it is the first *angelia* that brings Pentheus to the site of the second. The first messenger's narrative not only introduces the role of the messenger as hidden spectator; it also paints a picture of what it is Pentheus shortly after will so eagerly want to see. Or it offers an account of what Pentheus (mis)takes for *aiskhrourgia* (1062). Upon receiving the first messenger's report, Pentheus immediately orders an attack on the women. But this plan is short-lived. Dionysos intervenes, offering first to make a deal that Pentheus suspects is a trick, and then to provide Pentheus with a private viewing. It is, of course, this second offer that Pentheus latches onto, revealing his profound curiosity (811–12):

Δ.     βούλῃ σφ' ἐν ὄρεσι συγκαθημένας ἰδεῖν;
Π.     μάλιστα, μυρίον γε δοὺς χρυσοῦ σταθμόν.

D.     Do you want to see them sitting together in the mountains?
P.     Definitely. I'd give a lot of gold.

These lines have been much discussed, with attention paid to the verb of seeing and its implications for a psychological study of Pentheus.[27] If

27. Dodds remarks: "It is the answer, if not of a maniac, at least of a man whose reactions are ceasing to be normal: the question has touched a hid-

it is profitable to read Dionysos's offer with emphasis on the final word (*idein*), we should also remember that Pentheus has just been presented with a lengthy and marvelous portrait of σφ' ἐν ὄρεσι συγκαθημένας. Pentheus's fascination, well described by Dodds, seizes upon the possibility of seeing what he has just heard.[28]

Pentheus's desire to see for himself what the herdsman has already seen confirms what becomes clear in the second *angelia:* namely, that the status of spectator aimed at by Pentheus strongly resembles and is modeled on the privileged position of the messenger(s). The first messenger's narrative, then, occurs as the anticipation of Pentheus's desire; it not only gives rise and structure to his desire but makes it overwhelming: he must see what occasions the narrative and thereby recover the original moment witnessed by the herdsman. When we find, then, the second messenger succeeding where Pentheus fails, we realize that we have come full circle.[29] It is the privilege that the two messengers—and they alone—share that is the object of Pentheus's desire.

———

Inasmuch as metatheater enacts a form of commentary on the institution of theater per se, it thereby invites the examination of theatrical performance in the terms set forth by the metatheater. In this way we may consider, for example, the theatrical audience in terms of Pentheus's suffering and ask whether their/our experience is in some sense a metaphorical *sparagmos;*[30] or we may examine the festival context of the tragic performances in terms of *Bacchae*'s complex metatheatrical exploitation

———

den spring in Pentheus' mind, and his self-mastery vanishes" (1960 ad loc.). See Segal, 1982, 225, and Gregory 1985, 23.

28. McDonald, (1992, 233) comments: "Penthée ne peut tirer un enseignement d'une parabole ou de la parole. Il ne croit que ce qu'il voit."

29. As Foley (1985, 244) observes: "The first messenger-speech gives Pentheus the precise scenario for his own death." See also de Jong 1992, 574 and 579–80.

30. As Segal suggests (1982, 218 and 225); cf. Foley 1985, 220.

of festival and ritual themes.[31] Similarly, the metatheater's incorporation of the familiar figure of the messenger invites us to examine the conventional messenger as a tragic "institution" in terms of the play's presentation of the servant (and the herdsman). In this way, the metatheater here offers a model for how tragic messengers acquire the privilege of spectatorship that is so crucial to their successful functioning in their appointed role: the particular form of autopsy that makes the tragic messenger-speech possible relies upon the very principles of spectatorship evident in *Bacchae*'s metatheater. Specifically, the narrative strategies as here analyzed—the implicit claim of a virtually disembodied status; a comprehensive view of the events narrated; a position noticeably "outside" the drama (i.e., extradiegetic status); and, as discussed above, the borrowing of features of epic narrative—indicate the basis of the tragic messenger's claim to the privileged status of (invisible) spectator. As such, elements constitutive of the tragic messenger-speech appear in the metatheater underlined by the play's sharp focus on spectatorship as central to Dionysos's manipulation of Pentheus. Furthermore, in presenting a messenger outside the metatheater (the shepherd) who shares essential traits with and who, as I have argued, functions in some senses in tandem with the messenger within the metatheater (the servant), the play as a whole suggests that its metatheatrical interest in the messenger applies more broadly: the yoking of the two messengers to their shared status of unseen spectator encourages us to consider this status as one that goes beyond either of these figures as individuals.[32]

31. As Foley does so well (1985, 205–58).

32. It is possible, of course, to point to moments of explicit self-reference in tragic messenger-speeches, as it is possible to perform the kind of analysis found in de Jong 1991, discerning traces of any given messenger's focalization. My claim is not that tragic messengers always unproblematically achieve the status delineated in Euripides' play. Rather, I would suggest that one strategy of the tragic messenger is to *claim* such a status in a variety of ways, most of which remain implicit. (I hasten to add that this strategy is not the only one employed by tragic messengers. They must also, for example,

This analysis has limited itself to the status of the messengers in Euripides' play. In claiming that the metatheatrical performance represents the messenger as a "spectator-in-the-text," however, this argument also raises a question concerning what the play's metatheater says about the audience seated in the Theater of Dionysos: To what extent is the messenger an enlightening model of the audience in the theater? Although I have argued that within the metatheater of Euripides' play Pentheus stands out as a would-be or failed spectator, it remains true that in some ways he is a more compelling model of the audience in the theater than is the messenger. With respect to what the (first) messenger sees, we are in the same position as Pentheus: we, too, are excluded from recovering the original moment witnessed by the messenger; we, too, must remain satisfied with his narrative. Additionally, as Segal has argued, Pentheus's status as spectator-become-spectacle and victim of the *sparagmos* symbolically represents the experience of the audience in the theater: "In order for the 'sacrifice' at the center of the rite-spectacle to work for them [the audience], they too must relinquish some of their distance; they must become participants" (Segal 1982, 225).[33]

But if it is fruitful to consider Pentheus as a model of the theatrical audience, it is equally compelling to consider this group in terms of the messenger's status as spectator. The latter, that is, does contribute to the metatheater's construction of the audience's role. And as this doubling of metatheatrical spectators suggests, the audience in the theater experiences more than a symbolic *sparagmos*. Just as the servant appropriates the vocabulary of the theater (or pilgrimage) in order to buttress his claim of privileged spectatorship (θεωρία at 1047), so the metatheater reaffirms the status of the audience members as *theōroi* endowed with the qualities

---

establish their status as eyewitnesses to the events reported, and this imperative can conflict with the claim to the kind of spectatorship discussed here.) Nonetheless, the history of criticism shows that these claims have been remarkably successful.

33. Much the same might be said of the audience from an Aristotelian point of view: experiencing pity and fear is a form of such "participation."

displayed by the messenger. The theater audience, the metatheater tells us, is made up not only of a group of individuals succumbing to emotional and psychological "*sparagmos*"; it consists also of those engaged in a collective, tranquil contemplation of what is staged. That is, not only are the spectators in one sense required, like Pentheus, to become "actors"; they also command a comprehensive, masterful view while they are endowed with the invisibility and invulnerability of the messenger on Mt. Cithaeron.[34]

The metatheater, then, posits an audience with the twofold role of both participant and observer.[35] This double status reflects something of the ambiguity of performance in the theater: as a fiction capable of speaking truth;[36] as representation endowed with an immediacy; and as the performance of actors that manages to elicit the audience's "belief" in the action's reality.

If it seems unremarkable that the metatheater should present such a view of the theatrical audience, it is important to appreciate the significance of the inclusion of this twofold audience in the play-within-the-play. By incorporating the messenger as spectator, the metatheater extends its interest in the audience beyond the psychological and emotional, as it exhibits a keen awareness of the audience's civic role. Just as *theōria* implies a civic purpose expressed in the eyewitness's report, so the messenger shows himself to be adept at turning spectatorship into narrative. And as *theōria* is the distinctive mark of both messenger and audience, we may read the metatheater's treatment of spectatorship as including an indication of the civic charge inherent in such spectatorship: the audience members, as *theōroi*, are granted a privileged, contempla-

34. Speaking of the messenger in Euripides' *Suppliants*, Froma Zeitlin remarks: "The messenger, as always in Greek tragedy, stands in for the spectators, those both on and off the stage" (1994, 143).

35. This is perhaps appropriate for a drama so concerned with doubling. See Segal 1982, 27–54; Foley 1985, 241–43; Goldhill 1988a.

36. Cf. Segal 1982, 232–40.

tive view and are endowed with both the ability and the responsibility to "report" what they have seen. As such, the metatheater pictures tragedy both as an occasion of Dionysiac experience, however mediated in its theatrical form, and as the subject of contemplation and public discourse.[37]

As such, the metatheatrical handling of spectatorship posits a continuity between the experience of the audience in the theater and life in the city. And this continuity bridges to some extent the "gap between the power of illusion within the fiction and the power of the fiction to convey truth," which gap, Segal argues, "*Bacchae* refuses fully to close" (1982, 237). Segal sees this disjunction in Euripides' metatheater:

> Through his metatragic criss-crossing between actor and audience, participant and spectator, fiction and reality, Euripides also opens the distance between what can be lived and what can be said, what can be grasped by the symbolic fictions of poetic representation and what can be communicated in everyday language. How much of what we experience in the theater (of Dionysus) can we bring into the rest of our lives? Does the self that surrenders to the power of the Dionysiac illusion overlap with the self that performs the daily responsibilities of worker, citizen, spouse, parent, friend? Pentheus and Agave's experience does not leave us sanguine. (1982, 236–37)

But that of the messenger may. Having seen that the metatheater's presentation of spectatorship is more complex than hitherto appreciated, we

37. The herdsman announces as much soon after entering: "I have come because I must report both to you and to the city" (ἥκω φράσαι σοὶ καὶ πόλει χρῄζων, 666). Karen Bassi has argued that the spectators in the theater "assume a passive subject position inimical to the elite masculine ethos" (1998, 227–28). She speaks of Pentheus in Euripides' *Bacchae* as epitomizing "the gender-specific prejudices that characterize the male as spectator in Greek culture" (230). We can now redirect her comments to the messenger as (successful) spectator: if *Bacchae*'s metatheater implies a discursive role for the citizen-spectator, it also figures something of the complexity that constitutes his citizen status, as Bassi suggests. Cf. Zeitlin's analysis of Plato's critique of theater as a feminizing force (1996, 367–74).

are able to narrow Segal's "gap," insofar as the metatheatrical representation of the audience embraces both of the worlds separated by this gap. As "victim" of a "*sparagmos,*" the spectator "surrenders to the power of Dionysiac illusion"; as *theōros,* the spectator turns spectatorship into "narrative," transforming "experience in the theater" into a subject of public discourse, and brings it into the life of the city.

# FOUR

# Homer and the Art of Fiction in Sophocles' *Electra*

Sophocles may be read for and/or against but never without Homer.

*Simon Goldhill*, Reading Greek Tragedy

ὦδ' ὁ μῦθος ἐστάτω.

Let this be the story.

Orestes to the Paidagogos, Sophocles *Electra*

If Aeschylus's *Persians* reveals the Homeric underpinnings of the conventional tragic messenger and if Euripides' *Bacchae* displays the ideal form of spectatorship that is the province of this messenger, Sophocles' *Electra* joins these two defining characteristics. The play does this as it puts on stage the only fictitious *angelia* in the extant tragic corpus. Any study of the tragic *angelia* would have to take account of the false messenger-speech performed by the Paidagogos in Sophocles' play, if only because of its unique status. But insofar as this lengthy false narrative displays in metatheatrical form the practices of conventional tragic messengers in the theater, it provides a compelling case study for understanding the tragic messenger-speech more broadly. Moreover, the play's substantial reliance upon Homer both structures its metatheatrical interest and enables us to appreciate the value of the Homeric model in constructing the tragic messenger-speech.

This chapter, then, examines the Paidagogos's false narrative as a self-conscious staging of tragic convention. Even moreso than in the case of *Bacchae*, the metatheater of Sophocles' play locates the messenger at the center of its interest.[1] But the route to understanding just how the false *angelia* is constructed requires first an appreciation of the play's use of both the *Odyssey* and the *Iliad*. It is accordingly with the play's deployment of the Homeric material that I begin.

Immediately following the proem, the *Odyssey*'s narrator tells us that with Poseidon having gone off to visit the Ethiopians, the rest of the gods assembled on Olympos. Zeus begins the discussion that will set the ensuing plot in motion. In his mind, the narrator reveals, is the example of Aigisthos, "whom the widely known son of Agamemnon, Orestes, killed" (1.30). Citing the example of Aigisthos, Zeus scorns the idea that the gods are responsible for human suffering. He briefly recounts Agamemnon's death and the revenge exacted by Orestes. Athena then agrees with Zeus that Aigisthos died in a manner befitting his crime (46) and proceeds to turn the discussion to the fate of Odysseus. In this way does the return of Odysseus to Ithaka begin.

In thus prefacing the story of Odysseus with that of Aigisthos and Orestes, the poem announces the importance of the Oresteia story to the poem as a whole. This introduction, in fact, "sounds like the opening of an Oresteia" (Heubeck et al. 1988 *ad* 1.29–31). Such a program-

---

1. Although arguing that the play is permeated by metatheatrical elements, Mark Ringer states that the false *angelia* "stands at the apex of the *Electra*'s metatheatrical structure. That the playwright lavished over eighty lines on this section and assigned it to the exact center of the play suggests its importance" (1998, 161–62). Ringer studies metatheater in the Sophoclean corpus as a whole. On metatheater in Sophocles see also Falkner 1998 and 1999.

matic passage sets the stage for the repeated suggestion that the plot of the *Odyssey* finds important *comparanda* in the Oresteia story.[2]

Although this juxtaposition of plots is most commonly taken to suggest real or potential parallels between (1) Telemachus and Orestes, (2) Penelope and Clytemnestra, and (3) Odysseus and Agamemnon, the repeated invocation of the Oresteia story in the poem reveals more at work. As S. Douglas Olson has shown (1995), the Oresteia story fulfills a number of purposes. Although the presence of this story presents a rich field of possibilities, most relevant and informative here are the parallels suggested between Orestes and Odysseus.

The *Odyssey* allows for a good while that Odysseus's *nostos* may be modeled on that of Orestes. For example, Zeus's mention of Aigisthos's blunders and subsequent punishment suggests that "Odysseus may be preparing to play Orestes" (Olson 1995, 27). The revenge and *kleos* won by Orestes and held out by Athena/Mentes to be emulated by Telemachus (1.293–300) prove, finally, to belong more securely to Odysseus: those qualities of Orestes that make him an exemplary figure suitable for the use made of him by Athena/Mentes become the very traits that characterize Odysseus.[3]

But this need not surprise. Inasmuch as Athena/Mentes urges Telemachus to take revenge on the suitors as a task central to Telemachus's own maturation,[4] Orestes appears as a model for Telemachus in his effort to claim his patrimony. Telemachus's success at laying claim to what belonged to Odysseus requires his emulation of Orestes. In short, becoming like Orestes will enable him to become like Odysseus.

---

2. The poem refers to the Oresteia story at 1.29–43, 298–300; 3.193–98, 234–35, 248–75, 303–12; 4.90–92, 512–47; 11.387–89 (= 24.20–22), 405–39, 452–64; 13.383–84; 24.96–97, 192–200. See Olson 1995, 24 n. 2, for bibliography; cf. Slatkin 1996, 227–29.

3. Nestor in book 3 makes very much the same use of Orestes: 193–200; 303–16.

4. E.g., 1.296–97.

The goddess, furthermore, instructs Telemachus to travel to Pylos and to Sparta in order to find out if Odysseus is still alive. If he discovers that his father is dead, he is to make a tomb for him, offer sacrifice, and give his mother Penelope away in marriage. And invoking the act that will fulfill his emulation of Orestes, Athena/Mentes goes on to speak to Telemachus of killing the suitors (1.293–96):

αὐτὰρ ἐπὴν δὴ ταῦτα τελευτήσῃς τε καὶ ἔρξῃς,
φράζεσθαι δὴ ἔπειτα κατὰ φρένα καὶ κατὰ θυμόν,
ὅππως κε μνηστῆρας ἐνὶ μεγάροισι τεοῖσι
κτείνῃς, ἠὲ δόλῳ ἢ ἀμφαδόν.

Then once you have done these things, plan out in your mind and in your heart how you can kill the suitors in your house, whether by trickery or openly.

She goes on to add that Telemachus should emulate Orestes in doing this deed (1.298–302):

ἦ οὐκ ἀΐεις οἷον κλέος ἔλλαβε δῖος Ὀρέστης
πάντας ἐπ' ἀνθρώπους, ἐπεὶ ἔκτανε πατροφονῆα,
Αἴγισθον δολόμητιν, ὅ οἱ πατέρα κλυτὸν ἔκτα;
καὶ σύ, φίλος, μάλα γάρ σ' ὁρόω καλόν τε μέγαν τε,
ἄλκιμος ἔσσ', ἵνα τίς σε καὶ ὀψιγόνων ἐὺ εἴπῃ.

Or have you not heard what great fame *[kleos]* noble Orestes acquired among all people when he killed his father's murderer, the tricky Aigisthos, who killed his famous father? You, too, my friend—I see that you are strong and big—be courageous, and even those in the distant future will speak well of you.

Lines 295–96 are repeated nearly verbatim later in the poem. During their meeting in book 11, Teiresias tells Odysseus that if he manages to return to Ithaka he will find his house in trouble, beset by reckless men eating up his goods and courting his wife. They will pay, however, for their outrages, Teiresias says, repeating the lines spoken by Athena in book 1 (11.119–20):

αὐτὰρ ἐπὴν μνηστῆρας ἐνὶ μεγάροισι τεοῖσι
κτείνῃς, ἠὲ δόλῳ ἢ ἀμφαδόν . . .

Then once you kill the suitors in your house, whether by trickery or
openly . . .

Needless to say, this act of revenge is carried out by both father and son,
rendering this echo meaningful at the level of plot. What matters here
is simply that this convergence of father and son occurs via Athena's for-
mulation of this revenge in terms of Orestes.[5]

In these ways, then, the *Odyssey* makes use of the Oresteia story not
only to suggest broad parallels between its own story and that of the Ores-
teia myth, and, more specifically, to juxtapose Telemachus and Orestes;
it also suggests that Odysseus himself may be read with profit against the
model of Orestes. The structural similarities between their two stories
make such parallels perhaps inevitable, but Homer's text clearly charts
these waters for later writers.

As the Oresteia myth finds itself woven into the texture of the *Odys-
sey*, so, in turn, the epic holds important clues for our readings of fifth-
century tragic accounts of Orestes' revenge. Simon Goldhill, for ex-
ample, asserts that Aeschylus's Oresteia "is grounded in . . . the epic"
(1984b, 195) as he discusses Orestes' *nostos* as a reworking of that of Odys-
seus. More generally, he speaks of "the transformation of the Odyssean
discourse" in Aeschylus (194). Euripides also makes use of Odysseus as
model for his Orestes, as Theodore Tarkow (1981) and Barbara Goff
(1991) astutely show.[6] Goff speaks of "the general presence of Odysseus
within the *Elektra*," arguing that "the scar of Orestes operates . . . as a
trace of the scar of Odysseus" (261).[7]

---

5. Cf. Goldhill 1984a, 191–92. On the similarities between Telemachus
and Odysseus see Roisman 1994 and Olson 1995, chap. 4, esp. 78–82.

6. Cf. Dingel 1969; Goldhill 1986, 163–64.

7. Goff claims that even prior to the mention of the scar itself (at 573)
"Orestes already evokes Odyssean patterns of action" (1991, 260).

In looking at Sophocles' *Electra*, then, it may seem entirely predictable and unremarkable that his Orestes should somehow evoke the Homeric Odysseus as well. Although some critical attention has been directed toward examining Sophocles' exploitation of what proves fertile ground for both Aeschylus and Euripides,[8] much remains unexplored. This chapter takes up this issue anew, arguing that both the *Iliad* and the *Odyssey* occupy a central place in the constitution of the Sophoclean Orestes. I will argue that Sophocles' play draws substantially upon the Odysseus-Orestes parallel implicit in the *Odyssey*, as it presents an Orestes defined in terms of the *mētis-biē* opposition so central to Odysseus's own identity in the epic tradition. The use of this opposition reveals a peculiarly Odyssean element in the play in the form of the Paidagogos's false narrative—an element found in neither the Aeschylean nor the Euripidean account of Orestes' revenge. This fiction, I will argue, shows itself to be the most elaborate form of *mētis* in the play. And, like the fictions of Odysseus, this one proves to bear a metafictional charge. Sophocles' play, then, shows itself to contain the most elaborate of the tragic exploitations of the *Odyssey*.

## THE HOMERIC INHERITANCE

Critics have traced many borrowings from or echoes of Homer's *Odyssey* in Sophocles' text.[9] T. M. Woodard states the matter concisely:

> Homer's Odysseus shares all the dominant characteristics of Sophocles' Orestes. Both return from abroad, and seek to recover their

8. See, for example, Woodard 1964, 171–72; Davidson 1988, 53–58; and Batchelder 1995, 6–12, 37–39.

9. Whitman 1951, 150–52; Woodard 1964, 170–73; Jebb 1894.xli; Stinton 1990, 476 n. 74; Blundell 1989, 174. Davidson, who compiles a lengthy list, suggests that the *Odyssey* stands behind Sophocles' text *in extenso* (1988, 46). Batchelder (1995, chap. 1 passim) speaks of Orestes as a poet comparable to Odysseus (and others), but makes little use of the *Odyssey* parallel(s).

home, property, and prerogatives. . . . Both Orestes and Odysseus lie with zest to further their own just ends. Both are masters of *dolos*. The *doloi* of both are tied up with *mythoi*. Both are masters of effective speech. (1964, 171–72)

All of these parallels, however, are true of the Aeschylean and Euripidean Orestes as well: an Orestes described as such is not peculiar to Sophocles' play.[10] I will argue that Sophocles' play constructs the figure of Orestes with reference to Odysseus in yet other ways. The play's use of the *Odyssey*, however, is part of its broader inheritance from Homer.

It has been widely recognized that the Paidagogos's false report of Orestes' death draws upon the account of the chariot race that forms part of the funeral games for Patroklos in *Iliad* 23. The fictitious account borrows from Nestor's speech to his son Antilokhos. As the commentaries tell us,[11] lines 720–22, relating Orestes' superb execution of a turn at the post, and lines 743–46, describing his subsequent crash, are based upon *Iliad* 23.334–41, where Nestor outlines a smart racing strategy for Antilokhos. I give first the passage from the *Iliad*:

τῷ σὺ μάλ' ἐγχρίμψας ἐλάαν σχεδὸν ἅρμα καὶ ἵππους,
αὐτὸς δὲ κλινθῆναι ἐϋπλέκτῳ ἐνὶ δίφρῳ
ἦκ' ἐπ' ἀριστερὰ τοῖιν· ἀτὰρ τὸν δεξιὸν ἵππον
κένσαι ὁμοκλήσας, εἶξαί τέ οἱ ἡνία χερσίν.
ἐν νύσσῃ δέ τοι ἵππος ἀριστερὸς ἐγχριμφθήτω,
ὡς ἄν τοι πλήμνη γε δοάσσεται ἄκρον ἱκέσθαι
κύκλου ποιητοῖο· λίθου δ' ἀλέασθαι ἐπαυρεῖν,
μή πως ἵππους τε τρώσῃς κατά θ' ἅρματα ἄξῃς·

10. Just what Woodard means by the "*doloi* of both are tied up with *mythoi*" is unclear. As I will argue below, it is the innovation of Sophocles to bring into his play precisely Odysseus's uncanny ability to charm his listeners as well as the closely related thematic concern with false stories that permeates the *Odyssey*. Perhaps Woodard intends something along these lines.

11. Kells 1973 and Kamerbeek 1974 ad loc., for example.

Brushing [ἐγχϱίμψας] this [post], drive the chariot and horses close, while you yourself in the well-made chariot lean slightly to the left. Goading on the right-hand horse, encourage him with a shout and give him slack with the reins. But let the left-hand horse brush close [ἐγχϱιμφθήτω] to the post so that the nave of the well-made wheel will seem to touch it. But be careful not to smack into it lest you injure the horses and crash the chariot.

In Sophocles' play we learn that Orestes skillfully negotiated the turn on a number of laps, relying upon the very strategy outlined by Nestor (720–22):

κεῖνος δ' ὑπ' αὐτὴν ἐσχάτην στήλην ἔχων
ἔχϱιμπτ' ἀεὶ σύϱιγγα, δεξιὸν δ' ἀνεὶς
σειϱαῖον ἵππον, εἶϱγε τὸν πϱοσκείμενον.

And he [Orestes], driving close to the post, brushed [ἔχϱιμπτ'] the wheel against it each time, and, giving slack to the right-hand horse, he kept [the left-hand horse] close.

Later, however, he was not as successful (743–46):

ἔπειτα, λύων ἡνίαν ἀϱιστεϱὰν
κάμπτοντος ἵππου, λανθάνει στήλην ἄκϱαν
παίσας· ἔθϱαυσε δ' ἄξονος μέσας χνόας,
κἀξ ἀντύγων ὤλισθε·

Then, letting the left-hand rein go slack as the horse was rounding the turn, he inadvertently struck the edge of the post. He broke the axle's nave right through the center and fell from the chariot's rails.

The Orestes of the fiction proves to be a devoted "student" of Nestor.[12] And inasmuch as the disastrous crash results precisely from the mistake

12. Kells 1973 *ad* 720f.

about which Nestor warned Antilokhos, it is clear that the fictitious account stands as a revised version of the Homeric chariot race.[13]

In spite of the consensus about the fact of the borrowing, however, there has been little agreement about its significance. Richard Garner, in fact, comments that "there seems to be no special significance in the source from which the details are drawn" (1990, 119–20). Karl Reinhardt calls this false narrative "little more than a virtuoso display" (1979, 151). Charles Segal, on the other hand, sees a marked opposition in this account between "the high registers of epic and epinician poetry" and "the low registers of lie and deception" (1981, 282).[14] Although the contrast between registers indicated by Segal surely gains in force from the Homeric echoes, such a contrast might be created by borrowing from any number of Iliadic passages. An examination of how *Electra* makes use of the *Iliad* 23 passage in its specificity, I will argue, has implications for our understanding of the messenger.[15]

## MĒTIS / BIĒ

As a prelude to telling Antilokhos how to negotiate the turning post, Nestor gives "a sermon on the uses of *mētis*"(311–18):[16]

τῶν δ' ἵπποι μὲν ἔασιν ἀφάρτεροι, οὐδὲ μὲν αὐτοὶ
πλείονα ἴσασιν σέθεν αὐτοῦ μητίσασθαι.

13. An Attic vase painting of the sixth century B.C.E. illustrating this scene (Kossatz-Deissmann 1981, 219, no. 419; Friis Johansen 1967, 86–92) and Plato's citation of *Iliad* 23.335–40 (at *Ion* 537a–b) suggest that we may reasonably expect a fifth-century audience to have been familiar with this *Iliad* 23 passage.

14. Cf. Seale 1982, 66.

15. It is important to note that in addition to what is discussed here, there are a number of possible motivations for the use of a chariot race in the play. For example, this race recalls the chariot race of Pelops, referenced at 504–15 (echoing Aesch. *Cho.* 1022). Cf. Myrick 1994, 135–37.

16. Richardson 1993, 209.

ἀλλ' ἄγε δὴ σὺ φίλος μῆτιν ἐμβάλλεο θυμῷ
παντοίην, ἵνα μή σε παρεκπροφύγῃσιν ἄεθλα.
μῆτι τοι δρυτόμος μέγ' ἀμείνων ἠὲ βίηφι·
μῆτι δ' αὖτε κυβερνήτης ἐνὶ οἴνοπι πόντῳ
νῆα θοὴν ἰθύνει ἐρεχθομένην ἀνέμοισι·
μῆτι δ' ἡνίοχος περιγίγνεται ἡνιόχοιο.

Their horses are faster, but they don't know any more than you do
about the use of *mētis.* You, my son, must keep *mētis* of all sorts in
mind so the prizes don't escape you. It is by *mētis* that the wood-
cutter excels rather than by *biē;* it is by *mētis* that the captain keeps
his swift ship on course in the wind as it sails over the wine-dark sea;
it is by *mētis* that one charioteer surpasses another.

Five times within 7 lines Nestor uses the word *mētis* (once in a verb form,
μητίσασθαι). Not only does Nestor urge Antilokhos to use *mētis,* but he
recommends this in place of a reliance upon *biē* ("strength, force"), thus
elaborating what Gregory Nagy identifies as a traditional opposition
(1979, 47).[17] Nestor then goes on (319–25) to distinguish between the
careless charioteer and the one who knows *kerdea* ("shrewdness, guile").
By way of Nestor's emphatic introductory advice, Antilokhos's actual
behavior in the race, and Menelaos's charge at its conclusion (581–85),
the narrative of the chariot race is clearly structured in terms of *mētis:*
Nestor's speech provides the introduction of *mētis* as an ally capable of
guaranteeing victory even to one with a handicap; Antilokhos in the race
demonstrates both the daring and timing required to execute such a strat-
egy; and Menelaos's charge of cheating invokes the potential for ethical
ambiguity inherent in the use of *mētis.*[18]

Some have argued that the Orestes of the false narrative stands as a
reliable indicator of the nature of the Orestes who appears onstage in

17. See also Detienne and Vernant 1991, 12–13. Cf. Dunkle 1987, 3.
18. See Richardson 1993, 166. Dunkle shows well how the *mētis-biē* op-
position structures this episode (1987, 4–9).

Sophocles' play.[19] The status of "Orestes" as a "student" of Nestor in the false *angelia*, I suggest, betokens an aspect of the play's real Orestes; for the false narrative's interest in the *Iliad* passage points to the role of *mētis* in Orestes' successful return home.

The Paidagogos opens the play, addressing Orestes as the son of Agamemnon, "who once commanded the army at Troy" (τοῦ στρατηγή-σαντος ἐν Τροίᾳ ποτὲ). In naming him the son of Agamemnon, the Paidagogos invokes Orestes' burden of avenging his father's death. Further, he identifies Orestes as the son of the martial Agamemnon, commander of a *stratos*.

Following the Paidagogos's introduction of Orestes, his identification of the scene of action, and call to action (1–22), Orestes speaks of Apollo's oracle (32–37):

ἐγὼ γὰρ ἡνίχ' ἱκόμην τὸ Πυθικὸν
μαντεῖον, ὡς μάθοιμ' ὅτῳ τρόπῳ πατρὶ
δίκας ἀροίμην τῶν φονευσάντων πάρα,
χρῆ μοι τοιαῦθ' ὁ Φοῖβος ὧν πεύσῃ τάχα·
ἄσκευον αὐτὸν ἀσπίδων τε καὶ στρατοῦ
δόλοισι κλέψαι χειρὸς ἐνδίκους σφαγάς.[20]

When I arrived at the Pythian oracle to ask how I might get justice
for my father from those who slaughtered him, Phoibos gave me an
oracle that you will straightaway learn: that I myself with neither
arms nor army should secretly and cunningly carry out with my own
hands the justifiable slaughter.

Here Sophocles clearly follows Aeschylus (*Cho.* 555–59) in attributing to Apollo the command to carry out the revenge by means of *doloi* ("de-

19. Seale 1982, 66; Kamerbeek 1974 *ad* 735.
20. I depart from Lloyd-Jones and Wilson in keeping ἐνδίκους of the manuscripts.

ceit, trickery"). Sophocles' play, however, presents the *dolos* as a ruse spe-
cifically marked in terms that invoke Odysseus.[21]

If Aeschylus's Apollo ordered that the killing of the murderers take
place δόλῳ (*Cho.* 557), Sophocles' text expands the simple deceit into
an opposition between trickery and force, between *doloi* and weapons:
ἄσκευον αὐτὸν ἀσπίδων τε καὶ στρατοῦ (36). As Nagy has shown, this
opposition itself is traditional in the form of a rivalry between Odysseus
and Achilles and shows up in both the *Iliad* and the *Odyssey* (1979, 15–58,
esp. 45–49). This tradition casts one term of the opposition—namely,
*doloi* and *mētis*—as the province of Odysseus above all.[22] Whereas the
act of deception in Aeschylus appears as simple trickery, Sophocles' play
presents this strategy in terms that invoke a traditional opposition be-
tween deceit and force. Orestes thus appears as the practitioner of the
very strategies and talents that distinguish Odysseus.[23]

As Orestes explains Apollo's command, he implicitly rejects the fil-
iation proclaimed by the Paidagogos in the opening lines of the play:[24]

21. The text repeatedly recounts the role of *dolos* in the revenge: 649,
1392, 1396.

22. Nagy cites Nestor's advice to Antilokhos at *Iliad* 23.313–18 as a clear
example of the opposition between *mētis* and *biē* (1979, 47). Cf. Davidson
1988, 57.

23. The word *mētis* does not occur in the play. Nonetheless, *mētis* often
appears as *dolos,* and the successful implementation of *dolos* may be under-
stood as the effective practice of *mētis*. In this way I understand the tradi-
tional opposition between *mētis* and *biē* to include the opposition of trickery
and force, as Nestor at *Od.* 3.120–22 makes clear: skill in the realm of *dolos*
(which does appear in our play) implies a command of *mētis*. See also Men-
elaos's complaint against Antilokhos at *Il.* 23.585, where he speaks of An-
tilokhos's use of *mētis* as a *dolos*.

24. See Seale 1982, 80 n. 1; Segal 1981, 253; di Benedetto 1983, 162–63.
At his reappearance in the guise of a messenger, the Paidagogos echoes his
earlier lines at the play's beginning when he speaks of Orestes τοῦ τὸ κλεινὸν
Ἑλλάδος / Ἀγαμέμνονος στράτευμ' ἀγείραντός ποτε (694–95). His strat-

Orestes, armed with *doloi* rather than a *stratos*, rejects his father as model and emulates the more successful approach of Odysseus.[25] And as Orestes does so, the text offers an ironic commentary on the relationship between father and son and the role of Odysseus in mediating that relationship.

The opposition between trickery and force invoked by Orestes at 36–37 not only echoes a thematic concern of the *Odyssey*,[26] but also draws telling parallels between Orestes and Odysseus.[27] Like Orestes, "Odysseus" in Odysseus's false tales consults an oracle to find out whether to return home openly or secretly.[28] Odysseus tells Eumaios that the Thesprotian king told him about "Odysseus" (14.327–30):

τὸν δ' ἐς Δωδώνην φάτο βήμεναι, ὄφρα θεοῖο
ἐκ δρυὸς ὑψικόμοιο Διὸς βουλὴν ἐπακοῦσαι,

---

egy in delivering his false *angelia* would appear to include an effort to assimilate—for Clytemnestra's consumption—the fate of Orestes to that of his father and at the same time, perhaps, to allay any suspicion that Orestes may in fact be adopting another (more dangerous) model.

25. A parallel has long been seen between the opening of the play and *Odyssey* 13, where Athena introduces Odysseus to Ithaka. See the scholion on the opening lines with Davidson 1988, 56–57.

26. *Od.* 1.296, 9.408, 11.120, and 11.455, inter alia.

27. Davidson notes several of the following parallels and cites them as evidence to discredit the view that Orestes posed the wrong question to Apollo—asking *how*, not *whether*, he should take revenge. Davidson concludes that Orestes' methods "merely follow what is a perfectly acceptable pattern established by the epic hero of the *Odyssey*. Thus Orestes' consultation experience *can* be seen from one perspective as a relatively uncomplicated echo of Homer" (1988, 57). I hope to show that the echoes are more complicated than Davidson appreciates.

28. While the text does not explicitly state that Orestes' question to Apollo opposed openness and secrecy, these are the terms in which Apollo responded.

ὅπως νοστήσει' Ἰθάκης ἐς πίονα δῆμον,
ἤδη δὴν ἀπεών, ἢ ἀμφαδὸν ἦε κρυφηδόν.[29]

He said that he [Odysseus] had gone to Dodona in order to hear the
will of Zeus from the divine leafy oak tree, how he could get back to
the fertile land of Ithaka, being gone so long now, whether openly or
in secret.

Apollo's response to Orestes could very well have answered the ques-
tion put by this "Odysseus." In book 11, after recounting his own
wretched demise, Agamemnon warns Odysseus about his return to
Ithaka (11.454–56):

ἄλλο δέ τοι ἐρέω, σὺ δ' ἐνὶ φρεσὶ βάλλεο σῇσι·
κρύβδην, μηδ' ἀναφανδά, φίλην ἐς πατρίδα γαῖαν
νῆα κατισχέμεναι, ἐπεὶ οὐκέτι πιστὰ γυναιξίν.

I'll tell you another thing, and you take it to heart: bring your ship
to your dear homeland in secret, not openly, since women are no
longer trustworthy.

Here Agamemnon rehearses the thematic opposition between deceit
and openness in the *Odyssey* as he warns Odysseus not to repeat his own
mistake. The *Odyssey* repeatedly offers the cases of Agamemnon, Cly-
temnestra, and Orestes as *comparanda* for its own developing plot: just as
Orestes is held up to Telemachus as a model, so Agamemnon here offers
himself to Odysseus as an example of a fate to avoid. As Agamemnon
here says—and as we see come true in the poem—Odysseus's success in
returning home safely depends upon his following Agamemnon's ad-
vice, inasmuch as he does arrive in Ithaka κρύβδην, μηδ' ἀναφανδά.[30]

---

29. He repeats these lines nearly verbatim to Penelope at 19.296–99. Cf.
11.119–20 and 1.295–96, cited above.

30. Another point in Sophocles' play picks up this scene between Odys-
seus and Agamemnon, according to Garner. Referring to this passage in
*Odyssey* 11, he notes that in lines 95–99 Electra's "words and sentiments re-

But in returning home disguised and with false stories ready at hand, Odysseus demonstrates not so much his docile implementation of Agamemnon's advice as his fundamental difference from Agamemnon: indeed, Odysseus, it might be argued, could hardly do otherwise.[31] One result of the epic's ongoing juxtaposition of these two *nostoi*, then, is to define Odysseus's achievement against the failure of Agamemnon: the hero of *mētis* not only wins the envy of the paradigmatic representative of *biē*, Achilles (11.488–91), but he also negotiates a return home that displays his intellectual gifts. And it is the case of Agamemnon within the *Odyssey* itself that clarifies the nature of Odysseus's *nostos* in these terms.

When, after being introduced by the Paidagogos as the son of Agamemnon, Orestes proclaims that his reentry into Mycenae must be effected by stealth and deceit rather than with weapons (36–37), the text announces that he, too, will follow his father's advice to Odysseus. He, like Odysseus, will *not* repeat Agamemnon's mistake. He, like Odysseus, will proceed κρύβδην, μηδ' ἀναφανδά.

There are two ironies here. First, although Orestes repudiates his father's tactics, it remains true, of course, that the political authority and wealth he seeks derive from Agamemnon. The revenge as well, needless to say, is a kind of performance of the familial bond between father and son, inasmuch as it is that relationship that confers upon Orestes the responsibility to carry out the revenge. The path to the successful accomplishment of these goals, however, requires that Orestes abandon his father's lack of suspicion of and his trust in Clytemnestra as well as his status as one unskilled in the tactic of deceptive speech. Immediately after advising Odysseus not to repeat his own mistakes, Agamemnon urges him to use caution in what he reveals to Penelope (11.441–43):

---

call those expressed by Agamemnon himself to Odysseus in Hades" (1990, 121). He also adduces *Cho.* 324–26 and *Ag.* 1453–57, 1559, as echoes of the same Homeric passage and possible models for Sophocles.

31. Cf. Pratt 1993, 94.

μή ποτε καὶ σὺ γυναικί περ ἤπιος εἶναι
μηδ' οἱ μῦθον ἅπαντα πιφαυσκέμεν, ὅν κ' ἐὺ εἰδῇς,
ἀλλὰ τὸ μὲν φάσθαι, τὸ δὲ καὶ κεκρυμμένον εἶναι.

Don't you, too, be overly gentle with your wife, and don't tell her the whole story of all that you know; tell her some things, but let others remain hidden.

Agamemnon here effectively advocates the strategies that Odysseus has long ago mastered, and in the process judges his living self as deficient compared to the master of deceit, Odysseus. In adopting the course recommended by Agamemnon to Odysseus, then, Orestes, too, takes the path of Odysseus rather than that of his father in order to assert his right to inherit Agamemnon's power and household.

Second, while explicitly adopting the ways of Odysseus and departing from those of his father, Orestes in fact adheres to (the Odyssean) Agamemnon's advice. That is, as he enacts his own allegiance to the rival tradition of Odysseus, he remains the faithful son. This, of course, is the necessary result of Agamemnon's own embracing of Odysseus's methods, even if he himself seems oblivious of what he is doing in *Odyssey* 11. In retrospect, the *Odyssey* claims, all agree that Odysseus is, if not the best, at least the most enviable of the Achaians. As Sophocles' text, then, stages the assimilation of Orestes to Odysseus, it is able to show the son abandoning his paternal bequest in becoming "Odyssean," as it invokes the Agamemnon of the *Odyssey* and reveals the son to be in step with the father as he now is: in the underworld.[32] Indeed, Orestes'

32. Into the dialogue between Odysseus and Agamemnon in *Od.* 11 is woven Agamemnon's concern for Orestes, whom he mentions at 431, 452, and 458–61, as well as his interest in Telemachus, whom he mentions at 448–49: if the *nostoi* of both Odysseus and Agamemnon inevitably call to mind their sons, so are their strategies of homecoming articulated with respect to these children. Orestes, too, has a *nostos* that is here contextualized by the dialogue: his fate, this passage suggests, may depend on whether he adopts the *nostos* of Agamemnon or that of Odysseus as model.

success depends upon his ability to avoid becoming (too much) like his father.[33]

Further suggesting this parallel is a similarity between Orestes and the Odysseus of Sophocles' *Philoctetes*. Explaining his willingness to pretend to be dead, Orestes, at line 61, claims his allegiance to *kerdos* ("profit"): "I consider no word bad that is spoken with profit" (δοκῶ μὲν οὐδὲν ῥῆμα σὺν κέρδει κακόν). J. H. Kells compares this line to *Philoctetes* 111, where Odysseus urges Neoptolemos to overcome his hesitation to lie (to Philoctetes), saying: "When you do something for profit, you need not have any scruples" (ὅταν τι δρᾷς εἰς κέρδος, οὐκ ὀκνεῖν πρέπει). Kells comments that "these words of Odysseus . . . are a mere variation on Orestes'" (1973, 6). *Kerdos*, of course, is associated with trickery, and it is one of the domains of expertise that typically characterize Odysseus.[34] Orestes' commitment to *kerdos* here restates his adoption of the Odyssean model of trickery: what is a self-evidently appropriate pronouncement in *Philoctetes* finds propriety coming from Orestes figured as the practitioner of Odyssean *mētis*.[35]

Confirmation that the *mētis* of the *Iliad* 23 passage lurks behind our play arises also from the shared notion of *kairos* in both contexts. In his speech of advice to Antilokhos, Nestor introduces the notion of timing

---

33. In the final scene, which looks forward, perhaps portentously, to what is to come, Orestes claims skill as a *mantis*, which, Aigisthos remarks, was a clear failing of Agamemnon (1499–1500). Whether or not Orestes in fact does possess such a skill is at best in doubt. See, for example, Winnington-Ingram 1980, 225–28; Roberts 1988, 186, with references.

34. Segal 1994, 181–82. At *Od.* 19.285–86 Odysseus, in the guise of the Cretan Aithon, tells Penelope that Odysseus is supreme among mortals for his knowledge of *kerdea*. Cf. Roisman 1990, 225–30.

35. This identifiably Odyssean sentiment also acknowledges the inseparability of *kerdos* and *mētis*. See Roisman 1994, 10. A scholion on lines 62–64 cites the view that Orestes' boast refers to Odysseus. See Davidson 1988, 57–58.

as crucial to the successful use of *mētis* (322–25).[36] Both Orestes and the Paidagogos speak of their plan in terms of *kairos*.[37] The Paidagogos at line 22 opposes hesitation and the ἔργων ἀκμή ("the time for action"). Orestes then picks this up and amplifies its importance for the plan of deceit: he asks the Paidagogos for assistance εἰ μή τι καιροῦ τυγχάνω ("if I miss the mark," 31); again at 39 Orestes speaks of the "right moment" *(kairos)* for the Paidagogos to enter the palace; and finally he marks the moment that sets the plan in motion as *kairos* (75–76).

This shared concern, I suggest, underscores the common theme of *mētis*. Marcel Detienne and Jean-Pierre Vernant (1991) argue that the concern with timing in the *Iliad* 23 passage is indicative of how *mētis* was typically thought to function. Its appearance in *Electra*, then, conforms with their analysis and serves to confirm the importance of *mētis* for understanding this Homeric borrowing. Given an Orestes who claims an Odyssean identity and speaks of his own plan in terms of the opposition between deceit and force, the *Iliad* 23 passage may be more apposite than critics have recognized.[38]

———

οὔτ' οὖν ἀγγελίη ἔτι πείθομαι.[39]

I will no longer trust in messages.

The Sophoclean Orestes' return finds itself further likened to the *nostos* of Odysseus in a manner not found in Aeschylus: the prolonged anticipation of Orestes' arrival. On the one hand, Electra is analogized to Pe-

36. On *kairos* in the *Iliad* 23 passage see Detienne and Vernant 1991, 15.

37. Cf. Woodard 1964, 165.

38. Lest the attention drawn by our text to the role of Nestor's advice in the fictitious chariot race be thought to detract from the parallel between Odysseus and Orestes, it is worth noting that Nestor himself at *Od.* 3.120–29 defers in matters of *mētis* to Odysseus while claiming that he and Odysseus were "alike in mind and clever planning" (ἀλλ' ἕνα θυμὸν ἔχοντε νόῳ καὶ ἐπίφρονι βουλῇ, 128).

39. Telemachus to Eurymakhos, *Od.* 1.414.

nelope;[40] on the other hand, Orestes is analogized to Odysseus. In part, of course, the significance of this structural parallel results from Sophocles' focus on Electra and her sufferings: she suffers because Orestes has not (yet) returned. But the text amplifies what might have remained an implicit parallel, as it does in Aeschylus. At 169–70 Electra laments not only the absent Orestes, but the (apparently) deceptive reports about him that she has received:

> τί γὰρ οὐκ ἐμοὶ
> ἔρχεται ἀγγελίας ἀπατώμενον;

> What message do I receive that does not turn out to be deceptive?

Here Electra announces her ongoing distress at Orestes' absence, as well as the play's concern with false reports. And this latter concern recalls the *Odyssey*.

At 289–92 Electra rehearses Clytemnestra's verbal abuse and then comments that she makes such remarks unless she hears about Orestes (293–95):

> τάδ' ἐξυβρίζει· πλὴν ὅταν κλύῃ τινὸς
> ἥξοντ' Ὀρέστην· τηνικαῦτα δ' ἐμμανὴς
> βοᾷ παραστᾶσ'.

> She speaks these outrageous things except whenever she hears from someone that Orestes is coming; then she goes mad and approaches me, shouting.

---

40. See Davidson 1988, 55. Segal (1966, 512 n. 45) compares Electra's lament for Orestes and Agamemnon at 1150–51 (πάντα γὰρ συναρπάσας, / θύελλ' ὅπως, βέβηκας· οἴχεται πατήρ, "snatching up everything like a storm, you have gone; father has gone.") to Penelope's dejected appeal to Artemis at *Od.* 20.63–64 (ἢ ἔπειτά μ' ἀναρπάξασα θύελλα / οἴχοιτο προφέρουσα, "or later let a storm snatch me up and be gone, carrying me away"). Cf. Davidson 1988, 55.

Though here attributing the reports that Clytemnestra hears to "someone" (τινὸς), at 319 Electra attributes the reports that she receives to Orestes himself. Electra indicates that Orestes sent secret messages (1155), while Clytemnestra has merely heard rumors.[41] Only after the recognition is Electra prepared to recognize those messages as anything but deceptive. Aside from Orestes' promises to return, it seems that Electra has also heard reports *about* Orestes. At 951–53 she tells Chrysothemis that news about Orestes always gave her hope:

> ἐγὼ δ', ἕως μὲν τὸν κασίγνητον βίῳ
> θάλλοντ' ἔτ' εἰσήκουον, εἶχον ἐλπίδας
> φόνου ποτ' αὐτὸν πράκτορ' ἵξεσθαι πατρός·

As long as I heard that our brother was alive and well, I had hope
that one day he would come to avenge the killing of our father.

There are, then, numerous references to news about (or from) Orestes, and these reports figure prominently in the anticipation of Orestes' arrival.

The *Odyssey* constructs the story of Odysseus's return around a multitude of false stories, as it shows Penelope (and Telemachus) negotiating reports about Odysseus. Their experience, in fact, would seem to confirm Alkinoos's pregnant compliment of Odysseus, when he tells him that he does not seem like one of the wandering inventors of falsehoods (11.363–66). If Skheria is overrun with such people, so, it seems, is Ithaka. In response to Eurymakhos's line of inquiry about Athena/Mentes in book 1, Telemachus replies: οὔτ' οὖν ἀγγελίῃ ἔτι πείθομαι, εἴ ποθεν ἔλθοι ("I will no longer trust in messages, if one should come," 414). Not only does the entire world seem to be populated by lying strangers, but Penelope (and Telemachus) expect at every moment that news about Odysseus will be deceptive.[42]

---

41. So Jebb 1894 *ad* 293f.

42. See Penelope's account of her skepticism of strangers at 23.213–17; and 14.372–74, where Eumaios says he does not go to town unless Penel-

Having said that Sophocles departs from Aeschylus, I must acknowledge that *Choephoroi* does, of course, show an interest in false reports. Orestes, posing as a *xenos*, brings Clytemnestra the false news of his own death. Indeed, this play shares with that of Sophocles the commandment from Apollo to carry out the revenge by means of *doloi*, and Orestes' false announcement to Clytemnestra is his implementation of that plot. But two things mark this act of pretense on Orestes' part as qualitatively different from that of the Paidagogos in Sophocles' play. First, Aeschylus's play does not speak of Clytemnestra or Electra awaiting news of Orestes. Rather, the "news" appears unanticipated, and the link to the *Odyssey* effected in Sophocles' play as discussed above is here absent.[43]

Second, while Aeschylus's Orestes does indeed bring false news, he does not bring a story. The characteristic charm and danger of the false story in the *Odyssey* resides not simply in its falsity, but in its status as extended narrative capable of captivating the listener.[44] It is precisely this quality that the Paidagogos brings to his performance, and it is precisely this quality that is absent in Aeschylus.

-------

ope orders him "when a report arrives from somewhere" (ὅτ' ἀγγελίη ποθὲν ἔλθῃ). For Penelope's desire to hear news despite her skepticism see 17.508–11, and 17.549–50, where she confirms Eumaios' suggestion to Odysseus at 14.131–32 that he might get a cloak for telling a good story—a scenario that, in fact, gets played out soon after. The recurring interest in (false) news of Odysseus is more than a thematic concern of the *Odyssey*. The poem and its protagonist both are fashioned as collections of stories, and as the process of disentangling and interpreting those stories. See Olson 1995; Goldhill 1991, 37–56.

43. The absence of messages from or reports about Orestes is perhaps underscored by Electra's wish at 195 when contemplating the lock of hair found at Agamemnon's tomb: εἴθ' εἶχε φωνὴν ἔμφρον' ἀγγέλου δίκην. While there is no mention of rumors about the absent Orestes in Aesch. *Cho.*, Clytemnestra in *Ag.* conspicuously complains of having heard many false and worrying stories about Agamemnon while he was away at Troy (861–76).

44. See, for example, Eumaios's description of Odysseus as storyteller at 17.514–21. Cf. Walsh 1984, 14–21; Pucci 1987, 191–208.

*Choephoroi*, however, repeats its concern with false messages when the chorus intervene to change the message that Kilissa takes to Aigisthos (766–82). And Aigisthos himself shows a pronounced skepticism of what he has heard at a remove (838–54). He even wants to cross-examine the "messenger" (851). But for that he is too late, as the "messenger" has already performed. His skepticism, however, serves to underscore the absence of any such skepticism on Clytemnestra's part. Aigisthos claims that he would not be deceived by a false report (854), whereas Clytemnestra is taken in by a slender lie. In other words, there is nothing of Odysseus's characteristic ability to spin a convincing story in Orestes' false report, and Aigisthos's desire to confront the "messenger" only emphasizes this lack of confrontation between Orestes and Clytemnestra: nowhere does a fictitious *story* actually persuade or seduce in Aeschylus's play.

The importation of this concern in Sophocles' *Electra*, then, designates its Orestes' *nostos* as peculiarly Odyssean. In adopting this element from the *Odyssey*, Sophocles' text signals its interest in false reports and in the Odyssean use of such reports. All of this culminates, of course, in the Paidagogos's fictitious *angelia*.

## THE *ODYSSEY* AND THE PAIDAGOGOS: FICTION AND METAFICTION

δεδίδαχεν δὲ μάλιστα Ὅμηρος καὶ τοὺς ἄλλους ψευδῆ
λέγειν ὡς δεῖ.[45]

Homer most of all has taught the others [poets] how to
tell lies properly.

If the play effects the approximation of Orestes to Odysseus as a figure of *mētis*, the *angelia* itself remains the supreme example of *mētis* in the play.[46] It is, in fact, the play's most Odyssean element. In a context am-

45. Arist. *Poet.* 1460a.
46. The scene with Pylades and Orestes bringing in the urn (1098–1231), needless to say, also forms part of the ruse (and part of the metatheater).

ply qualified in terms of Odyssean *mētis*, this false narrative asks to be read against the false narratives that Odysseus himself tells in the *Odyssey*. The sustained curiosity and anxiety about news of Orestes prepare for the false narrative, as they mirror the comparable interest in news of Odysseus in Ithaka. And in the play, as in the epic, this interest is rewarded with a lie.

Writing of the false tales that Odysseus tells to Eumaios in *Odyssey* 14, Segal argues that "the poem insistently develops the irony that lies speak a form of the truth" (1994, 177).[47] Indeed, there is a lengthy and rich history of commentary on this topic within Greek poetry, and this body of commentary consistently provides self-conscious reflection on the nature of poetry itself.[48] Segal goes on to say of the irony mentioned above that it bears on the poem's "self-consciousness about its poetics, its exploration of how tales are fabricated, received, and believed or disbelieved" (177). Segal concludes with the claim that Odysseus is "a master of lies and disguise, who, like his poet, achieves his ultimate truth through devious paths and through a paradoxical mixture of truth and false appearances" (183). In its approximation of hero and bard, bard and beggar, the *Odyssey* displays its own fictionality, as it shows how truthful fiction can be.[49]

In a line much like the famous self-description offered by Hesiod's Muses (*Th.* 27), the Homeric narrator says of Odysseus at *Odyssey* 19.203: ἴσκε ψεύδεα πολλὰ λέγων ἐτύμοισιν ὁμοῖα ("He knew how to tell many lies like truth"). This comment, immediately following Odysseus's recounting of the false Cretan tale to Penelope, makes sense of what precedes in three ways. First, at the simplest level, it suggests that the lie Odysseus tells is indistinguishable, by Penelope at least, from what is

47. Cf. Goldhill 1991, 44–46, 68.

48. See, for example, Hes. *Th.* 27–28. See also Pucci 1977, 1980; Walsh 1984, 20–36; Segal 1994, 177–83; Goldhill 1988b; Pratt 1993.

49. See Segal 1994, 142–83; Goldhill 1991, 47–49, 54–56, 60–68; Olson 1995, 129–30, 139.

true. That is, it sounds plausible and convinces: nothing distinguishes it as false.[50] Second, it suggests that Odysseus manages to speak a kind of "truth" via the falsehood. His fiction contains as though in code a version of what is true such as to be intelligible to those who understand the code.[51] Third, as its kinship with the Hesiodic text suggests, this comment explicitly identifies Odysseus as an analogue of the bard: his (false) story is like the (true) story that contains it.[52] Odysseus's posture as "bard" models for us the dynamics of poetic performance, revealing the poem's exploitation of its own fictional status. This third form of being a "lie like truth" deserves some clarification.

In line with Pietro Pucci's comment that "Odysseus, as narrator, functions as the representative of the *Odyssey*'s poetics" (1998, 138), I would point to three aspects of Odysseus's stories that rehearse essential qualities of these poetics.[53] First, in a passage cited above, Alkinoos tells Odysseus that he does not resemble the horde of liars that wander the earth. Instead, he says, Odysseus resembles a more honorable type (11.367–68):

σοὶ δ' ἔπι μὲν μορφὴ ἐπέων, ἔνι δὲ φρένες ἐσθλαί,
μῦθον δ' ὡς ὅτ' ἀοιδὸς ἐπισταμένως κατέλεξας.

Your words have a form, and your mind is sharp, and you told your story with skill, just like a bard.

Odysseus's stories resemble those of a bard in that they possess (a certain) *morphē* ("form"). George B. Walsh suggests that one constituent of such a *morphē* is evidence of membership in a tradition of song, as indicated by the use of traditional language. Alkinoos takes the presence of

---

50. Cf. Walsh 1984, 27; Pratt 1993, 110–11.

51. Walsh calls the fictions told by Odysseus to Eumaios and Penelope "stories that are false in detail but true in substance" (1984, 27). Cf. Pucci 1977, 76; Nagy 1979, 234–42; Haft 1984, 300–303.

52. See Walsh 1984, 5.

53. These are not the only qualities shared by Odysseus's stories and the poem. See, for example, Pratt 1993, 85–89.

such *morphē* to indicate the truthfulness of the song.[54] Odysseus's story-telling clearly mimics a form that signifies authenticity.

Second, the stories of Odysseus, like poetry in general as conceived by the poem, "charm" their auditors. At 17.518–21 Eumaios speaks to Penelope of Odysseus, saying:

> ὡς δ' ὅτ' ἀοιδὸν ἀνὴρ ποτιδέρκεται, ὅς τε θεῶν ἒξ
> ἀείδῃ δεδαὼς ἔπε' ἱμερόεντα βροτοῖσι,
> τοῦ δ' ἄμοτον μεμάασιν ἀκουέμεν, ὁππότ' ἀείδῃ·
> ὡς ἐμὲ κεῖνος ἔθελγε παρήμενος ἐν μεγάροισι.

> Just as when a man looks at a bard, one who sings delightful songs
> for mortals with a skill from the gods, and they are always eager to
> hear him whenever he sings, in this way he enchanted me sitting in
> the hall.

The use of *thelgein* in this sense is characteristically and "exclusively Odyssean" (Pucci 1987, 193).[55] These two passages, then, which compare Odysseus to a bard, attribute to him the very qualities identified by the poem more broadly as belonging to song.[56]

Third, Odysseus's stories, like the poem that creates them, invoke and exploit the fictional status of the "truthful" story in which the "false" one is embedded. In so doing, the poem displays a keen interest in fictionality as such and in the poetics that generate notions of truth and fiction alike.[57] Concerning the scene in which Odysseus succeeds in getting a cloak from Eumaios by means of a false story (14.462–506, esp. 499–501), Pucci comments that this episode "shows the *Odyssey* poking fun at the epic principle" of poetry coming from the Muses. Instead, this story "declares ostentatiously that it is not the Muses but fic-

54. Walsh 1984, 12.

55. Cf. 1.337; 12.40, 44; 11.334 = 13.2. Poetry characterized by *thelxis* is not limited to the *Odyssey*, of course. See Pratt 1993, 73–81.

56. Cf. Pratt 1993, 65.

57. On fictionality in Eumaios's tale to Odysseus at 15.415–84 see Richardson 1996, 399.

tion . . . that brings the epic into being" (1998, 95). Odysseus's stories, like the *Odyssey* itself, delight in calling into question not only their own truthfulness, but also the very criteria that one might reasonably call upon to distinguish the true from the false.

All of these qualities of Odysseus's tales are implicit in Segal's observation that lies speaking a form of truth bear on the poem's "self-consciousness about its poetics, its exploration of how tales are fabricated, received, and believed or disbelieved" (1994, 177). And this observation, I submit, holds true for the Paidagogos's false narrative as well. This "lie like truth" presents itself as a thoroughly Odyssean form of fiction in that it reproduces the triple character of being a ψεῦδος ἐτύμοισιν ὁμοῖον ("a lie like truth"). This false narrative (1) is indistinguishable by Clytemnestra (and Electra) from a true report about Orestes, sounds plausible, and convinces; (2) speaks the truth concerning Orestes' act of revenge in progress that it is an act of *mētis;* and (3) is a "false" performance that is very much like a "true" one and thus comments self-reflexively on the play's own poetics. Enacting the very *mētis* of which it speaks and therefore speaking of what it enacts, the false *angelia* points to an even broader self-directed commentary that appears as meta-theater. Just as Odysseus fabricates a (false) story that stands meta-fictionally for the (true) story of the bard, so the Paidagogos performs a (false) scene that stands metatheatrically for the (true) play of the tragic poet.[58]

Here in the Paidagogos's performance we find not only a fiction-within-the-fiction, a play-within-the-play; we find a very specific form of fiction: the metatheater takes the form of a messenger-speech. Not only does the Paidagogos create within the fictional world of the play a false report about Orestes that is indistinguishable from a true one; he also creates within the real world of the theater a "false" *angelia* that is indistinguishable from a "true" one. In this sense the metatheater is double,

---

58. On the "reality" of the false *angelia* see Parlavantza-Friedrich 1969, 48.

inasmuch as it stages a specifically tragic form of theater as the play-within-the-play. We are invited, then, not only to contemplate the construction of pretense as theater but also to study the specific form and workings of the tragic *angelia*. And by reading the Paidagogos's fiction against the stories of Odysseus we can understand the quality and significance of its metafictional status.

Just as the stories of Odysseus bear a metafictional relationship to the *Odyssey* as a whole in the threefold manner described above, so the false *angelia* displays these very aspects in its status as metatheater: it is characterized by a certain *morphē*, it "charms" its auditors, and it exploits the confusion between truth and fiction as it displays a keen interest in fictionality as such.

If we follow Walsh's suggestion about the appearance of a certain *morphē*, it is possible to describe the Paidagogos's performance in similar terms. In the case of the Paidagogos, the *morphē* that identifies his performance as traditional is that which identifies it as an *angelia*. The *morphē* of the Paidagogos's false narrative clearly identifies his performance as a conventional messenger-speech, *in form*.[59] It is, in fact, this *morphē* that renders the metatheater double.

The *thelxis* so characteristic of both Odysseus's stories and Odyssean poetry in general appears also in the false *angelia*. Given that there is substantial overlap between that aspect of the fiction that makes it indistinguishable from truth and its power to "charm," critics have identified the power of the Paidagogos's fiction as one of its most remarkable features. Some, in fact, have argued that the false narrative actually convinces the theatrical audience of its reality, in spite of the fact that they know in advance that it is false.[60] It obviously affects Electra and Cly-

---

59. On the formal properties of tragic *angeliai* see above, note 34 in the introduction.

60. Wilamowitz-Möllendorff 1917, 190–94; Parlavantza-Friedrich 1969, 36; Kaibel cited by Ringer 1998, 228 n.59. Vickers calls it "a masterpiece of *verismo*" (1973, 569).

temnestra profoundly.[61] It is not merely a simple lie that accomplishes this; rather, it is an *angelia* that is "one of the most splendid and effective in Sophocles," full of "glitter and pageantry" (Kells 1973, 137).

This *thelxis*, moreover, stands metatheatrically both for the impact on the audience of theater per se and for the specific impact of the tragic *angelia*.[62] That theater, perhaps especially tragedy, can make an impact deserving to be called *thelxis* is suggested by more than our own experience.[63] And that this *thelxis* characterizes the tragic *angelia* in its "true" (i.e., conventional) form is evident from criticism.[64] The substantial amount of critical opinion—much of it unexpressed—that has read the tragic *angelia* precisely as the equivalent of epic produced by an omniscient third-person narrator is, I suggest, one effect of the *thelxis* characteristic of the tragic *angelia*.[65]

As for the keen interest in fictionality evident in the stories of Odysseus, this too we find in the false *angelia*. At one level, the Paidagogos's performance stages pretense as metatheater, inasmuch as it is a play-within-the-play. Here, the pretense that Orestes is dead corresponds to any form of pretense. As such it speaks only generally about theater as pretense. But in its capacity as a metatheatrical staging of a conventional tragic form, the false *angelia* shows not merely that the Paidagogos is ca-

61. See Kells 1973, 139.
62. Cf. Ringer 1998, 173.
63. E.g., Arist. *Poet.* 1449b.
64. See the introduction above.
65. Recall, for example, Rosenmeyer's comment: "The messenger is, as far as his message is concerned, omniscient. He is the equivalent of the epic bard" (1982, 197). Although I here highlight the role of the *angelia*'s epic affiliation in its exercise of *thelxis*, Greek tragedy explores its own powers of *thelxis* in a variety of ways. As critics have recognized, the tragic texts provide substantial commentary on the range of charms available in the theater. See, for example, Segal's study of Euripides' *Helen* (1986, 222–67, esp. 263–67) and Zeitlin 1994.

pable of pretense; it shows more importantly that he, like the tragic poet, has mastered the art of creating this particular form.[66] That is, just as Odysseus in his lies employs the same tools as the bard and thereby exposes the fictionality of the bard's poem, so does the Paidagogos's mastery of a specific tragic form reveal the artifice that produces both.

In order to understand better just how this artifice appears in the metatheater, I turn to an examination of the false *angelia* itself by way of a closer look at the Iliadic model exploited by the Paidagogos.

In a much-discussed passage, Nestor emphasizes the importance to Antilokhos of properly negotiating the turning post as he expresses his uncertainty about what the marker is (23.326–33). Although identified in such a way that Antilokhos will have no trouble recognizing it, the post remains highly ambiguous in spite of Nestor's qualification of it as a *sēma ariphrades* ("very clear marker"). Nestor, whose knowledge of history spans generations, can only guess the history of this turning post.[67]

This passage places an object notable for its status as unknowable at the focal point of attention for the race. The *sēma*, I suggest, functions as an appropriate indicator of a certain opacity essential to this scene. Just as at the center of Nestor's advice stands the inscrutable object as *sēma*, so at the center of the narrative of the chariot race stand the events that take place at or near the turning post, shrouded in doubt and dispute.

There has been some critical dispute concerning the location of the events described in lines 375–447. With respect to the intervention of Apollo and Athena, Diomedes gaining the lead, and the maneuver of Antilokhos that puts him ahead of Menelaos, some argue that these events

---

66. Similarly, the scene in Greek tragedy that offers the greatest rewards for a metatheatrical reading occurs in Euripides' *Bacchae*, where the theatricality of the pretense is so clearly marked.

67. On the implications of Nestor's ignorance see Dickson 1995, 219; Ford 1992, 141–46; Nagy 1990a, 209–22.

occur *after* the turn around the post; others argue that they take place *at* the turning post.[68] Either reading leaves gaps in the account. More important is the disagreement that arises between Idomeneus and Ajax. This episode (448–98) serves to suggest that the spectators themselves were unable to see the race clearly. The dispute concerns the relative positions of the chariots after the turn; it persists for 30 lines and nearly becomes violent. Only Achilles' intervention brings an end to the animosity.

Unable to see who is in the lead after the turning post, the spectators cannot be expected to agree on what happened at the post. In fact, the events preceding the race itself seem to presage such a dispute about events at the turn. At 359–61 Achilles sends Phoinix to the turning post as an observer so that he could "report the truth" (ἀληθείην ἀποείποι).

As it happens, there is a dispute between Menelaos and Antilokhos about who deserves second prize. Menelaos accuses Antilokhos of employing *dolos* and demands that he swear an oath stating that he did not use trickery. It appears, if briefly, that Phoinix's testimony may be needed. But the dispute is resolved when Antilokhos offers to yield the prize, and Menelaos then refuses to take it. This friendly resolution, however, conceals what Phoinix's testimony might have revealed: namely, whether Antilokhos does in fact use trickery.[69]

But the short-lived dispute recalls the mission of Phoinix and reminds us that the certainty of his privileged viewpoint remains ignored. Doubly, then, this passage speaks of the ignorance of the spectators: overtly in the form of the disagreement and dispute between Idomeneus and Ajax, and more subtly in creating an eyewitness who does not testify.

68. Roisman (1988) and Richardson (1993, 218) argue for the former; Gagarin (1983) the latter.

69. Some critics take it as self-evident that he does (e.g., Richardson 1993 *ad* 587–95). Others claim that he does not (e.g., Gagarin 1983, 38). It is worth noting that the word *dolos* occurs only in the mouth of Menelaos, while the narrator characterizes that which enabled Antilokhos to win as *kerdea*, picking up the word used by Nestor at 322. Even at the level of vocabulary some doubt remains.

And, as the critical controversy suggests, we readers may be as much without the benefit of Phoinix's knowledge as the Iliadic spectators. We know, of course, how Diomedes gains first place, and that Antilokhos heeds (in some form) Nestor's advice about using *mētis*. Nonetheless, the Homeric text hedges its account with enough opacity to make us admit some limitations on what we know and to make it perfectly clear that the spectators at the race know nothing more than the order in which the contestants finished. This opacity derives, in part, from the multiplicity of competing voices attempting to describe the race and the various points of view they represent: Nestor, Menelaos, Antilokhos, Idomeneus, Ajax (and Phoinix?). Equally, of course, this uncertainty is produced by the absence of the narrative voice: here, withdrawing his own privileged view, the narrator leaves us with nothing more than what the actors in the stands can see.

When we turn to the false *angelia* in Sophocles' play we find a rewriting of the *Iliad* passage that recasts the narrator's absence and the compromised vision of the spectators in such a way as to produce an *angelia* that is a "lie like truth." The Paidagogos offers his narrative as that of an eyewitness to the disaster that befell Orestes. That is, he presents his report as that of a spectator at the racetrack (762). Unlike his Homeric counterparts, however, this spectator has a uniquely privileged viewpoint. The Paidagogos's catalogue of competitors (701–8) announces even before the race begins that his account will be elaborate: whereas in Homer's contest there are five competitors, this fictional one features no fewer than ten. The scale of the epic race is doubled. But the scale of this invented competition does not at all hinder this narrator's ability to see and recount fine detail. Soon after the race begins, he reports (713–9),

ἐν δὲ πᾶς ἐμεστώθη δρόμος
κτύπου κροτητῶν ἁρμάτων· κόνις δ' ἄνω
φορεῖθ'· ὁμοῦ δὲ πάντες ἀναμεμειγμένοι
φείδοντο κέντρων οὐδέν, ὡς ὑπερβάλοι

χνόας τις αὐτῶν καὶ φρυάγμαθ' ἱππικά.
ὁμοῦ γὰρ ἀμφὶ νῶτα καὶ τροχῶν βάσεις
ἤφριζον, εἰσέβαλλον ἱππικαὶ πνοαί.

The entire racetrack was filled with the clang of rattling chariots,
and dust whirled up into the air. Tightly packed together, the driv-
ers all used their goads, trying to get ahead of the other chariots and
snorting horses. For about their backs and the spinning wheels the
horses foamed and heaved their breath.

This passage reveals the double perspective implicit in the Paidagogos's
narrative. On the one hand, his account speaks of the "entire track" fill-
ing with dust as the competitors take off, much as he will speak of the
"entire plain" at 729–30 (πᾶν δ' ἐπίμπλατο . . . πέδον). On the other
hand, he is able to describe what could only be sensed by one atop one
of the horses in the race (718–19): "The chariots were so close together
that the breath of the horses warmed the backs of the charioteers in
front" (Lloyd-Jones and Wilson 1990, 56).[70] While the foam may well
have been visible to a spectator, clearly the warmth of the horses' breath
could not have been. Here the Paidagogos claims to have knowledge
that is not only unavailable in principle, but that, as we have seen, is ex-
plicitly denied to the spectators in *Iliad* 23.

Similarly, the Paidagogos's account of Orestes as he rounds the turn-
ing post shows a remarkably keen and close-up view (720–22):

κεῖνος δ' ὑπ' αὐτὴν ἐσχάτην στήλην ἔχων
ἔχριμπτ' ἀεὶ σύριγγα, δεξιὸν δ' ἀνεὶς
σειραῖον ἵππον εἶργε τὸν προσκείμενον.

And he [Orestes], driving close to the post, brushed the wheel
against it each time, and, giving slack to the right-hand horse, he
kept [the left-hand horse] close.

70. Jebb compares this passage to *Il.* 23.380, where Eumelos is pursued
by Diomedes (1894 *ad* 718f.).

Comparable is the description of his final turn (743–46):

ἔπειτα, λύων ἡνίαν ἀριστερὰν
κάμπτοντος ἵππου λανθάνει στήλην ἄκραν
παίσας· ἔθραυσε δ' ἄξονος μέσας χνόας,
κἀξ ἀντύγων ὤλισθε·

Then, letting the left-hand rein go slack as the horse was rounding the turn, he inadvertently struck the edge of the post. He broke the axle's nave right through the center and fell from the chariot's rails.

As it stages its most explicit Homeric borrowing, the Paidagogos's account appears as "a marvel of direct observation" (Lesky 1983, 163), in sharp contrast to the confusion and disagreement among the spectators in *Iliad* 23. Whereas the Iliadic spectators argue about who is in the lead after the turn, this spectator sees everything that takes place at the turn.

Seen as the reworking of the Iliadic scene that it is, the false messenger-speech displays itself as the product of a privileged point of view at the racetrack. And in place of the limited vision and multiple voices of *Iliad* 23, the Paidagogos's fiction is spoken by a single, authoritative voice. Having presented himself as the equivalent of Ajax or Idomeneus, his clear, sure vision and his uncontested, persuasive voice stand out in sharp contrast to what appears in the Homeric account.

In borrowing from and modeling itself to a substantial degree on the *Iliad* 23 chariot race, the Paidagogos's fiction allows us to appreciate the highly "dramatic" character of the Homeric scene: the commanding third-person narrative of the false *angelia* throws the polyphony and dispute of the Homeric account into sharp relief. And in displaying its own distance from what any of the Iliadic spectators might be able to report, the Paidagogos's false narrative ironically shows itself to resemble the significantly absent voice of the narrator in the Homeric episode. That is, if the Paidagogos reveals himself to be epistemically and discursively distinct from the Iliadic spectators, he proves to be on these same grounds the equivalent of the Homeric narrator. It is precisely the absence of the familiar narrative voice that makes possible and is in turn signified by the disagreement and dispute between Ajax and Idomeneus; and it is this voice that is effectively appropriated by the Paidagogos. In borrowing from the *Iliad* 23 account, then, the false *angelia* invents and inserts that which is conspicuously absent in the Homeric passage. And the result is precisely the clarity that is missing in the epic.

The Homeric borrowing, then, shows up as more than the adoption of words and phrases that proclaim a literary pedigree.[71] This borrowing appears also as the appropriation of the privilege that inheres in the status of the Homeric narrator. And it is the metatheater, in its Odyssean form, that enables us to understand both the richness and the significance of the Homeric borrowings.

The fictitious *angelia* displays its claims of privilege as emphatically distinct from those of the "real" spectators in the *Iliad*. And this disjunction signals the relevance of the metatheatrical commentary to the institution of tragic theater. Understood on the model of the metafiction in the *Odyssey*, the Paidagogos's performance displays its powerful effects as those of the tragic *angelia*. That is, in its claims of privilege, the fiction of the Paidagogos metatheatrically suggests that such privilege inheres in the tragic *angelia* itself. Just as the Paidagogos speaks with a voice that stands out as peculiarly privileged when compared to the multiplicity of voices in *Iliad* 23, so, the metatheater suggests, does the tragic *angelia* more generally stand out as peculiarly privileged among the multiplicity of voices on the tragic stage. The Homeric borrowings, then, allow us to understand the specific privileges and powers claimed by the Paidagogos's fiction, as well as the status of these claims as the province of the tragic messenger.

The metatheater thus corroborates the lessons of Aeschylus's *Persians*, in specifying the role of Homeric narrative practice in the tragic *angelia*. Furthermore, in conjuring up an observer at a fictitious chariot race, the

---

71. In characterizing the fictitious *angelia* Kells (1973) speaks of "epic colouring" (*ad* 711f.), "epic and Homeric atmosphere" (*ad* 709), and "Homeric feel" (*ad* 746ff.). Cf. his comments on the use of στρατός *ad* 749.

fictitious messenger-speech confirms *Bacchae*'s metatheatrical presentation of the messenger as privileged spectator. Indeed, here the two are indistinguishable: the ideal spectator of *Iliad* 23 is the (missing) narrator. In creating a version of this Homeric scene, the Paidagogos's fiction distinguishes itself as a masterful fusion of these twin elements that underpin the conventional *angelia*.

Like the Homeric spectators, the characters of Sophocles' play who are not privy to the plot of the pretense inhabit a world of limited vision, partial knowledge, and disagreement. And into this world, this "rehearsal of imperfect knowledge or of blindness," steps the Paidagogos with his false *angelia* that "introduces the knowledge that liberates or kills" (Rosenmeyer 1982, 197). Testimony to the power of this performance is twofold: the Paidagogos's narrative "charms," overwhelms, and utterly convinces both Clytemnestra and Electra; and it stands as an edifice next to which the true report of Chrysothemis can appear to Electra only as foolish babbling (920, 935–36). This fiction is far more persuasive than the truth that Chrysothemis speaks. And inasmuch as the metatheater carefully marks this masterful and persuasive, but fictitious, narrative as an *angelia* built on its Homeric borrowings, it suggests that it is precisely in its status as an *angelia* so constructed that it wields such power. That is, the Paidagogos's narrative, the metatheater suggests, derives its authority and force not so much from its status as fiction, as from its status as an *angelia*. The artifice of the Paidagogos, the metatheater suggests, is the artifice of tragedy itself.

As discussed above in the introduction, many critics have read tragic messenger-speeches as though the implications of the metatheater outlined here hold true in general. Others—most notably Irene de Jong (1991)—have refuted such a view as naive. I think we can negotiate some of these difficulties by paying attention to the ramifications of what we find in Sophocles' play. It is, of course, the fictitiousness of the Paidagogos's performance that enables us to read it along the lines I have sketched. But its fictitious quality, together with the exposition of the artifice behind a "true" *angelia*, also enables us to appreciate that the claims to epistemic and discursive privilege of the tragic *angelia* in its conventional form remain "fictitious," too. In other words, it is part of tragedy's artifice to produce a figure who performs the fiction of speaking with the voice of epic. In short, the metatheater here tells us that the tragic messenger-speech is a form of "fiction"—insofar as it is not only theater but also a conventional form of theater—that *claims* the privileges I have identified. As the metatheater makes clear, however, it is within our powers to look behind the curtain and discover the artifice underpinning these claims.

# FIVE

# *Rhesos* and Poetic Tradition

> Recollection is a discarded garment that does not fit. . . . Repetition is an indestructible garment that fits closely and tenderly, neither binds nor sags.
>
> *Kierkegaard, "Repetition"*

The narrative practices on exhibit in the *angeliai* discussed in the preceding chapters are not, in fact, always adopted by tragic messengers. I have argued that the messenger makes competing, even contradictory, claims as eyewitness and narrator. The messenger's bodily presence as eyewitness—and as *dramatis persona*—competes to some extent with his claim to extradiegetic status. This contradiction is fundamental to the messenger's identity as conventionally conceived. There are, however, several moments at which tragic messengers either explicitly deny claims to knowledge or perform a narrative that implicitly makes no allowance for a claim to extradiegetic status. In short, in some cases messengers clearly fail to make one of the claims I have outlined above. The next two chapters address plays that present important and productive challenges to my general argument.

This chapter takes up the challenge posed by the charioteer who reports the death of Rhesos in the play of that name. The narrative of this messenger, while largely conforming to the formal patterns that identify an *angelia*, sharply diverges from the practices I have outlined. Specifically, this narrative bears recurrent, even insistent, signs of its own enunciation that emphasize the strong embodiment of the voice that speaks it. Further, the subject of the narrative itself is almost exclusively the narrator himself. So markedly does this messenger's narrative depart from conventional practice that one critic has said it leaves tradition behind.[1]

I will argue that this anomalous *angelia* serves the larger interests of the play in a way that it is uniquely able to perform. This messenger-speech, I will suggest, forms the centerpiece of the play's attention to treatment of Rhesos in the poetic tradition. Exploiting the incompatibilities between Iliadic and non-Iliadic traditions of the Rhesos myth, the play stages the confrontation of these divergent traditions. And in so doing the play assumes a critical posture, commenting on the fate of Rhesos as a figure whose claim to *kleos* is contested. In particular, the play directs its attention to the place of Rhesos within the Iliadic tradition and to the impact of this tradition on the fate of Rhesos as a mythic figure.

In presenting a messenger-speech that departs so strongly from conventional practice, then, the play makes productive use of this departure and shows that this anomalous feature is not gratuitous: the play does not rewrite this conventional form; rather, it demonstrates precisely what are the losses concomitant with such a departure. In adapting the conventional messenger-speech to its own ends, the play successfully elaborates its larger thematic interests as it proves in the end to be the exception that confirms what it so conspicuously seems to deny.

_____

Aside from the *angelia* of the charioteer in particular, the play as a whole is unique as well. It is, for example, the only play of dubious authentic-

1. Strohm 1959, 271.

ity in the manuscripts of Euripides.[2] More important for the discussion here, it is the only extant tragedy that stages a plot from Homer. In presenting the story told in *Iliad* 10, the play displays an obvious reliance upon the epic. But the extent of the borrowing may in fact be more extensive than is at first apparent. Robin Sparks Bond, for example, sees extensive parallels between the play and the *Iliad* as a whole, arguing that "the play's structure mirrors that of the entire poem." He concludes that the play constitutes "an effort to create a dramatic equivalent of the *Iliad*" (1996, 271–72).[3] However great the play's reliance upon the epic, it is clear that the play demands to be read against the *Iliad*.

At the same time, others have pointed to signs of the play's reliance upon non-Iliadic traditions about Rhesos. Bernard Fenik, while acknowledging the important influence of *Iliad* 10, speaks of the play's "basically non-Iliadic derivation" (1964, 28).[4] For him, Dolon as a non-functional character and the role of Athena are signs that the play is closer to the non-Iliadic story than it is to the *Iliad* (25).[5] A further sign of this, in Fenik's judgment, is Rhesos's status as a formidable figure in the play, together with multiple borrowings from the epic cycle (37). The play, then, relies upon elements from *Iliad* 10 as well as from traditions both different from and incompatible with what appears in the epic, producing what Fenik calls "a mixed version" (25).

From the Iliadic account of Rhesos's last hours one would never suspect that he might have led a more interesting life. Even his death in the

2. The charioteer's anomalous *angelia*, in fact, is cited by some as evidence that the play is not the work of Euripides. See Strohm 1959, 271–72, and Ritchie's response, 1964, 139–40.

3. Cf. Paduano 1973.

4. Cf. Ritchie 1964, 62–64, 79–81; Burnett 1985, 182 n. 60.

5. For Fenik, this lack of functionality derives from the fact that—unlike in the epic—Dolon does not tell Odysseus and Diomedes about Rhesos, since he leaves the Trojan camp prior to the Thracians' arrival. Consequently, Athena performs the function of informing the Greeks.

*Iliad* receives little attention and in and of itself is of no particular interest to the poem. Having killed twelve Thracian soldiers under Rhesos's command, Diomedes summarily dispatches their king with little comment from the narrator (10.494–97):

> ἀλλ' ὅτε δὴ βασιλῆα κιχήσατο Τυδέος υἱός,
> τὸν τρισκαιδέκατον μελιηδέα θυμὸν ἀπηύρα
> ἀσθμαίνοντα· κακὸν γὰρ ὄναρ κεφαλῆφιν ἐπέστη
> τὴν νύκτ' Οἰνείδαο πάϊς διὰ μῆτιν Ἀθήνης.
> τόφρα δ' ἄρ' ὁ τλήμων Ὀδυσεὺς λύε μώνυχας ἵππους.

When Tydeus's son reached the king, the thirteenth, he took the man's honey-sweet life as he gasped; for above his head that night, through the plotting of Athena, stood an evil dream, the grandson of Oineus. In the meantime enduring Odysseus was setting the single-hoofed horses free.

Turning immediately to the theft of the horses, the narrative abandons Rhesos himself with a speed that mirrors that of his killing.

Soon thereafter, with the two Greeks having been sent back to their ships by Athena, Apollo wakes Rhesos's nephew Hippocoon and brings him to the scene of the slaughter. Hippocoon is, of course, the counterpart of the play's charioteer, inasmuch as both report the events to the Trojan camp. It is worth noting, however, that Hippocoon's report remains implicit. Upon encountering the scene (522–25)

> ᾤμωξέν τ' ἄρ' ἔπειτα φίλον τ' ὀνόμηνεν ἑταῖρον.
> Τρώων δὲ κλαγγή τε καὶ ἄσπετος ὦρτο κυδοιμὸς
> θυνόντων ἄμυδις· θηεῦντο δὲ μέρμερα ἔργα
> ὅσσ' ἄνδρες ῥέξαντες ἔβαν κοίλας ἐπὶ νῆας.

he wailed and called out the name of his dear companion. The Trojans shouted loudly and made an enormous din as they swarmed together; and they gazed at the horrific deeds the men performed before returning to the hollow ships.

Here the text assimilates Rhesos to the entire group of Thracians, effectively minimizing the significance of his personal story. One commentator, noting the short shrift given both Rhesos and Dolon in these lines, calls these three lines "excessively laconic."[6] This silence, I would suggest, is of a piece with the more general exclusion of Rhesos as a figure with a story of his own.

Alternate versions of the myth, however, present a somewhat different picture.[7] Two elements of these other versions deserve mention. First, we are told that Pindar had Rhesos fighting one glorious day against the Greeks, killing many of them. He has, in other words, an *aristeia*. Pindar, we are told, also made Hera send Athena to orchestrate Rhesos's death at the hands of Odysseus and Diomedes. This she did frightened about the danger he posed to the Greeks.[8] In conjunction with the *aristeia*, this divine concern underscores the reality of the threat represented by Rhesos, itself an indication of his martial abilities. Second, the scholia report that Rhesos had received an oracle announcing that if he and his horses drank from the Scamander, and if his horses ate from the pasture there, he would be invincible. Although in no version does Rhesos ever achieve this invincible status, this version of the myth endows him with the potential to do so. With an *aristeia*, Rhesos claims not only an active role in the fighting, but a measure of success as well. As the recipient of the oracle, he has at least the potential to displace not only Hector as the rival of Achilles, but even Achilles himself. A Rhesos with such an oracle renders both Hector and Achilles potentially inferior. Indeed, he might well have upended divine plans and rewritten the story of the Trojan

6. Hainsworth 1993 ad loc. He comments further that "the focus of the poet is so firmly set on his two heroes that he is blind to the other side."

7. Preserved in the scholia on *Il.* 10.435 (A, B, and T); reproduced in Fenik 1964, 5–6. Schol. A = Pindar fr. 277 (Bowra).

8. Schol. A: δείσασα δὲ ῞Ηρα περὶ τῶν ῾Ελλήνων ᾿Αθηνὰν ἐπὶ τὴν τούτου [sc. Rhesos] διαφθορὰν πέμπει. See also the prologue contained in the anonymous hypothesis to the play ( = TrGF adesp. F81), where Hera speaks to Athena about intervening on behalf of the Greeks.

War.[9] Clearly this is a Rhesos quite different from the one we meet in the *Iliad*.

Following Fenik's claim that other versions of the Rhesos myth preserved in the scholia antedate the Iliadic version,[10] it is not hard to agree with him that the *Iliad* has radically rewritten these other versions, nearly pushing Rhesos from the horizon altogether. In place of a Rhesos who poses a serious threat even to Achilles, or one who successfully slaughters many Greeks, the *Iliad* presents a marginal figure whose chief accomplishment is dying in his sleep and making fabulous horses available for theft. The epic, then, deprives Rhesos not only of an *aristeia* or the potential to threaten the Greeks, but also of any claim to *kleos*. This Rhesos is a barely recognizable shadow of his pre-Iliadic forerunner.[11]

The play, then, insofar as it gives life to elements of the non-Iliadic traditions concerning Rhesos, implicitly challenges the epic's virtual exclusion of the Thracian king. In the wake of the *Iliad*, when the canonical version of the Rhesos myth denies him *kleos* and turns him into a pathetic figure who plays a minor role in a story no longer his own, a treatment of Rhesos such as is presented in the play inevitably contests

9. Burnett 1985, 13–14.

10. Fenik 1964; cf. Hainsworth 1993, 152. Burnett, though arguing that the oracle version is late, agrees that *Iliad* 10 constitutes a "rationalized telling" of an older version. She also concurs that the version of the myth found in Pindar, in which Rhesos has an *aristeia*, is "as old or older than" book 10 (1985, 182 n. 60). In disputing Fenik's claim about the age of the oracle version, however, she does not counter his suggestion that lines 600–605 of the play constitute "an unmistakable reworking of the oracle motif" (Fenik 1964, 26). Cf. Ritchie 1964, 64; Hainsworth 1993, 151–52. One need not, of course, conclude that these *traditions* antedate the Iliadic *tradition;* rather, the claim is only that they antedate *Iliad* 10 as we know it. On the basis of Fenik's work, it is a more reasonable assumption that all of these traditions coexisted prior to the writing of book 10.

11. "He can, indeed, hardly be called a person at all. He is a suit of armour labelled with a name, no more" (Leaf 1915, 1).

the Iliadic version's canonical status.[12] At the same time that the play conspicuously puts part of the *Iliad* onstage, it also cleverly presents a new focus. Whereas, for example, *Iliad* 10 opens in the Greek camp at night with the fires of the Trojan camp visible in the distance, the play opens in the Trojan camp at night with the fires of the Greek camp visible in the distance. And this act of reframing the familiar underpins much of the play.[13] To a significant degree, this interest in restating the familiar in altered form is directed toward staging an encounter between the Iliadic version of the Rhesos myth and the traditions that diverge from it. And in so doing, the play announces that one of its chief concerns is the fate of Rhesos in the poetic tradition.

As Anne Pippin Burnett has shown, however, the play is designed to evoke smiles from the spectators as they confront the absurdity and foolishness of the world portrayed onstage (1985, 49–50). One of the elements that support this project, I suggest, lies in the play's ironic anti-Iliadic stance. As it gestures toward reviving the Rhesos excluded by the *Iliad*, the play reveals this figure to be the hollow conjuring of its own sense of absurd humor. The play's attention to Rhesos as a figure with a story independent of his treatment in the *Iliad* proves finally to be an ironic pretense to tell that story. Although the play stages the encounter of the contradictory traditions surrounding Rhesos, it suggests via this encounter that any attempt to challenge the canonical status of the *Iliad* is doomed to fail. Its own challenge, that is, proves in the end to affirm the success of the Iliadic account in excluding earlier versions of the Rhesos myth.

The shepherd's announcement of Rhesos's arrival begins this ironic stance in opposition to the *Iliad*. Here Rhesos is proclaimed as the son of the Strymon (279) and then compared to a god (δαίμονα, 301). The

---

12. In this the play is not alone. I will return below to the Pindar fragment as a part of this "debate" between versions of the Rhesos myth. Cf. Hainsworth 1993, 151.

13. See Paduano 1973, esp. 12–17.

forces accompanying him, we are told, are too numerous to count (309–10). The shepherd then proclaims Rhesos's invincibility (314–16):

τοιόσδε Τροίᾳ σύμμαχος πάρεστ' ἀνήρ,
ὃν οὔτε φεύγων οὔθ' ὑποσταθεὶς δορὶ
ὁ Πηλέως παῖς ἐκφυγεῖν δυνήσεται.

Such a man is this ally of Troy, whom the son of Peleus will not be able to escape, whether he tries to flee or fight with a spear.

This is but the first rehearsal of Rhesos's martial abilities, calling up the non-Iliadic figure: like the Rhesos of the oracle, this one is invincible. The shepherd continues to make the case for such a Rhesos when he tells Hector that the Greeks will be terrified at the mere sight of their new ally (335): φόβος γένοιτ' ἂν πολεμίοις ὀφθεὶς μόνον. Fenik takes this line to recall Iris's suggestion that the appearance of Achilles would cause fear among the Trojans (*Iliad* 18.198–200). If he is right, the shepherd here implies an underlying similarity between Rhesos and Achilles.[14]

The chorus continue the themes of Rhesos's near-divine status, his martial abilities, and his invincibility. They expand on the shepherd's announcement in identifying Rhesos's mother as well as his father (346–54). Here for the first time we learn that his mother was one of the Muses. Unlike the unremarkable, mortal ancestry of the Iliadic figure, this Rhesos is endowed with divine parentage. This divine affiliation becomes an attribute of Rhesos himself when the chorus address him as Zeus Phanaios and Zeus Eleutherios (355–59). They then invoke Rhesos as the opponent of Achilles as they sing of his invincibility (375–79):

σὲ γὰρ οὔτις ὑποστὰς
Ἀργείας ποτ' ἐν Ἥ-
ρας δαπέδοις χορεύσει·

14. Fenik 1964, 26 n. 3. Cf. Bond 1996, 261. The Muse reasserts this similarity at the play's end (962–82).

ἀλλά νιν ἅδε γᾶ
καπφθίμενον Θρηκὶ μόρῳ
    φίλτατον ἄχθος οἴσει.

No one who opposes you will ever again dance on the plains of Ar-
give Hera. Rather, he will die at the hands of a Thracian, and this
land will gladly bear the burden of his weight.

The optimism of the chorus, like that of the shepherd, recalls the threat
to the Greeks represented by the non-Iliadic Rhesos, as it reflects their
exaggerated confidence in his abilities and in his divine pedigree. As
such, these invocations of an invincible Rhesos invite a reconsideration
of the Iliadic figure.

But the optimism of the shepherd and of the chorus prove, of course,
to be misplaced. As we know even before the play begins, Rhesos will
not, in fact, survive the night. And the text itself makes it quite clear that
the confidence of both shepherd and chorus are not only exaggerated,
but ludicrous as well.[15] The shepherd reminds us that Rhesos is a bar-
barian (294), as Hector rejects the claims about Rhesos's grandeur (319–
26) before reversing course. The ensuing choral song mimics the form
of a cletic hymn, but in a way that is "outrageous," "tasteless," and "com-
ical" (Burnett 1985, 26–27). These effects are compounded upon the
entrance of Rhesos himself, says Burnett in speaking of the "offensive
self-importance of this useless and tardy ally" (31).

In spite of the absurdity evident in the claims of both chorus and
shepherd, the figure they imagine derives from the Rhesos of the non-
Iliadic versions of the myth.[16] And these invocations of this figure suffice

15. Burnett has shown all of this well (1985, 25–32). I provide here a
brief summary.

16. Speaking of references to Rhesos's victory in "one single day," Bur-
nett comments that these "words remind us that the semidivine Rhesus of
the cletic hymn [lines 342–87] . . . ought to have a day in the field." She goes
on to say that in adhering to the Iliadic model of Rhesos rather than to the

to make clear the nature of his fate at the hands of the *Iliad*. The effect of the play in this regard is double and contradictory: on the one hand, the text gestures toward reclaiming the "lost" Rhesos; on the other hand, this gesture is shown to be hollow. In the end, I suggest, this juxtaposition of traditions ironically exemplifies the effects of the *Iliad*'s canonical status, as it demonstrates the permanent marginalization of Rhesos: no longer is he the subject of the story in which he appears. These expressions of confidence in the non-Iliadic Rhesos prove finally to display the naiveté and foolishness of both chorus and shepherd. For all of their insistence on the stature of Rhesos, they can recall only that he has lost this stature as they tell rather the story of their own limited understanding. A similar contradiction between the claim to tell the story of a non-Iliadic Rhesos and the impossibility of sustaining that claim, I will argue, is even more effectively established by the *angelia* of the charioteer.

Prior to this *angelia*, however, there is another invocation of the non-Iliadic Rhesos that does not arrive with the undermining irony of the earlier ones. With a frightened Odysseus and Diomedes on the verge of returning to their ships, Athena appears to urge them on to the killing of Rhesos (598–605):

ἄνδρα δ' οὐ πέπυσθε σύμμαχον
Τροίᾳ μολόντα Ῥῆσον οὐ φαύλῳ τρόπῳ;
ὃς εἰ διοίσει νύκτα τήνδ' ἐς αὔριον,
οὔτ' ἄν σφ' Ἀχιλλεὺς οὔτ' ἂν Αἴαντος δόρυ
μὴ πάντα πέρσαι ναύσταθμ' Ἀργείων σχέθοι,
τείχη κατασκάψαντα καὶ πυλῶν ἔσω
λόγχῃ πλατεῖαν ἐσδρομὴν ποιούμενον.
τοῦτον κατακτὰς πάντ' ἔχεις.

---

Pindaric, the poet "emphasized the inadequacy of his weaker principal by giving him the other's parentage and also by referring to the 'single fateful day' that could reasonably belong only to the creature he was not" (1985, 31–32). Burnett cites lines 443 and 455–57; but see 447, 464, and 600–604 with the discussion of these lines below.

Haven't you heard that Rhesos has arrived, a well-equipped ally
of Troy? If he survives through the night until morning, neither
Achilles nor the spear of Ajax will be able to prevent him from de-
stroying the entire Argive fleet, after tearing down the walls and
making a wide breach through the gates with a horde of spearmen.
Kill him, and you'll have complete control.

Here we face not the foolish imaginings of the chorus or the shepherd;
rather, it is Athena who speaks what is perhaps the clearest evocation of
the non-Iliadic Rhesos in the play. Whether or not we read this as a re-
working of the oracle motif,[17] we can only understand Athena's formu-
lation as recalling the Rhesos excluded by the *Iliad*. She, like the chorus
and the shepherd, insists on his near invincibility. Although there is an
important difference between her concern about what might happen
and their certainty about what will happen, both are founded on a view
of Rhesos as a figure endowed with great martial powers. While such a
Rhesos is not incompatible with the Pindaric figure who fights one glori-
ous day, he has more in common with the one who receives the oracle. But
in either case, this is a Rhesos unimaginable for the *Iliad*. And this com-
monality between Athena's warning and the earlier expressions of cer-
tainty affirms that the wild optimism of chorus and shepherd are neither
arbitrary nor entirely without justification: they derive from a Rhesos
familiar from non-Iliadic versions of the myth. In a context so strongly
determined by *Iliad* 10, then, the irony of their exaggerated confidence
in such a Rhesos nonetheless leaves some room for the non-Iliadic fig-
ure. Athena's warning reminds us that the Rhesos absent from *Iliad* 10 is
precisely the one imagined by the shepherd and by the chorus.

If, however, Athena suggests that such a Rhesos may yet appear, the
audience at least have every reason to be certain that he will not. And, to
be sure, the Rhesos who appears onstage bears little resemblance to any
of the more glorious figures of the non-Iliadic traditions. We have seen
him being led off to bed by Hector, and the fact that the action of the

17. See above, note 10, and Burnett 1985, 183 n. 74.

play takes place at night virtually ensures that Rhesos will not see the sunrise. Athena's invocation of this other Rhesos, therefore, ultimately serves to demonstrate the success of the Iliadic exclusion: it calls to mind a Rhesos whose absence will be announced in no unmistakable terms. And it is the charioteer's report that most clearly formulates the condition of the mythical Rhesos.

If the multiple suggestions of Rhesos's invincibility are proven hollow, the play does nonetheless honor him in a way the *Iliad* does not. If his life in the play is no more glorious than that of his Iliadic counterpart, his death receives far more attention than it does in the epic. While there is still no *aristeia* in the play, the lengthy narrative about his death distinguishes this Rhesos from his Iliadic counterpart. The play suggests that even if Rhesos can claim nothing more at Troy than a pathetic death while asleep, at least his death can be told in some detail. Whereas the *Iliad* summarily recounts his death in 4 lines, the play gives a continuous narrative of about 50 lines to the charioteer.

If the play reminds us in rather subtle ways that there is a Rhesos ignored by the *Iliad*, it does so even more strongly here by insisting that it will recount his pathetic end in full. Even as the play conforms to the larger pattern of *Iliad* 10, it seeks to insert into its telling a form of homage to, or least a more extensive memory of, the non-Iliadic figure. But just as it seems to assert Rhesos's claim to some degree of *kleos* against the grain of the *Iliad*, the play undermines that claim in a comic reaffirmation of the dead Thracian's fate in the post-Iliadic world.

Just after the Thracians have been slaughtered, and Diomedes and Odysseus have slipped into the night, a "moaning, singing, barbarian groom" arrives onstage to recount Rhesos's final moments "quite as if it were the pathos of an unquestionable tragedy" (Burnett 1985, 33).[18] Just

---

18. The charioteer shares much with the Phrygian in Euripides' *Orestes* (1369–1526). Like the Phrygian, the charioteer sings, if briefly; possesses only a highly flawed knowledge of what he attempts to report; is likewise a barbarian (see below); and is a comic figure whose performance mocks the convention it purportedly enacts. (On Euripides' Phrygian see Willink 1986

as this *angelia* ironically claims a tragic status for Rhesos, so it presents itself as a virtual mockery of a conventional messenger-speech.[19] Posing as a conventional figure of the tragic stage whose task is to report offstage events, the charioteer in the end tells us little if anything about Rhesos. The lengthy narrative that ostensibly informs both stage and theater audiences about the gruesome slaughter proves to be the flawed, self-absorbed lament of a man who slept through the events he supposedly narrates. After announcing that the Thracian soldiers and their leader are dead, he says (749–53):

ἆ ἆ ἆ ἆ
οἵα μ' ὀδύνη τείρει φονίου
τραύματος ἔσω. πῶς ἂν ὀλοίμην;
χρῆν γάρ μ' ἀκλεῶς Ῥῆσόν τε θανεῖν,
Τροίᾳ κέλσαντ' ἐπίκουρον;

Aaaaaaahhh! A bloody gash racks me deep with pain. How am I to die? Must I, along with Rhesos, die without fame, having come here to help Troy?

A few lines later he explains the double evil that both he and Rhesos suffer (758–61):

θανεῖν γὰρ εὐκλεῶς μέν, εἰ θανεῖν χρεών,
λυπρὸν μὲν οἶμαι τῷ θανόντι— πῶς γὰρ οὔ;—
τοῖς ζῶσι δ' ὄγχος καὶ δόμων εὐδοξία·
ἡμεῖς δ' ἀβούλως κἀκλεῶς ὀλώλαμεν.

Dying with fame, if you have to die, is painful for the one dying, I suppose—how could it not be?—but it's a mark of distinction and

---

*ad* 1366–1502, 1425, and 1473.) Compare also the comic guard of Sophocles' *Antigone* who, though hardly a barbarian, shares some traits with these two flawed messengers.

19. Cf. Strohm 1959, 272, quoted above; Pagani 1970, 38; Burnett 1985, 34.

honor for the survivors in the family. But as for us, we've died stupidly and without fame.

The charioteer announces that his pain is central to what he has to say and that his own lack of *kleos* is on a par with that of Rhesos. And the narrative that follows does not fail to live up to this introduction.

There are numerous indications that the charioteer's narrative aims to recount his own suffering rather than to memorialize or honor Rhesos. This is the only messenger in tragedy who reports not events, but a dream (780–86).[20] And although the charioteer's interest in his own dream indicates the degree to which he departs from conventional practice, it does more. Rhesos in *Iliad* 10, after all, dreams as well. Once more, then, does the play reframe something familiar from the epic account. In transferring Rhesos's dream to the charioteer, the play surely acknowledges its own inability to include the dream of a dead man.[21] But it also, to be sure, displaces one of the few elements that characterize the Iliadic Rhesos onto the charioteer.[22] The dream here not only signals the anomaly that is the messenger; it also marks the Rhesos of the play as one dispossessed of his own story.

Immediately following his dream of the horses being attacked by wolves, the charioteer recounts the moment of Rhesos's death (787–91):

ἐγὼ δ' ἀμύνων θῆρας ἐξεγείρομαι
πώλοισιν· ἔννυχος γὰρ ἐξώρμα φόβος.
κλύω δ' ἐπάρας κρᾶτα μυχθισμὸν νεκρῶν.
θερμὸς δὲ κρουνὸς δεσπότου παρὰ σφαγῆς
βάλλει με δυσθνῄσκοντος αἵματος νέου.

Frightened by the dream, I woke up trying to defend the horses. Lifting up my head, I hear the moaning of the dead, and a warm

20. Burnett 1985, 34.    21. Fenik 1964, 52.

22. Fenik (1964, 51–52) argues that the dream was a feature of traditions about Rhesos that antedate *Iliad* 10.

stream of fresh blood strikes me, spurting from my master, who was struggling with death.

Before telling of his own inept attempt to fight off the attackers and of the wound he receives, the charioteer thus concludes his account of Rhesos's death. Like the dream, Rhesos's last moments are transformed into the experience of the messenger. There is "no ultimate *aristeia* of resistance —there is not even a finite, indicative statement in which the end of his [Rhesos's] life is recorded" (Burnett 1985, 34). Instead, we learn that the blood that struck the charioteer was still warm.

With Rhesos now left behind and himself now at the center of his account, the charioteer attempts to become a combatant. This feeble effort is short-lived, however, as he proceeds to tell of his inability to find a spear and of the wound he receives while looking for one (793–97):

καί μ' ἔγχος αὐγάζοντα καὶ θηρώμενον
παίει παραστὰς νεῖραν ἐς πλευρὰν ξίφει
ἀνὴρ ἀκμάζων· φασγάνου γὰρ ᾐσθόμην
πληγῆς, βαθεῖαν ἄλοκα τραύματος λαβών.
πίπτω δὲ πρηνής.

As I look for a spear, a big brute slices my belly at the side with his sword. I felt the sword's cut making a deep wound, and I fell facedown.

After adding that the attackers fled on foot, he utters another moan. Then repeating his earlier lament that his wound pains him greatly, he says he can no longer stand upright. This account of the gruesome events is replete with pain and suffering, but it is principally the pain and suffering of the messenger himself that are on exhibit.

I have argued that a messenger-speech is typically spoken by an eyewitness who not only survives the disaster he reports but in fact commands a kind of invulnerability. This invulnerability stems in principle from the messenger's status as an idealized eyewitness who commands a virtually disembodied presence at the scene he describes. The charioteer, however, finds no distance at all between his status as narrator and his status as embodied Thracian. His announcement that he is badly wounded finds its narrative equivalent in his account of his own suffering. Just as his own pain and pathetic status effectively drive Rhesos from his thoughts, his vulnerable bodily presence in the Thracian camp anticipates Rhesos's exclusion from his narrative.

The significance of such an *angelia* is twofold. On the one hand, this narrative forms the culmination of the play's ironic commentary on the fate of the post-Iliadic Rhesos. In making a gesture toward rewriting *Iliad* 10, the play finally proves to reproduce the epic's exclusion of Rhesos: even the extended narrative of the only part of the story left to Rhesos in the *Iliad*—his death—turns out to be a pointed exercise in marginalizing him. So profoundly has Rhesos been dispossessed of his own story that even his pathetic death remains untold. On the other hand, the very qualities of the charioteer's narrative that carry out this exclusion of Rhesos are the same as those that mark this *angelia* as anomalous: in offering an account of his own experiences, the charioteer departs from one of the principal canons of conventional form. The messenger's exceptional performance, then, concisely expresses the play's ongoing commentary on the status of Rhesos in myth. As such, this *angelia* demonstrates that its violation of conventional form serves to underpin one of the play's larger thematic concerns.

That the charioteer's anomalous messenger-speech does not offer a competing model of conventional form is made clear in several ways. First, although performing what is formally marked as an *angelia*, the charioteer fails the crucial test of informing his audience about the events he claims to report. It is true that he reports *that* Rhesos died, but he does not know *how* he died. And it is a principal task of the messenger to report the latter.[23] Calling up this particular aspect of conventional practice, the charioteer uses a marked expression in confessing his failure (800–802):

23. De Jong 1991, 32–33.

καὶ ξυμφορὰν μὲν οἶδ' ὁρῶν, τρόπῳ δ' ὅτῳ
τεθνᾶσιν οἱ θανόντες οὐκ ἔχω φράσαι
οὐδ' ἐξ ὁποίας χειρός.

I know the disaster because I saw it, but how they died I cannot say,
nor by whose hand.

The messenger's expression here (τρόπῳ ὅτῳ) is one of several that serve
as formulaic markers typically introducing an *angelia:* messengers typi-
cally respond to a request to tell *how* the events occurred.[24] This mes-
senger thus distinguishes his report from those of conventional messen-
gers elsewhere.

Second, the charioteer's bodily wound starkly separates him from
messengers who successfully claim an ideal form of spectatorship. If the
disembodied status typically aimed at by messengers underpins the priv-
ilege they wield onstage, the charioteers's wound is a physical sign of his
failure successfully to perform the role of messenger: all too visible to
the Greek attackers, he was far from acquiring the spectator status that
characterizes tragic messengers elsewhere. Such a figure can make no
headway at all in claiming to escape the constraints of the stage; and this
claim, we have seen, is fundamental to the performance of the conven-
tional role. Instead, as his *angelia* and subsequent lines make clear,[25] this
messenger forgoes the privilege of the conventional messenger as he de-
parts from standard practice.

His bodily wound, furthermore, pushes the typically compromised
gender status of the messenger close to its limit: so far is he from the
masculine standard that his bodily presence—both in his narrative and
onstage—takes on a markedly feminine form.[26] The wound he receives,
that is, marks not only his failure as a messenger; it marks also his body

24. De Jong 1991, 33 with n. 81.
25. Cf. Burnett 1985, 35.
26. See above, chapter 2. For his body onstage see his lament at 750–51
and his comment that he cannot stand upright at 799.

as a vulnerable hindrance. Froma Zeitlin has argued that in tragedy "when the male finds himself in a condition of weakness, he too becomes acutely aware that he has a body. Then, at the limits of pain, is when he perceives himself to be most like a woman" (1996, 350). She cites several exemplary passages that admirably make the point. Toward the end of Sophocles' *Trachiniae*, for example, Herakles in great pain asks his son Hyllus for pity, saying that now as the result of his suffering he is found to be a woman (θῆλυς ηὕρημαι, 1075). The body in pain, the vulnerable and hindering body, is, in Zeitlin's analysis, a feminized body.[27] And it is such a body that the charioteer possesses.[28] The lesson taught here is that the messenger's position within the gender system is rather fragile: he must neither act nor suffer the actions of others. If the successful messenger cannot approach too closely the masculine standard of bodily strength, he must likewise avoid the feminized body that is only a "condition of weakness."[29] His wound, then, is the most concrete expression of his failure to perform the role of messenger. And the charioteer's failure in this regard proves to illustrate by negative example the very principles that define the conventional *angelia*.

———

I have argued that the play makes an ironic challenge to the Iliadic version of the Rhesos myth, reenacting the exclusion of Rhesos as it gestures toward restoring to him something of a claim to *kleos*. One of the principal sources for reconstructing the pre- or non-Iliadic Rhesos, how-

27. Cf. Loraux 1995, 43

28. It may be no coincidence that the charioteer (like Rhesos himself, of course) is a Thracian, that is, a barbarian. See Hall (1989, 102–33, esp.128), who catalogues tragic stereotyping of barbaric violence, mendacity, luxury, effeminacy, and so on. Part of the charioteer's characterization—and part of his feminization—derives from his status as a Thracian. In large measure, however, the stereotypical elements in his portrayal as a barbarian serve to reinforce his failure as a messenger—as is the case with the Phrygian in Euripides' play mentioned above.

29. Cf. Halperin 1990, 96–99, and the discussion above in chapter 2.

ever, is Pindar, who wrote, of course, in the wake of the *Iliad*. How, then, is it possible to speak of the Iliadic version of the myth effecting Rhesos's marginalization within the poetic tradition? If Pindar recounted the *aristeia* of Rhesos, is this not evidence that he remained very much a mythic figure with a firm place in his own story and that his status as a minor appendage in the *Iliad* reflects but one version of the myth?

It is true that the evidence from Pindar clearly establishes that into the fifth century a non-Iliadic Rhesos was a familiar figure. In fact, as I have argued, the play itself preserves the memory of such a Rhesos. (If we could date the play, this would be a substantial aid in charting the course of the non-Iliadic versions.) My argument, then, posits the continued existence of a non-Iliadic Rhesos. But the mere coexistence of multiple forms of a myth does not argue for their equality. Rather, I submit, the testimony of the play is that this non-Iliadic Rhesos has little, if any, chance to reclaim the status denied him in the *Iliad*.

The paucity of interest in Rhesos among extant sources suggests that the Iliadic account did, in fact, succeed in relegating Rhesos to the margins of the poetic tradition in general. And our play being the only work we know of to treat the myth in a sustained manner, its commentary can only support this suggestion. Nonetheless, some accounting must be given both of the Pindar fragment and of the play's own interest in a non-Iliadic Rhesos.

Because of the status of Homer—in both Pindar's time and the time of the play, whether it dates from the fifth or fourth century—poetic works that alter what appears in Homer must be understood as doing just that. Every act of (re)telling (part of) the *Iliad* or the *Odyssey* in the classical period—or, indeed, in the archaic period—necessarily asks that it be read against the Homeric version. Such intertextuality was, of course, widely practiced and used to greatly varying effect. Among the many works that perform this kind of operation, however, *Rhesos* is unique (for us) in being the only tragedy to stage a substantial portion of a Homeric poem. As such, its ironic challenge to the *Iliad* deserves careful attention as a commentary on a culturally privileged text.

The Iliadic version of the Rhesos myth, then, may be understood as the dominant version, while the Pindar fragment (and, to some degree, the play) demonstrates the persistence of a different, and perhaps older, tradition. A persistent element that poorly accords with the dominant version may be analogized to what Raymond Williams calls a "residual cultural element." Speaking of cultural production broadly conceived, Williams says that such a residual element "is usually at some distance from the effective dominant culture, but some part of it, some version of it—especially if the residue is from some major area of the past—will in most cases have had to be incorporated if the effective dominant culture is to make sense in these areas."[30] If we think of the war at Troy—including the role played by Rhesos—as a "major area of the past" of which the *Iliad* must make sense, this formulation is enlightening: the *Iliad* is under some constraint to incorporate the story of Rhesos, but only "some part of it, some version of it." In other words, the effective dominance of the Iliadic version does not demand absolute silence concerning Rhesos; in fact, it may lose some authority by failing to "make sense" of this particular episode of the war at Troy. And this act of incorporating (some part of) the non-Iliadic Rhesos myth, leaves room for this form of the myth to be told elsewhere. And, I suggest, both the Pindar fragment and our play testify to this. But as the play makes clear, the non-Iliadic version is overwhelmed by the *Iliad* and its telling relegated to the margins of a territory already well-mapped.[31]

30. 1977, 123. Williams's model incorporates a broad analysis of cultural production in its social and historical contexts, guided by a Gramscian notion of hegemony. As such, his model is far more inclusive than my brief discussion indicates. Carrying out a comprehensive analysis of Homeric dominance vis-à-vis *Rhesos* along the lines outlined by Williams is perhaps impossible on the evidence we have, and at any rate beyond the scope of this study. I mean simply to suggest that his model offers a framework that makes sense of the dynamic between these texts.

31. An alternate model for understanding this process is available in the concept of Panhellenization as articulated by Gregory Nagy. Nagy writes of

We do not know how Pindar used the non-Iliadic Rhesos. It is not out of the question, however, that his use paralleled that found in the play: it, too, may have addressed the marginalization of Rhesos carried out by the *Iliad*. His poetry does on occasion distance itself from Homer, and his treatment of Rhesos may have been another instance.[32] Insofar as Pindar does depart from the Iliadic account in his portrayal of Rhesos, however, there remain a number of possible motivations for doing so. Gregory Nagy, for example, argues that Pindaric song does not distinguish diachronic differences in the epic medium, and he suggests further that "there is in Pindaric song an ongoing nondifferentiation of epic traditions" (1990b, 416). This nondifferentiation, he claims, applies to Homeric and Cyclic poetry. On such a reading of Pindar, the inclusion of a "non-Iliadic" Rhesos becomes perhaps simply one of the multiforms of epic and acquires a rather less oppositional stance vis-à-vis the *Iliad*.

Nagy has also argued, however, that Pindar's poetry champions local traditions, sometimes against the treatments found in Homeric poetry. Such, for example, is his reading of *Nemean* 7.20–27. In its commitment to the local tradition surrounding Ajax, Pindaric song challenges not only the version that appears in Homer, but also the panhellenic status

poetry making a "bid for Panhellenic status." Poetry that succeeds in this attempt operates "not simply on the basis of local traditions suited for local audiences. Rather, Panhellenic poetry would have been the product of an evolutionary synthesis of traditions, so that the tradition that it represents concentrates on traditions that tend to be common to most locales and peculiar to none" (1990b, 53–54). In this scheme, the Iliadic version of the Rhesos story—along with the *Iliad* as a whole, of course—would represent the successfully Panhellenic, as opposed to a local, tradition. See the discussion of Pindar below. Although these two models offer rather different mechanisms for understanding the status of Rhesos in myth, they are not incompatible. If the model of Panhellenization is perhaps more ready to hand, it nonetheless may well exemplify a process that conforms generally to the dynamic outlined by Williams.

32. Most notably with respect to the *Odyssey* at *Nem.* 7.20–27. See Nisetich 1989, 15–23.

of that version (Nagy 1990b, 422–24). Is it possible that a similar concern led to his account of Rhesos?[33]

In staging a version of *Iliad* 10 that recalls the epic's exclusion of Rhesos, the play makes productive use of a messenger who "fails his tragic function" (Burnett 1985, 34). As the culmination of the play's commentary on the fate of Rhesos as a figure of myth, this exceptional *angelia* proves to be a cornerstone of the play's larger thematic interests. As others have argued, the play presents a world governed by uncertainty.[34] Guido Paduano, in fact, speaks of the play addressing an epistemological problem, claiming that the nighttime fires constitute a looming question mark that portends a crisis of understanding.[35] The charioteer's *angelia*, I suggest, does something similar: in a play populated by figures characterized by ignorance and folly, a messenger who does not know is perhaps the most pointed example of this crisis of understanding. Conventionally endowed with knowledge and a privileged voice, the messenger here stands out for his ignorance and readiness to hazard worthless guesses: so pervasive is this crisis in this play that it subordinates even tragic convention.

---

33. Another possible factor in the formation of both the *Iliad* tradition and subsequent versions of the Rhesos myth is the fact that Rhesos was not a Greek. His barbaric status is inseparable from his story and as such may figure in the uses made of him. One critic, for example, has called the Rhesos of the play a "vaunting barbarian monarch" (Hall 1989, 32; cf. 122–23).

34. Strohm (1959, 265 n. 4) suggests that the *koruphaios*'s comment at 736–37 could be a motto for the entire play: κατ' εὐφρόνην / ἀμβλῶπες αὐγαὶ κοὔ σε γιγνώσκω τορῶς ("At night the light is dim, and I cannot identify you clearly").

35. "I fuochi . . . sono anche insieme un angoscioso punto interrogativo, capace di mettere in crisi la capacità umana di capire" (1973, 13).

# SIX

# Sophocles'
# *Oedipus Tyrannus*
## Epistemology and Tragic Practice

Wenn einer in den Spiegel siehet, ein Mann, und siehet darinn
sein Bild, wie abgemahlt; es gleicht dem Manne. Augen hat des
Menschen Bild, hingegen Licht der Mond. Der König Oedi-
pus hat ein Auge zuviel vieleicht.

If someone looks into the mirror, a man, and in it sees his im-
age, as though it were a painted likeness; it resembles the man.
The image of man has eyes, whereas the moon has light. King
Oedipus has an eye too many perhaps.

*Hölderlin, "In lieblicher Bläue"*

If *Rhesos* shows how a play may distort the conventional form of an
*angelia* in the service of its thematic interests, Sophocles' *Oedipus Ty-
rannus* offers a parallel example of how a play may profit from manip-
ulating conventional form. The play's second messenger, the *exangelos*,
provides a lengthy account of Jocasta's death and Oedipus's self-blinding.
This *angelia*, however, is framed and punctuated by announcements of
its own insufficiency. Conspicuously departing from the practices I have
outlined above, this play offers a treatment of the messenger that brings

us face-to-face with the larger issues at stake in tragedy's use of this conventional figure. This "flawed" and highly self-referential *angelia*, I will argue, enacts important elements of the play's epistemological commentary.

There are, in fact, two messengers in this play, and correspondingly two manipulations of expectation. In addition to the *exangelos*, the Corinthian who delivers the news about the death of Polybos is identified in our manuscripts as a messenger. This "messenger," however, performs nothing resembling an *angelia*, announcing the play's idiosyncratic use of this conventional figure.

The Corinthian appears with a suddenness that seems to answer Jocasta's immediately preceding prayer.[1] Her plea to Apollo (919) stands in place of the familiar announcement of a messenger's arrival. As such, his arrival is a sudden irruption into the world of the drama, perhaps bringing the "release from pollution" requested by Jocasta.[2] Just what this figure's place in the play will be remains unclear. In fact, it is only with the Corinthian's first lines that the text signals his role. Indeed, his first words are entirely conventional and familiar, signaling that he comes as an *angelos*. And as Jocasta makes clear at 932–33, she understands his purpose very well: ἀλλὰ φράζ' ὅτου / χρῄζων ἀφῖξαι χὥτι σημῆναι θέλων. ("But say what you've come for and what you want to say"). If his entrance is abrupt, he immediately assumes a familiar pose that implies the preparation for an *angelia*.

But that this messenger will not produce an *angelia* is suggested certainly by line 940, and perhaps before.[3] Indeed, behind the facade of their exchange lies the suggestion of a departure from the familiar terrain ini-

---

1. Jebb 1893 *ad* 924.

2. Reinhardt speaks of "an incredible effect of an intrusion from the world outside" (1979, 121). Dawe calls this entrance "a piece of shameless dramaturgy" (1982, 18).

3. Jocasta's σημῆναι at 933 may well hint that this messenger will not perform according to conventional expectation. Cf. Segal 1995, 149.

tially staked out by the Corinthian. Their dialogue initiates several false starts and ambiguities that find resolution only in being abandoned.

At 932–33 Jocasta asks the Corinthian two questions: what he is after and what he has to report. The Corinthian does not answer the first question,[4] and his answer to the second prompts Jocasta to request clarification (935). This "clarification" (936–37) is no improvement, as he claims the news will bring both joy and grief. Jocasta asks again at 938: τί δ' ἔστι; ποίαν δύναμιν ὧδ' ἔχει διπλῆν; ("What? What is the double effect it has?"). Thus far, his speech has become only more opaque.

At 939–40 the herdsman abandons his riddling manner:

τύραννον αὐτὸν οὑπιχώριοι χθονὸς
τῆς Ἰσθμίας στήσουσιν, ὡς ηὐδᾶτ' ἐκεῖ.

Those in the Isthmian land will establish him as *tyrannos.* So it is rumored there.

Here, to be sure, the indirection of the messenger gives way to a clear announcement. But this clarity concerns the future: he brings not a report of what has happened, but a claim about what will happen. In fact, he brings not an eyewitness account, but a report of rumor (ὡς ηὐδᾶτ' ἐκεῖ).[5]

Jocasta then asks about Polybos, and the Corinthian answers that Polybos is not in power (941–42). But again his indirection proves to be opaque to Jocasta. This series of questions and answers culminates in the emphatic yet evasive declaration of the messenger at 944: εἰ μὴ λέγω τἀληθές, ἀξιῶ θανεῖν ("If I do not speak the truth, I deserve to die"). Jocasta has certainly understood that Polybos is dead, and yet she has come to know this by a sinuous route.

But that the Corinthian messenger and Jocasta understand the substance of his news differently—a matter already implicit—is brought immediately to the fore. While he thinks he reports that Oedipus will be

4. Bollack 1990 *ad* 934; others read his response differently, as Bollack catalogues.

5. Cf. Dawe 1982 *ad* 940; Ahl 1991, 159–61.

king of Corinth, Jocasta (and Oedipus, of course) knows that what matters in his report is that Polybos has died. Little does the Corinthian know that he brings (false) news about the reliability of Apollo's oracle. What might have been a simple report of Polybos's death thus becomes an announcement that suffers more than one interpretation. This discrepancy is both emblematic of this messenger's distance from the conventional norm and indicative of how both messengers in this play speak a language that is as self-referential as any other in the play.[6]

This process continues in the Corinthian's encounter with Oedipus, who appears from the palace at 950. In response to the latter's demand for clarification, the Corinthian says that Polybos has died (958–59). Oedipus then asks at 960 for an account of how this happened: πότερα δόλοισιν, ἢ νόσου ξυναλλαγῇ; ("Was it through trickery or the workings of an illness?"). "Here, surely, is the moment for the classical messenger speech" (Ahl 1991, 164). In its place, of course, appears an ambiguous, metaphorical reply (961): σμικρὰ παλαιὰ σώματ' εὐνάζει ῥοπή ("A small tilt of the scale puts old bodies to sleep"). This formulation does not rule out either possibility mentioned by Oedipus, as it substitutes a gnomic utterance for a narrative account of the old man's death.[7] And Oedipus's reply underscores the inconclusiveness of the Corinthian's metaphoric pronouncement (962): νόσοις ὁ τλήμων, ὡς ἔοικεν, ἔφθιτο ("The poor man died from sickness, it seems"). Though we may take Oedipus as a guide and conclude that Polybos died of illness, this conclusion nonetheless remains the product of interpretation, as Oedipus himself makes clear ("it seems"). His question that invites an *angelia* in a nearly formulaic manner underscores the fact that in place of a clear account stands an uncertain inference based upon oblique metaphor.

6. Goldhill comments that "the ironic tension between the messenger's ostensible news and the significant facts which this news is capable of producing, marks the exchange of language as a contestation of the possibility of the simple, transparent transmission and reception of signals" (1984a, 193).

7. Ahl 1991, 164–65.

As Oedipus and Jocasta then work out the significance of Polybos's death, the silence of the old man suggests the discontinuity between his purpose and their interest. It is also with this silence that the Corinthian leaves behind his treading on the edges of an *angelia*. He reenters the dialogue at 989 with a series of questions that turn into a dialogue about Oedipus's origins. The hints that the Corinthian would offer an *angelia*, then, give way to a sharp cleavage between his purpose and that of his auditors, in which he assumes a new role and the scene becomes one far from what was implied at his entrance. Thus we are introduced to a "messenger" in such a way that we see not only that he does not fulfill conventional expectations but also that his message is diverted to other purposes. This, I suggest, is not an isolated frustration of convention, but part of a pattern that in the end resumes a major theme of the play as a whole.

The *exangelos* who enters at 1223 performs on the whole along familiar conventional lines: he informs the chorus (and the audience) that Jocasta has died by hanging and that Oedipus has put out his eyes. And indeed, in line with what I have argued above, he tells at great length *how* the events he reports transpired, quite unlike the Corinthian. At 1235 he gives the "headline" version of what happened offstage, and then at 1237 he launches into a 50-line narrative telling how it all happened. In broad terms, he performs as expected.

And yet the narrative itself contains several conspicuous lacunae and also offers some reflection on itself as a narrative of events offstage. This *angelia* contains a self-reflexive element that goes to the heart of what a messenger's narrative conventionally seeks to do, and thus poses challenges to my argument. Abandoning the practices I have identified as crucial to the success of the conventional messenger, the *exangelos* here goes out of his way to call attention to his narrative as flawed, incomplete, and idiosyncratic. That is, he presents his report as the product of his own particular viewing—flawed as it was—of the horrendous events offstage. In short, he drives a wedge between the reality of what transpired and the account he gives of it.

The *exangelos* enters sounding a remarkable note (1223–25):

ὦ γῆς μέγιστα τῆσδ' ἀεὶ τιμώμενοι,
οἷ' ἔργ' ἀκούσεσθ', οἷα δ' εἰσόψεσθ', ὅσον δ'
ἀρεῖσθε πένθος . . .

You who are forever most honored in this land, what deeds you will
hear and what you will see, what grief you will feel . . .

The common gesture of a messenger authenticating his narrative on the
basis of eyewitness experience is here displaced onto the audience. In
place of the explicit distinction between the seen and the heard at the
original scene (the locus of the offstage witnessing), on the one hand,
and a silent avoidance of that distinction as operative at the scene of nar-
ration (i.e., onstage), on the other, here we find this distinction empha-
sized as definitive of the audience's experience of pathos. As such, the
demarcation between the seen and the heard onstage invites interest in
the discrepancies between the narrative to follow and the events it re-
ports. Thus, the rhetorically powerful disjunction between seeing and
hearing here serves not to authorize the *exangelos*'s narrative by marking
his testimony as that of one who saw; rather, it serves to suggest to the
audience that this discontinuity is operative in the theater as well. But
the *exangelos* has only just arrived onstage.

In response to a question from the *koruphaios*, the *exangelos* replies
that, in brief, Jocasta is dead (1234–35). This headline version he marks
as one of the *logoi*, the most brief (ὁ μὲν τάχιστος τῶν λόγων). In re-
sponse to the next question, "How did it happen?" (1236), the *exangelos*
again qualifies his report as discontinuous with the events offstage. "She
died by her own hand," he responds (1237) and then frames the account
of her end with the following (1237–40):

τῶν δὲ πραχθέντων τὰ μὲν
ἄλγιστ' ἄπεστιν· ἡ γὰρ ὄψις οὐ πάρα.
ὅμως δ', ὅσον γε κἀν ἐμοὶ μνήμης ἔνι,
πεύσῃ τὰ κείνης ἀθλίας παθήματα.

But the most painful of what has been done is absent, since the spectacle is not present. Still, as much as my memory allows, you will learn the wretched woman's sufferings.

Here the *exangelos* doubly disturbs the conventional form of authorization. First, he extends his earlier exposure of the gap between seeing and hearing by qualifying his report as the absence of *opsis*. *Logos* in place of *opsis*, he says, spares us the most painful part. But also, he cannot help but say, *logos* is something other than the deeds themselves, and therefore he calls attention to its status as a means of representation. As such, the *logos* is far from transparent and here becomes self-referential to a surprising degree, in that it hints at its status as a theatrical creation: the messenger is one who speaks precisely because ἡ γὰρ ὄψις οὐ πάρα ("the spectacle is not present"). Further, his use of the term *opsis* would appear to augment this effect, inasmuch as it can denote a contemplative viewing such as might occur in the theater.[8] All of which serves to draw attention to the verbal account itself as a mediated representation of the "spectacle." This introduction frames the narrative as an account closely attached to its speaker, both as one of the *dramatis personae* and as a theatrical institution.

Second, the *exangelos* suggests not only that the account he is about to produce will be a verbal rendering of *his* experience of events offstage, but also that those events themselves as they appear in his account are mediated by his memory. And further, he suggests that his memory is incomplete, or at least not entirely capable of producing an adequate account. R. D. Dawe is perhaps right that the "messenger could hardly have forgotten already,"[9] but we should recall, with Charles Segal, that

8. Dawe remarks: "In his ἡ γὰρ ὄψις οὐ πάρα he speaks with the crispness of one who might almost be thought anachronistically to have read Aristotle's *Poetics*" (1982 *ad* 1237–40).

9. Dawe argues further that μνήνης ought not be translated as "memory": "Mnemosyne was the mother of the Muses, and as the messenger ap-

this "emphasis on memory is striking when one considers how much memory in the play has distorted the recollection of the past" (1995, 156).[10] In emphasizing his own mediating function in the constitution of his narrative, the *exangelos* marks his report as selective, flawed, and unconventional.

After this telling introduction, the *exangelos* proceeds to the narrative proper. Jocasta, he says, rushed into the house and then into her bedroom, tearing out her hair with both hands (1241–43). Then, he says (1244–45),

πύλας δ' ὅπως εἰσῆλθ' ἐπιρράξασ' ἔσω,
καλεῖ τὸν ἤδη Λάιον πάλαι νεκρόν.

She slammed the doors shut when she went in and called on Laios, long since a corpse.[11]

The qualifications of the narrative offered by the *exangelos* assume now a tangible, structural form: the *logos* he provides in place of *opsis*, mediated as we have seen by his memory, derives ultimately from an earlier *opsis* that, we now learn, was abbreviated. Jocasta's closing of the doors to the bedroom into which she had gone cuts off even the *exangelos* from the source of his story; not only is the audience deprived of *opsis*, but the messenger himself was almost immediately deprived as well. What follows is an account of what Jocasta *said*, as heard, we are to understand, by the *exangelos* through the doors. She laments her marriage(s), children, and the dreadful doubling of generations.

_____

proaches his epic recital he depreciates his own poetic ability to do justice to his theme" (1982 *ad* 1239).

10. Kamerbeek, following Jebb, states that the *exangelos* implies "that their [the chorus's] own memory, had they been witnesses, would have procured them a more vivid picture of the horrors than his memory by his story" (1967 *ad* 1239).

11. Critics construe these lines variously. I follow Dawe 1982. See Bollack 1990 ad loc.

After these 6 lines, in which he recounts what Jocasta said, the *exangelos* speaks the remarkable χὤπως μὲν ἐκ τῶνδ' οὐκέτ' οἶδ' ἀπόλλυται ("And how after that she died, this is a further point on which I have no knowledge," 1251 [trans. Dawe 1982 *ad* 115]). Dawe's translation augments the force of this statement, inasmuch as the declaration of ignorance about the heart of what would seem to be the matter at hand — as 1235 makes clear — comes perhaps as the crown of this *exangelos*'s inability to report the events offstage, but certainly not as the only constituent of it. He heard Jocasta's lament, he says, but he does not know what chain of events led from what he heard to the moment of her death.[12] In any event, he here prevents the audience from thinking that his narrative is in any sense a verbal equivalent of what happened in the palace; again, his account speaks of its own inadequacy.

One might want to read this, along with 1239, as mere hyperbole. But here, I would suggest, we are beyond the realm of hyperbole in that the *exangelos* does not say that his powers of description pale in comparison with the scale of the pathos (as does, for example, the messenger in *Persians*); rather, he says he simply does not know. It is not a matter of degree; it is simply a matter of the *exangelos* not having *seen* what transpired.

He goes on to explain why he did not see (1252–54):

βοῶν γὰρ εἰσέπαισεν Οἰδίπους, ὑφ' οὗ
οὐκ ἦν τὸ κείνης ἐκθεάσασθαι κακόν,
ἀλλ' εἰς ἐκεῖνον περιπολοῦντ' ἐλεύσσομεν.

Because Oedipus shouting out burst in, on account of whom it was impossible to watch her suffering through to the end, but rather we trained our eyes on him as he rushed about.

---

12. Kamerbeek remarks: "Strictly speaking the man overstates his ignorance of the truth" (1967 *ad* 1251). While this is true—he knows, presumably, that she died by hanging—the rhetorical force of his exaggeration is telling. This messenger not only drives a wedge between his narrative and its referent, but he exaggerates the gulf separating the two.

Here, as Jean Bollack remarks, Oedipus displaces his mother,[13] and as he does so he stands as the sign of the messenger's deflected vision. If the pathos of Jocasta's death gives way to Oedipus's raving (1258) and self-blinding, the track of the messenger's narrative—following his vision—finds itself redirected and to some extent frustrated, as line 1253 makes clear: οὐκ ἦν τὸ κείνης ἐκθεάσασθαι κακόν ("It was impossible to watch her suffering through to the end").

But this frustration is, in fact, doubly determined in a way that has created a substantial amount of difficulty for critics, for if Oedipus's bursting in is what made it impossible for the servants to watch Jocasta, what are we to think would have happened if he had not arrived on the scene? After all, were not the doors to the bedroom closed? As so often, Bollack conveniently summarizes a plethora of views, from those that suggest that Sophocles simply made a mistake to those that imagine a hole in the door through which the servants might have watched. I propose no novel reconstruction of the scene. Rather, I would suggest that inasmuch as the text emphatically underscores the removal of the *exangelos* from the scene of Jocasta's death, this twofold barring of the narrator from the ostensible subject of the narrative serves to augment the sense of distance and difference between word and deed. The closed doors literally bar his view, and Oedipus distracts it, redirects it. Thus the impetus of the narrative is not only stopped; it is also deflected elsewhere. Consequently, the narrative itself appears as something other than an impartial account that simply records what happened offstage; it becomes rather an account of the *exangelos*'s experience. And as something susceptible to the vagaries of this experience, the narrative appears more starkly as the product of an intentional observer who in this case is thwarted. As his account of Jocasta breaks off it becomes evident that the narrative appears not as a simple report of events offstage, but rather as a record of the servant's vantage point. Again the *exangelos* underscores

---

13. "Oedipe se substitue à sa mère" (1990 *ad* 1251–53).

the difference between what happened and what he reports, here by emphasizing the limitations of his vision.[14]

As the narrative then proceeds to track the movements of Oedipus asking first for a sword and then for direction in his search for Jocasta, it curiously takes us back to that which was so suddenly cut off before. Oedipus is led by "one of the *daimones*" (1258) to the bedroom that holds Jocasta, and he breaks through the doorway and into the room (1261–62). At this moment, the servant's vision regains its earlier object, namely, Jocasta and her *kakon* (1253). The trajectory of Oedipus's interference in the servant's witnessing comes to coincide, finally, with that of the witnessing itself as both Oedipus and the servant (and the audience by means of the narrative) behold the hanged Jocasta. But again, as suddenly as before, the gaze of the servant yields to Oedipus's intervention. This time, however, the seam is nearly invisible. Oedipus bursts into the bedroom, where (1263–65)

> κρεμαστὴν τὴν γυναῖκ' εἰσείδομεν,
> πλεκταῖσιν αἰώραισιν ἐμπεπλεγμένην.
> ὁ δ' ὡς ὁρᾷ νιν . . .

> we saw the woman hanging, twisted up in the swinging noose. And when he saw her . . .

As suddenly as Oedipus's bursting through the doors reveals Jocasta to the servant's view, the dead woman becomes again the object of Oedipus's gaze. The irony constituted by the fact that Oedipus's interruption of the servant's witnessing leads circuitously to a resumption of that witnessing is quickly erased as Oedipus once again becomes the author of the pathetic vision. Or so it might appear.

In fact, the subtle irony of the text interweaves these multiple points of view in such a way as to reclaim much of the narrative authority the

---

14. Tonelli comments that the *exangelos*'s report is "doomed to narrate only the story of its narrating subject" (1983, 154).

*exangelos* so conspicuously jettisoned earlier. By staging the revelation of the corpse in this way, the narrative presents the horrific tableau of Jocasta hanging as that which is seen and reacted to by Oedipus. εἰσείδομεν of 1263 reestablishes the scene in the bedroom within the frame of the *exangelos*'s narrative as the object of his interest, thereby bringing a tenuous completion to the narrative, which was, after all, announced as the answer to the question, How did Jocasta die? Line 1251 declares an ignorance, which now at 1263 is revisited and to some extent replaced. But this tenuous sense of narrative completion instantly gives way to perhaps an even greater imperative, that of reclaiming narrative authority, which this *exangelos* achieves by quickly substituting the third-person for the first with ὁ δ' ὡς ὁρᾷ νιν.

The *exangelos*'s account, which he announces as lacking that which is most distressing, in that it is *logos* and not *opsis*, up to this point preserves a sense of modesty vis-à-vis the shocking in part by "hiding" the gruesomeness of Jocasta's death behind closed doors as well as behind the intruding Oedipus. If *logos* can never shock as much as *opsis*, it seems to say, this particular *logos* can claim to shock even less than it might: the double remove of Jocasta's death illustrates something of the kinds of terrain that can separate a narrative from its referent.

But what follows Oedipus's discovery of the hanged Jocasta dispenses with all pretense to such modesty, for the most gruesome and disturbing of all that happens offstage is Oedipus's self-blinding. Introducing this gruesome account, he says (1267): δεινά γ' ἦν τἀνθένδ' ὁρᾶν ("What followed then was awful to see"). He goes on to describe Oedipus snatching the pins from Jocasta's clothing and piercing them into his eyes while proclaiming that his eyes would now be cut off from the evils he had brought about. Accompanying this eerie chant (ἐφυμνῶν, 1275), Oedipus (1275–79),

> πολλάκις τε κοὐχ ἅπαξ
> ἤρασσ' ἐπαίρων βλέφαρα. φοίνιαι δ' ὁμοῦ
> γλῆναι γένει' ἔτεγγον, οὐδ' ἀνίεσαν

φόνου μυδώσας σταγόνας, ἀλλ' ὁμοῦ μέλας
ὄμβρος χαλάζης αἱματοῦς ἐτέγγετο.[15]

not once but often struck his eyes, arm aloft. His bloody eyeballs
stained his chin not with mere drops of blood, but all about a storm
of black gore rained down.

Here the impeding doors and distractions foregrounded in the earlier
part of the narrative give way to an unobstructed view of a scene more
disturbing in its graphic horror than the (absent) description of Jocasta's
death could have been. The metaphor and repetition at this point stand
apart as such from the rest of the narrative, bringing both a sense of im-
mediacy and heightened pathos: if the *exangelos* has announced that τὰ
μὲν / ἄλγιστ' ἄπεστιν (1237–38), here he arrives at the greatest source
of *algos* in his account. Indeed, it might seem at this moment that his pre-
amble was a largely ineffective rhetorical ploy.

It is surely no coincidence that the moment in the narrative that at-
tains this gruesome level coincides with the *exangelos*'s retreat from his
virtual transgression of the boundaries that contain and define the con-
ventional messenger. With 1265 he withdraws his own gaze as a subject
of his narrative, substituting that of Oedipus. Although ὁρᾶν in 1267
clearly implies his own status as spectator of the self-blinding to come,
the impersonal construction is not without effect: we are invited to con-
template what follows as a scene as much for our own viewing as for that
of the *exangelos*. In fact, this introduction would seem flatly to contradict
1238 insofar as by detaching the spectacle from a particular gaze the nar-
rative offers it as something still visible. That is, as the object of the *ex-
angelos*'s gaze, Oedipus's self-blinding differs substantially—on the *ex-
angelos*'s own testimony at 1237–38—from the verbal account he offers;
but to the extent that the spectacle remains unattached to the *exangelos*

15. Editors have proposed numerous readings of 1279. Lloyd-Jones and
Wilson bracket 1278–79. I follow Jebb, Kamerbeek, and Bollack. See Bol-
lack for a convenient summary of views.

himself—and hence to anyone in particular—the distinction between word and deed diminishes because we are invited to imagine ourselves "seeing" what we hear.

As such, there is a double movement in this narrative, on the one hand aiming at the scene of Jocasta's death, and on the other tracking Oedipus and his self-blinding. I separate these two elements only as a convenience, as these two strands of the *exangelos's* narrative enable us to identify a twofold concern. First, we find a frustrated and displaced narrative that shows a provocative awareness of its own status as narrative: as it tries to tell how Jocasta died, it finds instead closed doors and interruption.[16] And second, we find a very explicit description of Oedipus's gruesome self-blinding following a strategic manipulation of narrative point of view. At once, we find a strong insistence that word and deed are far apart, as well as a quiet dismissal of the dynamics implied by this distinction.

If this contradictory aspect of the *angelia* finds any solution, it does so in the *exangelos's* closing words. In response to the *koruphaios's* question about whether Oedipus has found "some respite from evil" (1286), the *exangelos* says that Oedipus (1287–89)

βοᾶ διοίγειν κλῇθρα καὶ δηλοῦν τινα
τοῖς πᾶσι Καδμείοισι τὸν πατροκτόνον
τὸν μητρός, αὐδῶν ἀνόσι' οὐδὲ ῥητά μοι.

calls out to open the doors and to reveal to all the Cadmeans the father-killer, his mother's—saying unholy things, things unspeakable for me.

These lines blur the distinction between the two parts of the narrative identified above. The *exangelos* reminds us that, unlike what the stage itself can and will do, his account has not revealed (δηλοῦν) Oedipus. More important, his aposiopesis in 1289 signals a return of the lacunae so persistent in the narrative about Jocasta. Although the earlier silence about the death of Jocasta arises as a consequence of the *exangelos's* frus-

16. Cf. Goldhill 1984a, 195.

trated vision, and here he presents his silence as a sign of his respect for the dead queen, both serve the same purpose of interrupting the narrative.[17] What had appeared as an account marked by a sense of immediacy becomes at this point another truncated report of events offstage.

And as δηλοῦν at 1287 and δείξει at 1294 suggest, the distinction between the seen and the heard operates not only with respect to what is offstage; it will be enacted onstage as well. Indeed, at 1295–96 the *exangelos* announces that the doors are opening, and adds:

θέαμα δ' εἰσόψῃ τάχα
τοιοῦτον οἷον καὶ στυγοῦντ' ἐποικτίσαι.

Soon you will see a spectacle such as to make even one full of hate feel pity.

Here as the *exangelos* leaves the stage, he reestablishes the cleavage between the visible and the audible with a force comparable to that of his opening remarks. And in so doing, he once again underscores the gap between his own narrative and the events it purports to relate. Not only does his *logos* fail to capture τὰ ἄλγιστα, but in order to illustrate this claim, the text proceeds to enact it. The self-referential narrative of the messenger, parading its own status as representation, yields now to the horrific, blinded Oedipus. And this *theama*, says the *exangelos*, will move even one who feels hate. Again he suggests that *opsis* is more powerful than *logos*.

How, then, are we to explain the appearance of a messenger without an *angelia* and that of an *exangelos* who repeatedly insists that his narrative diverges sharply from the events it relates? I will argue that we can make sense of these two figures by understanding them as part of the play's larger commentary on the limitations of human knowledge and speech. This I will do principally by examining the figure of Oedipus in the play as I argue that he and the *exangelos* are analogues of one another.

17. There may well be, of course, other causes for this silence; see Clay 1982.

The philosophical concerns of this play, expressed primarily through the experience of Oedipus, so permeate it that they extend to the performance of the *exangelos*. I will suggest that the messenger reproduces in theatrical terms the intellectual journey of Oedipus.

———

It has been said that Oedipus is characterized by a "passion for disclosure of being."[18] His defeat of the Sphinx, offered by the text as emblematic of his identity, establishes Oedipus as a figure endowed with a talent for rendering the enigmatic transparent. And the text represents this defeat as both an intellectual and a linguistic feat. In "solving" the Sphinx's enigmatic riddle, Oedipus turned opaque, self-referential language into clear, unambiguous speech. This act, furthermore, stands as a model for understanding his quest first for the killer of Laios and then for his own parentage. That is, the action of the play consists largely in Oedipus's attempt to repeat his mastery over the Sphinx.

The text suggests in several ways that Oedipus's defeat of the Sphinx stands as a token of his identity. First, the punning on Oedipus's name serves on a number of occasions to link him both with his pierced feet and with his victory over the Sphinx, that victory seen as the solution of her riddle about feet. As the Corinthian says at 1036, referring to the maiming of Oedipus's feet, ὠνομάσθης ἐκ τύχης ταύτης ὃς εἶ ("From this chance event you were named who you are"). In other words, Oedipus is the person his name suggests: his identity is tied to (his) feet. And his expertise in feet is precisely what enabled him to defeat the Sphinx.

Second, Oedipus opens the play with a solicitation of the suppliants that includes an introduction of himself at line 8 as ὁ πᾶσι κλεινὸς Οἰδίπους ("Oedipus, the one known to all"). For the audience in the theater, Oedipus was famous for all the things that he himself comes to know during the course of the play: in an extreme case of dramatic irony Oe-

18. Heidegger 1959, 107. Flashar speaks of the play's "Entdeckungshandlung" (1976, 356). Goldhill (1984a) has extended this thought beyond the figure of Oedipus to the play as a whole.

dipus announces himself as the famous subject of myth.[19] Within the fiction, however, and for Oedipus to be sure, he is famous principally for his deliverance of Thebes by means of his victory over the Sphinx.[20] Oedipus's self-description, then, invokes his distinction as Sphinx-killer (1198–99) and reminds us that as a figure defined by his *kleos*, he is first and foremost the vanquisher of the Sphinx.[21]

But perhaps most important, his encounter with the Sphinx is invoked as the analogue of his task in the current crisis. The priest, at least, sees the plague as a reappearance of the crisis represented by the Sphinx and calls upon Oedipus to save the city again, as he did when the "harsh singer" (σκληρᾶς ἀοιδοῦ, 36) terrorized the city (52–53):

ὄρνιθι γὰρ καὶ τὴν τότ' αἰσίῳ τύχην
παρέσχες ἡμῖν, καὶ τανῦν ἴσος γενοῦ.

You gave us then an auspicious good fortune; so now become
the same.

Oedipus has, of course, already sent Creon to Delphi to consult the oracle. But the priest's request reiterates the fact that it is the plague that sets the action of the play into motion. Oedipus's search, which will lead from tracking down the murderer of Laios to tracing his own genealogy, begins in response to the crisis of the plague. The famous solver of the Sphinx's riddle now faces a new riddle, and the priest calls for a reprise of that past performance.[22]

---

19. Cf. Antiphanes fr. 189 (Kassel-Austin), with the comment of Pucci (1992, 190 n. 4). See Kamerbeek 1967, 1–7, for a summary of Oedipus in myth prior to the play.

20. Denniston, referring to this line, remarks that "κλεινός is a regular title of royalty" (1939 *ad* 327). Nonetheless, Oedipus's status as *tyrannos* of Thebes follows as a consequence of his defeat of the Sphinx. See Kamerbeek 1967, 10.

21. Cf. Knox 1957, 116–17.

22. Knox speaks of "not one Oedipus but two" (1957, 149–50).

This act of defeating the Sphinx betokens the supreme intelligence of Oedipus, as already Pindar memorializes (τὰν Οἰδιπόδα σοφίαν, *Pyth.* 4. 263). As such, this defeat serves well as a model for the current crisis: as in the case of the Sphinx's riddle, now Thebes stands in need of an intellectual feat. And as Bernard Knox has shown (1957, esp. 116–58), Oedipus's search in the play is consistently represented as an intellectual one. In characterizing Oedipus's journey as intellectual, then, the text affirms the analogy established by the priest.

It has often been noted that both Oedipus and the other *dramatis personae* conceive of the solution to the present crisis in terms of metaphors of vision.[23] When Oedipus asks why there had been no investigation into the death of Laios, Creon responds (130–31):

ἡ ποικιλῳδὸς Σφὶγξ τὸ πρὸς ποσὶ σκοπεῖν
μεθέντας ἡμᾶς τἀφανῆ προσήγετο.

The riddling Sphinx forced us to look at what lay at our feet and to ignore what was obscure.

Creon here employs two metaphors of vision (σκοπεῖν and τἀφανῆ). And the response of Oedipus is equally emphatic (132): ἀλλ' ἐξ ὑπαρχῆς αὖθις αὔτ' ἐγὼ φανῶ ("Then I myself will bring these things to light from the beginning"). At this moment Oedipus announces that he will carry out the search for Laios's killer, as he formulates the solution to the present crisis in terms of rendering the hidden visible.

These lines may in fact further mark the link between Oedipus's defeat of the Sphinx and his search for Laios's killer as parallel projects. The scholia preserve two interpretations of these lines, one understanding τἀφανῆ to refer to the details of Laios's death, the other taking it to refer to the riddle of the Sphinx.[24] Indeed, ἀφανές would be an apposite descriptive term for the Sphinx's enigma, as J. C. Kamerbeek notes: "At

23. Knox (1957, 131–35) catalogues these metaphors.
24. The latter reading requires us to construe τὸ πρὸς ποσὶ σκοπεῖν with μεθέντας, as Bollack (1990 ad loc.) notes.

first sight these lines seem to set us a Sphinx's riddle, but Oedipus' φανῶ (132) makes it clear that by τἀφανῆ are meant the mysteries connected with the murder" (1967 *ad* 130–31). Even though all modern editors follow the equation of τἀφανῆ with the events surrounding the death of Laios, the vocabulary of the text invites an extension of the reference to the riddle of the Sphinx.

Similarly, although I have not translated it as such, some read αὖθις at 132 as meaning "once more," that is "as he had done in the case of the Sphinx" (Jebb 1893 ad loc.).[25] On Jebb's reading, Oedipus himself conceives of the present search as a reprise of his former triumph, and furthermore he casts both as processes of rendering the obscure clearly visible. Of course, we may choose a somewhat open-ended reading that allows the reference both to the Sphinx and to the original, frustrated attempt to discover who killed Laios. At a minimum, the meaning understood by Jebb remains implicit in Oedipus's words, expressing the link between the Sphinx and the plague through a metaphor of vision.

The textual thread of representing the solution of Laios's death as a rendering visible continues during the exchange between Oedipus and the *koruphaios* following Oedipus's proclamation of the curse. The *koruphaios* suggests that Oedipus consult Teiresias (283–86):

ἄνακτ' ἄνακτι ταῦθ' ὁρῶντ' ἐπίσταμαι
μάλιστα Φοίβῳ Τειρεσίαν, παρ' οὗ τις ἂν
σκοπῶν τάδ', ὦναξ, ἐκμάθοι σαφέστατα.

I know Lord Teiresias sees most of all as does Lord Phoebus, and from him, my lord, one might clearly learn these things by looking.

This is, of course, one of many ironic exploitations of the fact that only the blind Teiresias truly "sees." His "vision" stands as the nearest approximation to divine knowledge. The vision of Teiresias, perhaps the

25. Others read it differently. Dawe says that "Oedipus means that what became ἀφανής will now be rendered φανερός again" (1982 ad loc.). Cf. Bollack 1990 ad loc.

play's most potent metaphor, marks in the words of the *koruphaios* the nearest source of truth. Aside from the wisdom of Teiresias, he says, "in whom alone among men truth is inborn" (298–99), "the other things said [about Laios] are mute and ancient" (290).[26] Oedipus then asks about "the other things" (291–93):

> O.   τὰ ποῖα ταῦτα; πάντα γὰρ σκοπῶ λόγον.
> X.   θανεῖν ἐλέχθη πρός τινων ὁδοιπόρων.
> O.   ἤκουσα κἀγώ· τὸν δ' ἰδόντ' οὐδεὶς ὁρᾷ.[27]
>
> O.   Which things? I look into every report.
> C.   He was said to have died at the hands of some travelers.
> O.   I, too, have heard this, but no one sees the one who saw it.

With σκοπῶ in 291 Oedipus picks up the *koruphaios*'s use of this verb at 286, as he says that he will subject these *logoi* to visual inspection. The opposition in this passage between seeing and hearing culminates in the next two lines. At Oedipus's insistence the *koruphaios* repeats the rumor about Laios's end and marks this as mere talk with his use of the passive (ἐλέχθη). Oedipus then recognizes the limitation of this rumor, which he himself has heard, emphasizing precisely its status as something heard and not seen. And as though to amplify the gulf between the two, the text puts the rumor at a double remove: not only did no one see Laios die (or so he thinks), but no one has even seen the one who saw. Again, certainty of meaning is imagined as the province of vision, and making the unknown known as a process of rendering visible.[28]

---

26. There is disagreement about how to understand τὰ γ' ἄλλα at 290. See Bollack 1990 ad loc.

27. Many editors (including Lloyd-Jones and Wilson, and Dawe) change τὸν δ' ἰδόντ' of the manuscripts into τὸν δὲ δρῶντ' in order to avoid the apparent change of subject in the following two lines; but see Kamerbeek 1967 and Bollack 1990 ad loc.

28. Metaphors of vision permeate the play, as Knox as shown (1957, 131–35).

This distinction between seeing and hearing rehearses a familiar opposition in Greek thought. As it does so, it forms part of the play's strong thematic interest in knowledge, in part because the vocabularies of knowing and seeing overlap: "I know" (οἶδα) means literally "I have seen." And, as has been often noted, the play makes much of this vocabulary, in part through puns on Oedipus's name.[29] It is perhaps not an exaggeration to say that much of the play's commentary on knowledge is expressed in terms of sight and blindness: Oedipus's attempt to render the hidden visible is an attempt to "see" and thus to know, while his "blindness strikes at the terms of his claims to knowledge and insight" (Goldhill 1986, 220).

But the play's insistent framing of Oedipus's search and intellectual journey in terms of vision does more. The play's extensive vocabulary of sight finds an analogue in the messenger: in his attempt to render the hidden visible, Oedipus seeks the status of (metaphorical) eyewitness. Represented in these terms, his task becomes parallel to that of the messenger. Such a parallel would perhaps be of little interest were it not for the fact that it is so extensive: not only is Oedipus's charge characterized in terms that suggest the parallel, but the performance of the *exangelos* reproduces the intellectual journey of Oedipus. As Oedipus discovers himself to be the object of his search, the *exangelos*'s narrative places its speaker at its focus: both Oedipus and the *exangelos* prove to be central participants in what they come to know as "eyewitnesses."[30]

The parallel between these two as compromised eyewitnesses finds elaboration, of course, in the *exangelos*'s report: his own emphatic interest in distinguishing the seen from the heard, and the hidden from the revealed, recalls the same persistent concern of Oedipus. Indeed, the *ex-*

29. See, for example, Knox 1957, 127–28, 183–84; Goldhill 1986, 217–20; Pucci 1992, 66–72.

30. In a play that has been read as a commentary on theater, such parallels deserve particular attention. See, for example, Tonelli 1983; Goldhill 1986, 220–21; Ringer 1998, 78–90.

*angelos* presents his report as part of the process that will bring to light (ἐς τὸ φῶς φανεῖ) the ills that lie hidden (κεύθει) in the house (1228–29). He defines his own project, both in its successes and in its failures, in terms that recall the metaphorical descriptions of Oedipus's task.

But the text itself encourages even more explicitly the reading of these two figures as analogues. On two occasions Oedipus acts in place of a messenger. First, at the play's opening he declares to the Thebans gathered before the palace (6–7):

> ἀγὼ δικαιῶν μὴ παρ' ἀγγέλων, τέκνα,
> ἄλλων ἀκούειν αὐτὸς ὧδ' ἐλήλυθα.
>
> Not thinking it right to hear these things from messengers, at second-hand, I have come myself.[31]

Here the absent messenger is "produced" intentionally by Oedipus as a sign of his concern and of the immediacy of his inquiry: the lack of mediation by a messenger testifies to his devotion to the city and to the level of his sensitivity to its difficulties.[32] Additionally, the text here first states its interest in the opposition between seeing and hearing, one term of which is central to Oedipus's emphatic rejection of both messengers and hearsay. Oedipus announces not only that he is acting in place of a messenger; he recalls the distinction between presence and absence—seeing and hearing—that the tragic messenger relies upon in establishing his own authority. Furthermore, while marking the inauguration of Oedipus's search for the city's deliverance as that which displaces or stands in for a messenger's performance, these lines also set in motion the text's reflections on the lack of immediacy involved in an *angelia*. Here at the outset the distinction between one's own presence (αὐτὸς) and the account of another is already operative, a distinction that, as we have seen, looms large in the account of the *exangelos*.

---

31. "at second-hand" I take from Jebb 1893.
32. Much as he explicitly claims at 60–64.

More explicitly, the text stages Oedipus's search for Laios's killer as
the consequence of an absent *angelia* concerning the murder: Oedipus
embarks on his search because there was no messenger, no account of
what happened. Only by taking up the matter anew and conducting an
inquiry into the murder can Oedipus hope to recover what happened on
the highway; only in this way can he hope to fill the void left by the ab-
sent *angelia*. In speaking with Creon, Oedipus learns that Laios was
killed on the highway. At 116–17 Oedipus asks:

οὐδ' ἄγγελός τις οὐδὲ συμπράκτωρ ὁδοῦ
κατεῖδ', ὅτου τις ἐκμαθὼν ἐχρήσατ' ἄν;

Was there not some messenger, or a fellow traveler who saw what
happened, from whom one might have learned something useful?

Oedipus's search begins as an effort to find out what an *angelos* would
have reported immediately following Laios's death; he marks his inquiry
as an effort to produce a narrative to take the place of the absent one.
Creon replies that there was indeed one survivor of the massacre, but
that he was able to tell only that Laios had died at the hands of many rob-
bers. There was, then, an eyewitness, but his report is not only absent
from our text; what survives of it—here in Creon's summary—proves
to be thin and unsatisfactory, to Oedipus at least. Oedipus's dissatisfac-
tion is perhaps not insignificant given the *angeliai* in our text: one that
does not deserve the name; another that violates conventional expecta-
tions and leaves lacunae that serve to question its status. These examples
would seem to be anticipated by the account of Laios's death: an eye-
witness in this play does not guarantee a (felicitous) report. Needless to
say, the original direction of Oedipus's search is deflected, but it begins
as the desire to compensate for the lost eyewitness report.

A fragment of Aeschylus's *Oedipus* (387a Radt) appears to preserve
part of such an *angelia*. If this fragment does derive from the lone sur-
vivor's report, it suggests that the exclusion of this account, together
with the notice of this exclusion, in our text is an important clue. Karl

Reinhardt argues, in fact, that the Aeschylean fragment "is enough to show what it was that Sophocles displaced by his diversion and its consequences, so as to make room for other things" (1979, 99). Although Reinhardt has other "other things" in mind,[33] the absent *angelia* surely makes room for much of Oedipus's pursuit of Laios's killer.

As the text's vocabulary of vision and knowledge suggests that Oedipus's intellectual journey constitutes a quest for "eyewitness" status, the play's interest in the Sphinx suggests yet another parallel between Oedipus and the messenger. "No play is more about language than the *Oedipus Tyrannus*," writes Segal (1981, 241), and the lesson of the Sphinx forms a crucial part of the play's interest in this subject.

From Athenaeus (456b) we know that Asclepiades of Thrace wrote a *Tragoidoumena* in the mid-fourth century B.C.E. in which he recorded the enigma of the Sphinx. The enigma in this form—the familiar one about an animal with one voice but two, three, and four feet—made its way into a number of the extant manuscripts of the play.[34] The enigma in this form may in fact be older than Sophocles' play.[35] There has been a lengthy critical tradition identifying the enigma of the Sphinx with this particular riddle, and concomitantly identifying Oedipus's defeat of the Sphinx with his solving of the riddle.

In Sophocles' play, however, the relationship between Oedipus and the Sphinx remains somewhat elusive. The text skirts not only the issue of what the enigma was, but also the question of what constituted Oedipus's victory over the Sphinx. We know from the text of the play neither what the Sphinx sang (ἀοιδοῦ, 36) nor whether it is appropriate to speak

33. For Reinhardt, this "diversion" is Oedipus's suspicion of a conspiracy: the absence of a messenger in Sophocles' play makes such a suspicion possible. It is, however, possible that the Aeschylus fragment appeared late in the play, thus leaving room for such a suspicion there as well.

34. A scholion on Eur. *Phoen.* 50, along with one of our manuscripts, records the solution of the enigma as well.

35. See Knox 1957, 237 n. 31; Kamerbeek 1967, 4.

of Oedipus "solving" a riddle. In short, the text does not reveal whether or not, in fact, the enigma was—as usually imagined—a question that Oedipus answered.[36] Indeed, there is textual support for reading Oedipus's victory not only as an intellectual act, but also as a linguistic one, a form of translation, so to speak. In line with this suggestion of the text, Oedipus's intellectual gifts acquire a specifically linguistic, or discursive, form.

Our text recalls Oedipus's meeting with the Sphinx on a number of occasions, but never does it say that he "solved" the enigma. In fact, the first explicit mention of Oedipus's victory draws us very close to a characterization of that victory as a solving of the riddle before suddenly averting its course and turning to metaphor. Invoking the defeat of the Sphinx, the priest calls upon Oedipus to come to the aid of Thebes (35–36):

ὅς γ' ἐξέλυσας ἄστυ Καδμεῖον μολὼν
σκληρᾶς ἀοιδοῦ δασμὸν ὃν παρείχομεν.

You who came to the city of Cadmus and freed us from the tax we paid to the harsh singer.

The translation does not capture the teasing in the original. The verb translated here as "freed" (ἐξέλυσας) is a compound of what is nearly a technical term for "solving" a riddle or a problem (λύω).[37] This verb also means "bring to an end" or (with the prefix ἐκ) "make the final pay-

36. Marie Delcourt speaks of Oedipus's defeat of the Sphinx as "un fait nu." Speaking about the entire mythological tradition and not only of our play, she says: "Nous n'en avons pas un récit. Nous ne savons même pas exactement en quoi elle [the victory] consiste" (1981, 105). She does, however, take it for granted that Oedipus "eut prononcé le mot décisif" and that it was this "mot" that effected his victory somehow.

37. As the language of Aristophanes' hypothesis indicates, speaking of Oedipus (line 7): Σφιγγὸς δὲ δεινῆς θανάσιμον λύσας μέλος. Jebb remarks: "The notion is not, 'paid it in full,' but 'loosed it,'—the thought of the tribute suggesting that of the riddle which Oed. solved" (1893 *ad* 35). Cf. Segal 1981, 232; Dawe 1982 *ad* 394.

ment," as it does here being construed with *dasmon*. But used with reference to Oedipus's defeat of the Sphinx, it would seem to suggest a solving of her riddle, only to supplant that suggestion with a resolving of the burden she represented, expressed through a financial metaphor. At once, this line calls to mind Oedipus's victory as a solving and withdraws that suggestion: the expected and seemingly well-understood vocabulary is displaced, thereby bracketing the familiar conception of Oedipus's encounter with the Sphinx.

Elsewhere in connection with the Sphinx, Oedipus stops her (397), he is by nature the best at discovering the enigmatic (*ta ainikta*, 440), he is wise (507–10), he destroys her (1197–1200), and he understands the enigmas (1525).[38] Two of these state merely that Oedipus put an end to the Sphinx (397, 1197–1200), without specifying how this happened. Three others mark the defeat with references to Oedipus's intellect (440, 507–10, and 1525). These indications of how Oedipus managed to defeat the Sphinx, in representing the victory as an intellectual feat, conform with the common understanding of it as the solving of the riddle.[39]

In one passage, however, where Oedipus upbraids Teiresias for having been of no help during the crisis of the Sphinx, the matter appears differently. These lines are important in that they are the only ones in our text that speak explicitly of what Oedipus actually did in response to the enigma. He asks Teiresias (391–94):

πῶς οὐχ, ὅθ᾽ ἡ ῥαψῳδὸς ἐνθάδ᾽ ἦν κύων,
ηὔδας τι τοῖσδ᾽ ἀστοῖσιν ἐκλυτήριον;
καίτοι τό γ᾽ αἴνιγμ᾽ οὐχὶ τοὐπιόντος ἦν
ἀνδρὸς διειπεῖν, ἀλλὰ μαντείας ἔδει.

Why, when the rhapsode-dog was here, did you not speak something to deliver the citizens? The enigma, indeed it was not for a

38. If lines 1524–30 are authentic; some regard them as spurious.
39. Cf. the scholion on Eur. *Phoen.* 1760, which speaks of the Sphinx as an oracle-monger (χρησμολόγος) speaking things difficult for the Thebans to understand (δύσγνωστα τοῖς Θηβαίοις λέγουσα).

man happening by to speak it distinctly; rather, it was the task of a seer.

The verb διειπεῖν, translated here as "to speak distinctly," has caused a substantial amount of difficulty for critics. On the one hand, many expect it to mean "solve," assuming that this is what Oedipus did to the enigma. On the other hand, Dawe remarks that "the choice of word is odder than it looks," noting that elsewhere in Sophocles (*Trachiniae* 22 and in our play also at 854) the word means "tell clearly" or "tell with precision" (1982 ad loc.).[40] Bollack's incisive comment deserves quotation at length:

> The idea of "solution" can be retained for this verb without having to alter the clear meaning if the "parole" and the distinctions that it makes are opposed to the "rhapsodic" recitation of the Sphinx who expresses herself by means of symbols. Her song remains opaque as long as that which is absent is not circumscribed by the introduction of a subject in a predicative proposition that makes the referents explicit. "To speak the enigma" is to have control over the representation of it that allows one to appropriate it through language. The fact that Oedipus can "speak" . . . shows that he was able to assimilate the song, while for the others, including the prophet, it remained unassimilable and therefore unspeakable.
>
> At the same time, τὰ κλείν' αἰνίγματ' ἤδη in the final lines [1525] may mean not only that Oedipus knew the solution, but that he knew how to say what was required. The "text," then, is not, as in the lines that have transmitted the enigma to us, the "song" of the monster, but its transposition articulated in language that makes an effective response to it, composed in order to master it.[41]

40. Kamerbeek (1967 ad loc.) claims the unusual meaning of "to interpret"; Jebb maintains the ambiguity in opting for "to declare, to solve," which would appear to be two rather different actions (1893 ad loc.).

41. "L'idée de solution peut être retrouvée dans le verbe, sans qu'on en modifie l'acception obvie, si la 'parole,' et les distinctions qu'elle établit, sont opposées à la récitation 'rhapsodique' de la Sphinge, qui s'exprime par

Bollack's formulation of Oedipus's victory is at once richer than what a willful translation of διειπεῖν as "solve" can produce, and also more telling as a model for understanding Oedipus's search staged in our play. By contrasting the clear statement expressed by the verb διειπεῖν with the song of "the rhapsode-dog" one understands Oedipus's feat as a specific kind of linguistic act, that of "translating" the sung into the spoken, the metaphorical into the literal.

Similarly, the other occurrence of the verb διειπεῖν in the play suggests that it means "to speak without ambiguity or possibility of misunderstanding." At 842 Oedipus, in explaining his eagerness to interview the old shepherd who witnessed Laios's death, seizes on what Jocasta said more than 100 lines earlier, namely, that Laios was reported to have been killed by robbers, plural in number.[42] And if in fact Laios was killed by more than one, Oedipus reckons, he himself could not have been the killer. Jocasta reassures him that the story was as he has heard, that there were a number of people involved in Laios's death. And, she goes on, if

---

symboles. Son chant reste confus tant que la chose absente n'est pas cernée par l'introduction d'un sujet dans une proposition prédicative qui explicite les références. 'Dire l'énigme,' c'est donc en posséder la représentation qui permet de se l'approprier par le langage. Le fait qu'Oedipe puisse 'parler' . . . montre que la parole chantée a pu être assimilée par Oedipe, alors que pour les autres, dont le devin, elle était restée inassimilable, et donc indicible.

"De même, dans les derniers vers, τὰ κλείν' αἰνίγματ' ἤδη peut ne pas signifier seulement qu'Oedipe connaissait la solution, mais qu'il sut dire ce qu'il fallait. Le 'texte' n'est pas alors, comme dans les vers qui nous ont transmis l'énigme, le 'chant' du monstre, mais sa transposition articulée dans le langage qui en fait une réponse efficace, composée pour le maîtriser" (1990 *ad* 393f.).

42. As Dawe (1982 *ad* 841) notes, Oedipus conflates what he heard from Creon at 118–23 with what Jocasta says at 715–16: she speaks of ἡ φάτις, whereas Creon speaks of the sole survivor of the attack who reported to Thebes. In the end, Jocasta's φάτις will derive from the survivor whom Creon mentions.

the original eyewitness should try to change his story, he will not get away with it, since the whole city heard what he said earlier. But even more significantly, she says, if he does say something a bit different the next time, he will never be able to show that the death of Laios happened in accordance with prophecy. The prophecy was unmistakable concerning Laios (853–54),

ὄν γε Λοξίας
διεῖπε χρῆναι παιδὸς ἐξ ἐμοῦ θανεῖν.

whom Loxias clearly said was destined to be killed by my child.

Just when issues of meaning and interpretation are at stake—at the moment of establishing the significance of the shepherd's report in determining what happened at the time of Laios's death—Jocasta claims that Apollo's declaration about how Laios was to die at any rate (γε) was beyond misunderstanding. Other elements in the prophecy may be open to doubt or misinterpretation, but on this point, she says, there can be only one meaning. She uses the verb διειπεῖν, then, in a context of establishing the clarity of Apollo's pronouncement.[43]

The text, then, invites us to think of Oedipus's victory over the Sphinx as an act characterized by clear, unambiguous speech, much as Bollack suggests for reading line 394. At the same time, it must be emphasized, the text studiously avoids revealing anything substantial about that encounter, and we must not imagine retrieving the "reality" of Oedipus's victory somewhere behind the text: the meeting of these two itself remains enigmatic. Yet while the text will always shroud that meeting in darkness, it makes it clear that the traces of their encounter bear on issues at stake during the course of the play.

43. Curiously, here Jocasta eschews the distinction she makes at 711–12 between Apollo and his servants: now, it seems, Apollo himself is as unreliable as the prophets. See Knox 1957, 173.

The principal legacy of this meeting, I suggest, is its characterization of Oedipus's talents. As I have argued, it is this encounter that stands as the exemplary victory that he attempts to repeat in his search for the killers of Laios. And Oedipus's victory proves to be not only an intellectual feat, but a linguistic, or discursive, one as well. In this way, the text identifies the talents that Oedipus attempts to use in his search: he seeks not only to know as one who has seen, but also to speak that knowledge distinctly and unambiguously (διειπεῖν).

The play's oblique treatment of Oedipus's victory, silencing both the Sphinx and Oedipus, does more than keep from us their words. It also preserves the status of the riddle as an enigma nearly impenetrable for being so self-referential: its enigmatic opacity itself becomes its referent; the text simultaneously preserves the status of Oedipus's solution as the ideal opposite of the Sphinx's speech, perfectly clear and distinct and utterly unmarked by self-reference. Against the inevitably compromising force of reality, this silence protects both pronouncements as ideal types. Much as the *Odyssey* preserves the ideal status of the Sirens' song by allowing us to hear them sing only about their song, Sophocles' play surrounds both riddle and solution with a silence that enables them both to wield the power of an imaginary language.[44]

This is important principally because it clarifies just what Oedipus in the play fails to do: seen as attempting to repeat his previous victory, he is held to an ideal standard and can only fall short. Oedipus says, for example, more than he understands in uttering the curse (236–43); he speaks a language far different from the one he is imagined to have spoken to the Sphinx. Here, what he says may be clear to the audience, but for everyone onstage Oedipus hardly speaks without ambiguity or possibility of misunderstanding. Unlike in his confrontation with the Sphinx,

44. Pucci notes that "the text's reticence in leaving the Sirens' song forever unsung, forever unknowable, is precisely what endows it with the force of sublimity" (1987, 211).

the Oedipus of the play "does not understand the secret speech that, without his realizing, lurks at the heart of what he says" (Vernant 1988c, 116).

Both in his quest for certain knowledge, conceived as the product of vision, and in his attempt to speak in an ideally unambiguous manner, Oedipus, of course, falls short: the exhaustive inquiry aimed at making the hidden visible ends with Oedipus's self-blinding; and the master of "translating" the Sphinx's opacity into unambiguous clarity proves to speak far more than he understands. These two aspects of Oedipus's failure in the play, in fact, have a common basis, in that both are marked by self-reference. As "eyewitness," Oedipus discovers himself to be the observed as well as the observer: his status as murderer (and son) of Laios is the hidden that he comes to "see." And his pronouncements, which he imagines to refer to others, prove in the end to speak principally about himself.

The text reaps great benefits from the absence of an *angelia* reporting the death of Laios as well as from the exclusion of Oedipus's defeat of the Sphinx: the former defines the status of the eyewitness's knowledge as ideal, while the latter does the same for the status of Oedipus's discursive mastery. And Oedipus's experience in the play demonstrates that both this ideal knowledge and this ideal speech are beyond (even) his reach. Oedipus finds that what he comes to know and what he says inevitably reproduce his own subjectivity: for mortals, at least, the dream of knowledge gained from mere observation as an eyewitness, like the dream of speech that is not self-referential, is just that, a dream. The knowledge that Oedipus acquires insistently (re)inserts him into what he expected simply to observe; and his speech proves to have something of the Sphinx's opacity, frustrating attempts to understand it as a transparent medium.

Oedipus's failures parallel those of the *exangelos* and in so doing illuminate the significance of the latter's unusual *angelia*. The *exangelos*'s explicit testimony that he was unable to see what happened offstage not only marks him as a compromised messenger; it also mimics the absence of a report about Laios. His emphatic insertion of his own frustration as an observer, together with his repeated insistence that his report is a mediated and inadequate substitute for events offstage, not only measures the extent of his departure from conventional practice; it also reproduces the self-referentiality of Oedipus's own speech. In short, the *exangelos*'s performance of his conventional role is sharply limited and reshaped in this play precisely along the lines established by Oedipus's own project of (self-) discovery.

In a play that explores the limitations of human knowledge through the metaphor of vision, it is appropriate that a figure whose authority derives from his eyewitness status finds this authority conspicuously curtailed. Similarly, in a play that expresses its strong interest in the limitations of language partly through contrasting the real speech of the play with (excluded) ideal forms, it is perhaps no surprise that a figure whose success relies upon the discursive privilege of one of these ideal types finds this privilege conspicuously curtailed. In a play that insists that both human knowledge and speech incorporate, or even reproduce, our own subjectivities, it is perhaps no surprise that the messenger proves to be a far from ideal spectator. As his own insistent embodiment impedes his attempt to observe, and as his own insistence on the gap between seeing and hearing serves to mark his narrative as a highly mediated product of his own limited experience, his performance as a whole restates the lessons of Oedipus's intellectual journey. In short, the *exangelos*'s departure from conventional practice demonstrates that such practice proves to be malleable in the service of the play's thematic interests.

It is possible, then, to make sense of the *exangelos*'s idiosyncratic performance as a significant element of the play's philosophical purpose. As in *Rhesos*, a substantially nonconventional *angelia* proves to be far from gratuitous and finally confirms the importance of the conventional claims of the messenger, as I have described them above. At the same time, these plays illustrate the value to be derived from sophisticated use of what has often been seen as a static conventional form. Perhaps most important, however, Sophocles' play provides the most astute commentary on what is at stake in the performance of the tragic *angelia*. In enlisting the *ex-*

*angelos* in the service of the play's larger thematic interests, the text not only displays its own rigor and thoroughness; it also reveals the artifice behind the conventional messenger's privilege, as it puts into question the philosophical premises on which this convention is built.

But the play goes even farther. As others have noted, Sophocles' play includes the audience in its challenging epistemological critique. Just as the *exangelos*'s use of theatrical vocabulary constitutes a metatheatrical commentary of sorts, so does the play's treatment of knowledge and spectatorship extend to the audience.[45] "What does it mean," asks Simon Goldhill, "for a spectator to watch or listen to a play which seems to equate sight and ignorance?" (1986, 220). Part of the answer, in Segal's words, is that the "external observer is also drawn into the action of self-discovery and becomes, with Oedipus, both the searcher and the one who is discovered" (1995, 160).

If the play does in fact encompass the audience in this fashion, the role of the *exangelos* forms a central part of its efforts to do so, for, as I have argued in earlier chapters, the exemplary observer in the tragic texts—namely, the messenger—constitutes a potent theatrical representation of the audience. And as this figure in Sophocles' play does in fact find himself following Oedipus, the implications for the audience are made even more explicit. Not only, then, does the play question the philosophical premises on which the tragic *angelia* is built; it also suggests that the lessons produced by this questioning apply to the audience as well. As a site of experimentation, the tragic *angelia* speaks to a range of issues that extend far beyond the confines of the theater itself.

45. On his use of *opsis* (1238) and *theama* (1295) and the significance of the final scene see Hay 1978, 76–77; Tonelli 1983, 151–66; Goldhill 1984a, 195, and 1986, 220–21.

# Messengers in Greek Tragedy

Please see the discussion in chapter 2 regarding the problem of identifying messengers in the tragic texts. In producing the following list I have largely followed the criteria of de Jong (1991, 179–80): (1) the figure in question is not one of the principal characters, and in fact most often is identified in our manuscripts by function (messenger, servant, shepherd, etc.); (2) the narrative of this figure contains verbs in past tenses; and (3) there is usually dialogue involving the figure preceding the *angelia* itself. Note, however, that this list is intended principally as a guide to which narratives may with profit be read as engagements with the conventional practice as examined in this study. For this reason, I include figures such as Hyllus in Sophocles' *Trachiniae* and the guard in Sophocles' *Antigone*, for example. There are in this list also figures identified in our manuscripts as messengers who, nonetheless, hardly perform according to conventional expectations (the Phrygian in Euripides' *Orestes*, for example). One might also with profit consider the *"angelia"* of Odysseus at lines 375–436 in Euripides' satyr-play, *Cyclops*, as a narrative that is produced against the model of the *tragic* messenger. I include *Rhesos* in the list of Euripidean texts only because of its traditonal place in our manuscripts. I intend no judgment about its authenticity.

## AESCHYLUS

| | |
|---|---|
| *Agamemnon* | 503–680 |
| *Persians* | 302–514 |
| *Septem* | 375–652 |

## SOPHOCLES

| | |
|---|---|
| *Ajax* | 719–802 |
| *Antigone* | 223–440, 1155–1256, 1278–1316 |
| *Electra* | 660–763 |
| *OC* | 1579–1669 |
| *OT* | 1223–96 |
| *Trachiniae* | 180–199, 229–90, 749–820, 899–946 |

## EURIPIDES

| | |
|---|---|
| *Alcestis* | 141–98 |
| *Bacchae* | 660–774, 1024–1152 |
| *Electra* | 761–858 |
| *Hecuba* | 484–582 |
| *Helen* | 597–621, 1511–1618 |
| *Heracl.* | 784–866 |
| *HF* | 909–1015 |
| *Hippolytus* | 1153–1254 |
| *IA* | 1532–1612 |
| *Ion* | 1106–1228 |
| *IT* | 238–339, 1284–1419 |
| *Medea* | 1121–1230 |
| *Orestes* | 852–956, 1369–1502 |
| *Phoen.* | 1067–1263, 1335–1479 |
| *Rhesos* | 264–316, 729–803 |
| *Suppliants* | 634–730 |

# WORKS CITED

Ahl, Frederick. 1991. *Sophocles' "Oedipus": Evidence and Self-Conviction.* Ithaca, N.Y.: Cornell University Press.

Allison, June W. 1997. *Word and Concept in Thucydides.* Atlanta: Scholars Press.

Bakewell, Geoffrey W. 1998. "*Persae* 374–83: Persians, Greeks, and *peitharkho phreni.*" *Classical Philology* 93: 232–36.

Bakhtin, M. M. 1986. *Speech Genres and Other Late Essays.* Translated by Vern W. McGee. Austin: University of Texas Press.

Barlow, Shirley A. 1971. *The Imagery of Euripides. A Study in the Dramatic Use of Pictorial Language.* London: Methuen.

Barthes, Roland. 1968. "L'effet de réel." *Communications* 11: 84–89.

Bassi, Domenico. 1899. "Il nunzio nella tragedia greca." *Rivista di Filologia e d'Istruzione Classica* 27: 50–89.

Bassi, Karen. 1998. *Acting Like Men: Gender, Drama, and Nostalgia in Ancient Greece.* Ann Arbor: University of Michigan Press.

Batchelder, Ann G. 1995. *The Seal of Orestes: Self-Reference and Authority in Sophocles' "Electra."* Lanham, Md.: Rowman and Littlefield.

Belloni, Luigi. 1988. *Eschilo: I Persiani.* Milan: Vita e Pensiero.

Benveniste, Emile. 1971. *Problems in General Linguistics.* Translated by M. E. Meek. Coral Gables, Fla.: University of Miami Press.

Bergson, Leif. 1953. "The Omitted Augment in the Messengers' Speeches of Greek Tragedy." *Eranos* 51: 121–28.

————. 1956. "L'épithète ornamentale dans Eschyle, Sophocle et Euripide." Diss., Uppsala.

————. 1959. "Episches in den ΡΗΣΕΙΣ ΑΓΓΕΛΙΚΑΙ." *Rheinisches Museum für Philologie* n.f. 102: 9–39.

Bierl, Anton F. H. 1991. *Dionysos und die griechische Tragödie: Politische und "meta-theatralische" Aspekte im Text.* Tübingen: Gunter Narr.

Blomfield, Carolus Jacobus. 1830. *Persae.* 4th ed. London: B. Fellowes.

Blundell, Mary Whitlock. 1989. *Helping Friends and Harming Enemies: A Study in Sophocles and Greek Ethics.* Cambridge: Cambridge University Press.

Bollack, Jean. 1990. *L' "Oedipe Roi" de Sophocle: Le texte et ses interprétations.* Lille: Presses Universitaires de Lille.

Bond, G. W. 1988. *Euripides: Heracles.* Oxford: Oxford University Press.

Bond, Robin Sparks. 1996. "Homeric Echoes in *Rhesus.*" *American Journal of Philology* 117: 255–73.

Bremer, J. M. 1976. "Why Messenger-Speeches?" In *Miscellanea Tragica in Honorem J. C. Kamerbeek,* edited by S. L. Radt, J. M. Bremer, and C. J. Ruijgh, 29–48. Amsterdam: Hakkert.

Broadhead, H. D. 1960. *The "Persae" of Aeschylus, Edited with Introduction, Critical Notes, and Commentary.* Cambridge: Cambridge University Press.

Brown, Norman O. 1969. *Hermes the Thief: The Evolution of a Myth.* New York: Vintage.

Browne, Nick. 1986. "The Spectator-in-the-Text: The Rhetoric of *Stagecoach.*" In *Narrative, Apparatus, Ideology: A Film Theory Reader,* edited by Philip Rosen, 102–19. New York: Columbia University Press.

Bundy, Elroy L. 1972. "The 'Quarrel Between Kallimachos and Apollonios,' Part I: The Epilogue of Kallimachos' *Hymn to Apollo.*" *California Studies in Classical Antiquity* 5: 39–94.

Burian, Peter. 1997. "Myth into *Muthos:* The Shaping of the Tragic Plot." In *The Cambridge Companion to Greek Tragedy,* edited by P. E. Easterling, 178–208. Cambridge: Cambridge University Press.

Burnett, Anne Pippin. 1985. "*Rhesus:* Are Smiles Allowed?" In *Directions in Euripidean Criticism,* edited by Peter Burian, 13–51. Durham, N.C.: Duke University Press.

Bushnell, Rebecca. 1988. *Prophesying Tragedy: Sign and Voice in Sophocles' Theban Plays.* Ithaca, N.Y.: Cornell University Press.

Buxton, R. G. A. 1982. *Persuasion in Greek Tragedy: A Study of Peitho.* Cambridge: Cambridge University Press.

————. 1991. "News From Cithaeron: Narrators and Narratives in the *Bacchae*." *Pallas* 37: 39–48.

Cahen, E. 1924. "Sur quelques traits du récit de 'Salamine' dans les *Perses* d'Eschyle." *Revue des Études Anciennes* 26: 297–313.

Calvino, Italo. 1981. *If on a Winter's Night a Traveler*. Translated by William Weaver. New York: Harcourt Brace.

Carrière, Jean. 1948. *Théognis: Poèmes élégiaques*. Paris: Les Belles Lettres.

Chantraine, Pierre. 1970. *Dictionnaire étymologique de la langue grecque*. Paris: Klincksieck.

Chatman, Seymour. 1978. *Story and Discourse: Narrative Structure in Fiction and Film*. Ithaca, N.Y.: Cornell University Press.

Clay, Diskin. 1982. "Unspeakable Words in Greek Tragedy." *American Journal of Philology* 103: 277–98.

Clay, J. S. 1974. "Demas and Aude: The Nature of Divine Transformation in Homer." *Hermes* 102: 129–36.

————. 1983. *The Wrath of Athena: Gods and Men in the "Odyssey."* Princeton: Princeton University Press.

Collard, Christopher. 1975. *Euripides: Supplices*. Groningen: Bouma's Boekhuis.

Craig, J. D. 1924. "The Interpretation of Aeschylus' *Persae*." *Classical Review* 27: 41–45.

Crane, Gregory. 1996. *The Blinded Eye: Thucydides and the New Written Word*. Lanham, Md.: Rowman and Littlefield.

Curtius, E. R. 1953. *European Literature and the Latin Middle Ages*. Translated by W. R. Trask. Princeton: Princeton University Press.

Dale, A. M. 1954. *Euripides: Alcestis*. Oxford: Oxford University Press.

Davidson, J. F. 1988. "Homer and Sophocles' *Electra*." *Bulletin of the Institute of Classical Studies* 35: 45–72.

Davies, Malcolm. 1991. *Sophocles: Trachiniae*. Oxford: Clarendon Press.

Dawe, R. D. 1982. *Sophocles: Oedipus Rex*. Cambridge: Cambridge University Press.

de Jong, Irene J. F. 1987. "The Voice of Anonymity: *Tis*-Speeches in the *Iliad*." *Eranos* 85: 69–84.

————. 1989. *Narrators and Focalizers: The Presentation of the Story in the "Iliad."* Amsterdam: B. R. Grüner.

————. 1991. *Narrative in Drama: The Art of the Euripidean Messenger-Speech*. Leiden: E. J. Brill.

———. 1992. "Récit et drame: Le deuxième récit de messager dans *Les Bacchantes.*" *Revue des Études Grecques* 105: 572–83.

Delcourt, Marie. 1981. *Oedipe ou la légende du conquérant.* Paris: Les Belles Lettres.

Denniston, J. D. 1939. *Euripides: Electra.* Oxford: Oxford University Press.

———. 1954. *The Greek Particles.* 2d ed. Oxford: Clarendon Press.

Detienne, Marcel, and Jean-Pierre Vernant. 1991. *Cunning Intelligence in Greek Culture and Society.* Translated by Janet Lloyd. Chicago: University of Chicago Press.

Dewald, Caroline. 1987. "Narrative Surface and Authorial Voice in Herodotus' *Histories.*" *Arethusa* 20: 147–70.

———. 1999. "The Figured Stage: Focalizing the Initial Narratives of Herodotus and Thucydides." In *Contextualizing Classics: Ideology, Performance, Dialogue (Essays in Honor of John J. Peradotto),* edited by Thomas M. Falkner, Nancy Felson, and David Konstan, 221–52. Lanham, Md.: Rowman and Littlefield.

Di Benedetto, Vicenzo. 1983. *Sofocle.* Florence: La Nuova Italia.

Dickson, Keith. 1992. "Kalkhas and Nestor: Two Narrative Strategies in *Iliad* 1." *Arethusa* 25(3): 327–58.

———. 1995. *Nestor: Poetic Memory in Greek Epic.* New York: Garland.

Di Gregorio, Lamberto. 1967. *Le scene d'annuncio nella tragedia greca.* Milan: Vita e Pensiero.

Dingel, Joachim. 1969. "Der 24. Gesang der *Odysee* und die *Elektra* des Euripides." *Rheinisches Museum für Philologie* 112: 103–9.

Dodds, E. R. 1960. *Euripides' "Bacchae."* 2d ed. Oxford: Oxford University Press.

Dunkle, Roger. 1987. "Nestor, Odysseus, and the μῆτις-βίη Antithesis: The Funeral Games, *Iliad* 23." *Classical World* 81: 1–17.

Easterling, P. E. 1982. *Sophocles: Trachiniae.* Cambridge: Cambridge University Press.

Edwards, Mark W. 1987. *Homer: Poet of the "Iliad."* Baltimore: Johns Hopkins University Press.

Else, Gerald. 1965. *The Origin and Early Form of Greek Tragedy.* Cambridge, Mass.: Harvard University Press.

Erdmann, G. 1964. "Der Botenbericht bei Euripides: Struktur und dramatische Funktion." Diss., Kiel.

Falkner, Thomas M. 1998. "Containing Tragedy: Rhetoric and Self-Representation in Sophocles' *Philoctetes.*" *Classical Antiquity* 17: 25–58.

———. 1999. "Madness Visible: Tragic Ideology and Poetic Authority in Sophocles' *Ajax.*" In *Contextualizing Classics: Ideology, Performance, Dialogue (Essays in Honor of John J. Peradotto)*, edited by Thomas M. Falkner, Nancy Felson, and David Konstan, 173–201. Lanham, Md.: Rowman and Littlefield.

Fenik, Bernard. 1964. *"Iliad" X and the "Rhesus": The Myth.* Brussels: Latomus.

Fischl, J. 1910. "De Nuntiis Tragicis." Diss., Vienna.

Flashar, Hellmut. 1976. "Die Handlungsstruktur des König Ödipus." *Poetica* 8: 355–59.

Foley, Helene. 1985. *Ritual Irony: Poetry and Sacrifice in Euripides.* Ithaca, N.Y.: Cornell University Press.

Ford, Andrew. 1985. "Theognis, Poet of Megara." In *Theognis of Megara: Poetry and the Polis*, edited by Thomas J. Figueira and Gregory Nagy, 82–95. Baltimore: Johns Hopkins University Press.

———. 1992. *Homer: The Poetry of the Past.* Ithaca, N.Y.: Cornell University Press.

Foucault, Michel. 1979. *Discipline and Punish: The Birth of the Prison.* Translated by Alan Sheridan. New York: Random House.

Fraenkel, Eduard. 1950. *Aeschylus: Agamemnon.* Oxford: Oxford University Press.

Friis Johansen, H. 1959. *General Reflection in Tragic Rhesis: A Study of Form.* Copenhagen: Munksgaard.

Friis Johansen, Knud. 1967. *The "Iliad" in Early Greek Art.* Copenhagen: Munksgaard.

Gagarin, Michael. 1983. "Antilochus' Strategy: The Chariot Race in *Iliad* 23." *Classical Philology* 78: 35–39.

Garner, Richard. 1990. *From Homer to Tragedy: The Art of Allusion in Greek Poetry.* London: Routledge.

Genette, Gérard. 1980. *Narrative Discourse: An Essay in Method.* Translated by Jane E. Lewin. Ithaca, N.Y.: Cornell University Press.

Gerber, Douglas E. 1999. *Greek Elegiac Poetry: From the Seventh to the Fifth Centuries B.C.* Loeb Classical Library. Cambridge, Mass.: Harvard University Press.

Gildersleeve, Basil L. 1965. *Pindar: The Olympian and Pythian Odes.* Reprint of 1890 ed. Amsterdam: Hakkert.

Goff, Barbara E. 1990. *The Noose of Words: Readings of Desire, Violence, and Language in Euripides' "Hippolytos."* Cambridge: Cambridge Univerity Press.

———. 1991. "The Sign of the Fall: The Scars of Orestes and Odysseus." *Classical Antiquity* 10: 259–67.

Goldhill, Simon. 1984a. "Exegesis: Oedipus (R)ex." *Arethusa* 17: 177–200.

————.1984b. *Language, Sexuality, Narrative: The Oresteia*. Cambridge: Cambridge University Press.

————. 1986. *Reading Greek Tragedy*. Cambridge: Cambridge University Press.

————. 1988a. "Doubling and Recognition in the *Bacchae*." *Metis* 3: 137–56.

————. 1988b. "Reading Differences: The *Odyssey* and Juxtaposition." *Ramus* 17: 1–31.

————. 1991. *The Poet's Voice: Essays on Poetics and Greek Literature*. Cambridge: Cambridge University Press.

————. 1996. "Collectivity and Otherness—The Authority of the Tragic Chorus: Response to Gould." In *Tragedy and the Tragic: Greek Theatre and Beyond*, edited by M. S. Silk, 244–56. Oxford: Oxford University Press.

Gould, John. 1996. "Tragedy and Collective Experience." In *Tragedy and the Tragic: Greek Theatre and Beyond*, edited by M. S. Silk, 217–43. Oxford: Oxford University Press.

Greenberg, Nathan A. 1990. *The Poetic Theory of Philodemus*. New York: Garland.

Gregory, Justina. 1985. "Some Aspects of Seeing in Euripides' *Bacchae*." *Greece & Rome* 32: 23–31.

Griffin, Jasper. 1995. *Homer: Iliad Book Nine*. Oxford: Clarendon Press.

Griffith, Mark. 1995. "Brilliant Dynasts: Power and Politics in the *Oresteia*." *Classical Antiquity* 14: 62–129.

————. 1999. *Sophocles: Antigone*. Cambridge: Cambridge University Press.

Groeneboom, Petrus. 1930. *Aeschylus' "Persae."* Groningen: J. B. Wolters.

Groningen, B. A. van. 1957. "Theognis 769–772." *Mnemosyne* 10: 103–9.

Haft, Adele J. 1984. "Odysseus, Idomeneus, and Meriones: The Cretan Lies of *Odyssey* 13–19." *Classical Journal* 79: 289–306.

Hainsworth, Bryan. 1993. *The "Iliad": A Commentary*. Vol. 3, *Books 9–12*. Cambridge: Cambridge University Press.

Hall, Edith. 1989. *Inventing the Barbarian: Greek Self-Definition through Tragedy*. Oxford: Clarendon Press.

————. 1996. *Aeschylus: Persians, Edited with an Introduction, Translation, and Commentary*. Warminster: Aris & Phillips.

Halliwell, Stephen. 1986. *Aristotle's "Poetics."* Chapel Hill: University of North Carolina Press.

Halperin, David M. 1990. *One Hundred Years of Homosexuality*. New York: Routledge.

Hartog, François. 1982. "L'oeil de Thucydide et l'histoire 'véritable.'" *Poétique* 49: 22–30.

Hay, John Gaylord. 1978. *"Oedipus Tyrannus": Lame Knowledge and the Homosporic Womb.* Washington, D.C.: University Press of America.

Heath, Malcolm. 1987. *The Poetics of Greek Tragedy.* Stanford: Stanford University Press.

Heidegger, Martin. 1959. *An Introduction to Metaphysics.* Translated by Ralph Manheim. New Haven: Yale University Press.

Henning, Erich. 1910. "De Tragicorum Atticorum Narrationibus." Diss., Göttingen.

Herington, C. J. 1985. *Poetry into Drama: Early Tragedy and the Greek Poetic Tradition.* Berkeley: University of California Press.

———. 1986. *Aeschylus.* New Haven: Yale University Press.

Heubeck, Alfred, Stephanie West, and J. B. Hainsworth. 1988. *A Commentary on Homer's "Odyssey."* Vol. 1, *Introduction and Books I–VIII.* Oxford: Clarendon Press.

Hölderlin, Friedrich. 1980. "In lieblicher Bläue . . ." ("In Lovely Blueness . . ."). In *Poems and Fragments,* translated by Michael Hamburger, 600–605. Cambridge: Cambridge University Press.

Janko, Richard. 1991. "Philodemus' *On Poems* and Aristotle's *On Poets.*" *Cronache Ercolanesi* 21: 5–64.

Jebb, Richard C. 1893. *Sophocles: The Plays and Fragments.* Pt. 1, *Oedipus Tyrannus.* Cambridge: Cambridge University Press.

———. 1894. *Sophocles: The Plays and Fragments.* Pt. 6, *Electra.* Cambridge: Cambridge University Press.

Jens, Walter, ed. 1971. *Die Bauformen der griechischen Tragoedie.* Munich: W. Fink.

Joerden, Klaus. 1971. "Zur Bedeutung des Ausser- und Hinterszenischen." In *Die Bauformen der griechischen Tragödie,* edited by Walter Jens, 369–412. Munich: W. Fink.

Kamerbeek, J. C. 1967. *The Plays of Sophocles.* Pt. 4, *Oedipus Tyrannus.* Leiden: E. J. Brill.

———. 1974. *The Plays of Sophocles.* Pt. 5, *Electra.* Leiden: E. J. Brill.

Kannicht, Richard. 1969. *Euripides: Helena.* Heidelberg: C. Winter.

Keller, J. 1959. "Struktur und dramatische Funktion des Botenberichtes bei Aischylos und Sophokles." Diss., Tübingen.

Kells, J. H. 1973. *Sophocles: Electra.* Cambridge: Cambridge University Press.

Kierkegaard, Søren. 1983. "Repetition." In *Fear and Trembling; Repetition,* edited and translated by Howard V. Hong and Edna H. Hong, 131–231. Princeton: Princeton University Press.

Kirk, G. S. 1985. The "Iliad": A Commentary. Vol. 1, Books 1–4. Cambridge: Cambridge University Press.

Knox, Bernard M. W. 1957. Oedipus at Thebes. New Haven: Yale University Press.

———. 1979. "The Ajax of Sophocles." In Word and Action: Essays on the Ancient Theater, 125–60. Baltimore: Johns Hopkins University Press ( = "The Ajax of Sophocles," Harvard Studies in Classical Philology 65 [1961]: 1–37).

Kossatz-Deissmann, Anneliese. 1981. Lexicon Iconographicum Mythologiae Classicae (s.v. Achilleus). Zurich: Artemis.

Lacroix, Maurice. 1976. Les "Bacchantes" d'Euripide. Paris: E. Belin.

Lanata, Giuliana. 1963. Poetica pre-Platonica. Testimonianze e frammenti. Florence: La Nuova Italia.

LaRue, Jene. 1968. "Prurience Uncovered: The Psychology of Euripides' Pentheus." Classical Journal 63: 209–14.

Leaf, Walter. 1915. "Rhesos of Thrace." Journal of Hellenic Studies 35: 1–11.

Lesky, Albin. 1983. Greek Tragic Poetry. Translated by Matthew Dillon. New Haven: Yale University Press.

Létoublon, Françoise. 1987. "Le messager fidèle." In Homer, Beyond Oral Poetry: Recent Trends in Homeric Interpretation, edited by I. J. F. de Jong, J. Kalff, and J. M. Bremer, 123–44. Amsterdam: B. R. Gruner.

Lloyd, Michael. 1992. The Agon in Euripides. Oxford: Clarendon Press.

Lloyd-Jones, H., and N. G. Wilson. 1990. Sophoclea: Studies on the Text of Sophocles. Oxford: Oxford University Press.

Löhrer, Robert. 1927. Beiträge zur Kenntnis der Beziehungen von Mienenspiel und Maske in der griechischen Tragödie. Paderborn: F. Schöningh.

Loraux, Nicole. 1995. The Experiences of Tiresias: The Feminine and the Greek Man. Translated by Paula Wissing. Princeton: Princeton University Press.

Lowe, N. J. 2000. The Classical Plot and the Invention of Western Narrative. Cambridge: Cambridge University Press.

Luther, Wilhelm. 1935. Wahrheit und Lüge im ältesten Griechentum. Leipzig: Noske.

Lynn-George, Michael. 1988. Epos: Word, Narrative, and the "Iliad." Atlantic Highlands, N.J.: Humanities Press International.

Martin, Richard. 1989. The Language of Heroes: Speech and Performance in the "Iliad." Ithaca, N.Y.: Cornell University Press.

Massenzio, Marcello. 1969. "Cultura e crisi permanente: La 'xenia' dionysiaca." Studi e Materiali di Storia delle Religioni 40: 27–113.

Mastronarde, Donald J. 1994. *Euripides: Phoenissae, Edited with Introduction and Commentary.* Cambridge: Cambridge University Press.

McClure, Laura. 1999. *Spoken Like a Woman: Speech and Gender in Athenian Drama.* Princeton: Princeton University Press.

McDonald, Marianne. 1992. "L'extase de Penthée: Ivresse et représentation dans *Les Bacchantes* d'Euripide." *Pallas* 38: 227–37.

Metz, Christian. 1982. *The Imaginary Signifier: Psychoanalysis and the Cinema.* Translated by Celia Britton, Annwyl Williams, Ben Brewster, and Alfred Guzzetti. Bloomington: Indiana University Press.

Michelini, Ann N. 1974. "Makran gar exeteinas." *Hermes* 102: 524–39.

———. 1982. *Tradition and Dramatic Form in the "Persians" of Aeschylus.* Leiden: E. J. Brill.

Mondi, Robert J. 1978. "The Function and Social Position of the *Kêrux* in Early Greece." Ph.D. diss., Harvard University.

Myrick, Leslie Diane. 1994. "The Way Up and Down: Trace Horse and Turning Imagery in the Orestes Plays." *Classical Journal* 89: 131–48.

Nagy, Gregory. 1979. *The Best of the Achaeans: Concepts of the Hero in Archaic Greek Poetry.* Baltimore: Johns Hopkins University Press.

———. 1985. "Theognis and Megara: A Poet's Vision of His City." In *Theognis of Megara: Poetry and the Polis*, edited by Thomas J. Figueira and Gregory Nagy, 22–81. Baltimore: Johns Hopkins University Press.

———. 1990a. *Greek Mythology and Poetics.* Ithaca, N.Y.: Cornell University Press.

———. 1990b. *Pindar's Homer: The Lyric Possession of an Epic Past.* Baltimore: Johns Hopkins University Press.

Nash, Laura L. 1990. *The Aggelia in Pindar.* New York: Garland.

Nightingale, Andrea Wilson. 2001. "On Wandering and Wondering: *Theōria* in Greek Philosophy and Culture. *Arion* 9: 23–58.

Nisetich, Frank J. 1989. *Pindar and Homer.* Baltimore: Johns Hopkins University Press.

Nünlist, René. 1998. *Poetologische Bildersprache in der frühgriechischen Dichtung.* Stuttgart: Teubner.

Ober, Josiah, and Barry Strauss. 1990. "Drama, Political Rhetoric, and the Discourse of Athenian Democracy." In *Nothing To Do with Dionysos? Athenian Drama in Its Social Context*, edited by John J. Winkler and Froma I. Zeitlin, 237–70. Princeton: Princeton University Press.

Olson, S. Douglas. 1995. *Blood and Iron: Stories and Storytelling in Homer's "Odyssey."* Leiden: E. J. Brill.

Oranje, Hans. 1984. *Euripides' "Bacchae": The Play and Its Audience.* Leiden: E. J. Brill.

O'Regan, Daphne. 1992. *Rhetoric, Comedy, and the Violence of Language in Aristophanes' "Clouds."* New York: Oxford University Press.

Paduano, Guido. 1973. "Funzioni drammatiche nella struttura del *Reso* I: L'aristia mancata di Dolone e Reso." *Maia* 25: 3–29.

———. 1978. *Sui "Persiani" di Eschilo: Problemi di focalizzazione drammatica.* Rome: Edizioni dell' Ateneo & Bizzarri.

Pagani, Guido. 1970. "Il *Reso* di Euripide, il drama di un eroe." *Dioniso* 44: 30–43.

Page, D. L. 1938. *Euripides: Medea.* Oxford: Oxford University Press.

Parlavantza-Friedrich, Ursula. 1969. *Täuschungsszenen in den Tragödien des Sophokles.* Berlin: Walter de Gruyter.

Peradotto, John J. 1969. "Cledonomancy in the Oresteia." *American Journal of Philology* 90: 1–21.

Pfister, Manfred. 1988. *The Theory and Analysis of Drama.* Translated by John Halliday. Cambridge: Cambridge University Press.

Pratt, Louise H. 1993. *Lying and Poetry from Homer to Pindar: Falsehood and Deception in Archaic Greek Poetics.* Ann Arbor: University of Michigan Press.

Pucci, Pietro. 1977. *Hesiod and the Language of Poetry.* Baltimore: Johns Hopkins University Press.

———. 1980. "The Language of the Muses." In *Classical Mythology in Twentieth-Century Thought and Literature,* edited by W. M. Aycock and T. M. Klein, 163–86. Lubbock: Texas Tech University Press.

———. 1987. *Odysseus Polutropos: Intertextual Readings in the "Odyssey" and the "Iliad."* Ithaca, N.Y.: Cornell University Press.

———. 1992. *Oedipus and the Fabrication of the Father: "Oedipus Tyrannus" in Modern Criticism and Philosophy.* Baltimore: Johns Hopkins University Press.

———. 1998. *The Song of the Sirens: Essays on Homer.* Lanham, Md.: Rowman and Littlefield.

Rabel, Robert J. 1997. *Plot and Point of View in the "Iliad."* Ann Arbor: University of Michigan Press.

Rassow, J. 1883. "Quaestiones Selectae de Euripideorum Nuntiorum Narrationibus." Diss., Gryphiswald.

Rehm, Rush. 1996. "Performing the Chorus: Choral Action, Interaction, and Absence in Euripides." *Arion* 6: 45–60.

Reinhardt, Karl. 1979. *Sophocles*. Translated by Hazel Harvey and David Harvey. Oxford: Blackwell.

Reiss, Timothy J. 1980. *Tragedy and Truth: Studies in the Development of a Renaissance and Neoclassical Discourse*. New Haven: Yale University Press.

Richardson, Nicholas, ed. 1993. *The "Iliad": A Commentary*. Vol. 6, *Books 21–24*. Cambridge: Cambridge University Press.

Richardson, Scott. 1990. *The Homeric Narrator*. Nashville: Vanderbilt University Press.

———. 1996. "Truth in the Tales of the *Odyssey*." *Mnemosyne* 49: 393–402.

Rijksbaron, A. 1976. "How Does a Messenger Begin His Speech? Some Observations on the Opening Lines of Euripidean Messenger-Speeches." In *Miscellanea Tragica in Honorem J. C. Kamerbeek*, edited by S. L. Radt, J. M Bremer, C. J. Ruijgh, 293–308. Amsterdam: Hakkert.

Ringer, Mark. 1998. *Electra and the Empty Urn: Metatheater and Role Playing in Sophocles*. Chapel Hill: University of North Carolina Press.

Ritchie, William. 1964. *The Authenticity of the "Rhesus" of Euripides*. Cambridge: Cambridge University Press.

Roberts, Deborah. 1988. "Sophoclean Endings: Another Story." *Arethusa* 21: 177–96.

Roisman, Hanna M. 1988. "Nestor's Advice and Antilochus' Tactics." *Phoenix* 42: 114–20.

———. 1990. "The Messenger and Eteocles in the *Seven Against Thebes*." *L'Antiquité Classique* 59: 17–36.

———. 1994. "Like Father Like Son: Telemachus' κέρδεα." *Rheinisches Museum für Philologie* 137: 1–22.

Rosenmeyer, Thomas G. 1982. *The Art of Aeschylus*. Berkeley: University of California Press.

Roux, Jeanne. 1970 and 1972. *Euripide: Les Bacchantes*. Paris: Les Belles Lettres.

Rutherford, Ian. 1994/95. "Apollo in Ivy: The Tragic Paean." *Arion* 3: 112–35.

Sale, William. 1972. "The Psychoanalysis of Pentheus in the *Bacchae* of Euripides." *Yale Classical Studies* 22: 63–82.

Sbordone, Francesco. 1969. *Ricerche sui papiri ercolanesi*. Vol. 1, *Il quarto libro del Peri Poiematon di Filodemo*. Naples: Giannini.

Schadewaldt, Wolfgang. 1966. *Iliasstudien*. 3d ed. Darmstadt: Wissenschaftliche Buchgesellschaft.

Scully, Stephen P. 1986. "Studies of Narrative and Speech in the *Iliad*." *Arethusa*. 19: 135–53.

Seaford, Richard. 1996. *Euripides: Bacchae.* Warminster: Aris & Phillips.

Seale, David. 1982. *Vision and Stagecraft in Sophocles.* Chicago: University of Chicago Press.

Segal, Charles. 1966. "The *Electra* of Sophocles." *Transactions of the American Philological Association* 97: 473–545.

———. 1981. *Tragedy and Civilization: An Interpretation of Sophocles.* Cambridge, Mass.: Harvard University Press.

———. 1982. *Dionysiac Poetics and Euripides' "Bacchae."* Princeton: Princeton University Press.

———. 1986. "Greek Tragedy: Writing, Truth, and the Representation of the Self." In *Interpreting Greek Tragedy: Myth, Poetry, Text,* 75–109. Ithaca, N.Y.: Cornell University Press.

———. 1994. *Singers, Heroes, and Gods in the "Odyssey."* Ithaca, N.Y.: Cornell University Press.

———. 1995. *Sophocles' Tragic World: Divinity, Nature, Society.* Cambridge, Mass.: Harvard University Press.

———. 1996. "The Chorus and the Gods in *Oedipus Tyrannus.*" *Arion* 6: 20–32.

———. 1997. *Dionysiac Poetics and Euripides' "Bacchae."* Expanded ed. Princeton: Princeton University Press.

———. 1998. "Messages to the Underworld: An Aspect of Poetic Immortalization in Pindar." In *Aglaia: The Poetry of Alcman, Sappho, Pindar, Bacchylides, and Corinna,* 133–48. Lanham, Md.: Rowman and Littlefield.

Seidensticker, Bernd. 1972. "Pentheus." *Poetica* 5: 35–63.

———. 1982. *Palintonos Harmonia: Studien zu komischen Elementen in der griechischen Tragödie.* Göttingen: Vandenhoeck & Ruprecht.

Silk, Michael. 1998. "Style, Voice, and Authority in the Choruses of Greek Drama." In *Der Chor im antiken und modernen Drama,* edited by Peter Riemer and Bernhard Zimmermann, 1–26. Stuttgart: Metzler.

Silverman, Kaja. 1983. *The Subject of Semiotics.* Oxford: Oxford University Press.

Slatkin, Laura M. 1996. "Composition by Theme and the *Metis* of the *Odyssey.*" In *Reading the Odyssey: Selected Interpretive Essays,* edited by Seth L. Schein, 223–37. Princeton: Princeton University Press.

Smethurst, Mae J. 1989. *The Artistry of Aeshylus and Zeami: A Comparative Study of Greek Tragedy and No.* Princeton: Princeton University Press.

Stanley-Porter, D. P. 1968. "Messenger-Scenes in Euripides." Diss., London.

Stehle, Eva. 1997. *Performance and Gender in Ancient Greece: Nondramatic Poetry in Its Setting.* Princeton: Princeton University Press.

Stevens, P. T. 1971. *Euripides: Andromache, Edited with Introduction and Commentary.* Oxford: Clarendon Press.

Stewart, Andrew. 1997. *Art, Desire, and the Body in Ancient Greece.* Cambridge: Cambridge University Press.

Stinton, T. C. W. 1990. "The Scope and Limits of Allusion in Greek Tragedy." In *Collected Papers on Greek Tragedy*, 454–92. Oxford: Oxford University Press.

Strohm, Hans. 1959. "Beobachtungen zum *Rhesus*." *Hermes* 87: 257–74.

Svenbro, Jesper. 1976. *La parole et le marbre: Aux origines de la poétique grecque.* Lund: Studentlittaratur.

Szondi, Peter. 1987. *Theory of the Modern Drama.* Translated by Michael Hays. Minneapolis: University of Minnesota Press.

Tarkow, Theodore A. 1981. "The Scar of Orestes: Observations on a Euripidean Innovation." *Rheinisches Museum für Philologie* 124: 143–53.

Thalmann, William G. 1984. *Conventions of Form and Thought in Early Greek Epic Poetry.* Baltimore: Johns Hopkins University Press.

Tonelli, Franco. 1983. *Sophocles' Oedipus and the Tale of the Theater.* Ravenna: Longo.

Verrall, A. W. 1910. *The "Bacchants" of Euripides and Other Essays.* Cambridge: Cambridge University Press.

Vernant, Jean-Pierre. 1988a. "The Historical Moment of Tragedy in Greece: Some of the Social and Psychological Conditions." In *Myth and Tragedy in Ancient Greece*, edited by Jean-Pierre Vernant and Pierre Vidal-Naquet and translated by Janet Lloyd, 23–28. New York: Zone Books.

———. 1988b. "Tensions and Ambiguities in Greek Tragedy." In *Myth and Tragedy in Ancient Greece*, edited by Jean-Pierre Vernant and Pierre Vidal-Naquet and translated by Janet Lloyd, 29–48. New York: Zone Books.

———. 1988c. "Ambiguity and Reversal: On the Enigmatic Structure of *Oedipus Rex*." In *Myth and Tragedy in Ancient Greece*, edited by Jean-Pierre Vernant and Pierre Vidal-Naquet and translated by Janet Lloyd, 113–40. New York: Zone Books.

Vickers, Brian. 1973. *Towards Greek Tragedy: Drama, Myth, Society.* London: Longman.

Walsh, George B. 1984. *The Varieties of Enchantment: Early Greek Views of the Nature and Function of Poetry.* Chapel Hill: University of North Carolina Press.

West, M. L. 1989. *Iambi et Elegi Graeci.* Vol. 1. 2d ed. Oxford: Clarendon Press.

Whitman, Cedric H. 1951. *Sophocles: A Study of Heroic Humanism.* Cambridge, Mass.: Harvard University Press.

Wilamowitz-Möllendorff, Tycho von. 1917. *Die dramatische Technik des Sophokles.* Berlin: Weidmann.

Wilamowitz-Möllendorff, Ulrich von. 1895. *Euripides: Herakles.* Berlin: Weidmann.

Williams, Raymond. 1977. *Marxism and Literature.* Oxford: Oxford University Press.

Willink, C. W. 1986. *Euripides: Orestes.* Oxford: Clarendon Press.

Winnington-Ingram, R. P. 1980. *Sophocles: An Interpretation.* Cambridge: Cambridge University Press.

Woodard, T. M. 1964. "The *Electra* of Sophocles: The Dialectical Design (1)." *Harvard Studies in Classical Philology* 68: 163–205.

Zeitlin, Froma I. 1994. "The Artful Eye: Vision, Ecphrasis, and Spectacle in Euripidean Theatre." In *Art and Text in Ancient Greek Culture,* edited by Simon Goldhill and Robin Osborne, 138–96, 295–304. Cambridge: Cambridge University Press (excerpted as "Art, Memory, and *Kleos* in Euripides' *Iphigenia in Aulis,*" in *History, Tragedy, Theory: Dialogues on Athenian Drama,* ed. Barbara Goff, 174–201 [Austin: University of Texas Press]).

——1996. "Playing the Other: Theater, Theatricality, and the Feminine in Greek Drama." In *Playing the Other: Gender and Society in Classical Greek Literature,* 341–74. Chicago: University of Chicago Press (= *Representations* 11 [1985] 63–94).

# INDEX LOCORUM

| | | | |
|---|---|---|---|
| 1161–62 | 94n67 | *Supp.* | |
| 1161–66 | 94 | 650–52 | 75 |
| 1166 | 94n67 | **Herodotus** | |
| 1166–70 | 95 | 1.125 | 49n42 |
| 1173–75 | 95 | 8.88 | 37 |
| 1222–30 | 93 | | |
| *Or.* | | **Hesiod** | |
| 1261 | 85n48 | *Theog.* | |
| 1266–67 | 85n48 | 27 | 154 |
| 1369–1526 | 179n18 | 27–28 | 68n23 |
| 1425 | 90n58, 97n73 | 81–84 | 58 |
| *Phoen.* | | 94–97 | 58 |
| 638–75 | 53–54 | 265–69 | 29n13 |
| 819 | 54 | | |
| 1219–58 | 83 | **Homer** | |
| 1222 | 83n44 | *Il.* | |
| 1238–39 | 83 | 1.188–92 | 1–2 |
| 1248–53 | 84 | 1.194 | 2 |
| 1334 | 26n8 | 1.198 | 2 |
| 1356–1424 | 83 | 1.334 | 57 |
| 1370–71 | 84 | 2.8–10 | 25 |
| 1371 | 85 | 2.10 | 56 |
| 1384–89 | 85–86 | 2.271 | 87 |
| 1388–89 | 86 | 2.484–90 | 40–41 |
| 1427–79 | 83 | 2.485–86 | 43 |
| 1760 | 215n39 | 2.597–600 | 60 |
| *Rhes.* | | 3.297 | 88 |
| 279 | 174 | 4.81 | 87 |
| 294 | 176 | 4.85 | 88 |
| 301 | 174 | 5.353 | 29n13 |
| 309–10 | 175 | 5.368 | 29n13 |
| 314–16 | 175 | 9.182–96 | 5 |
| 319–26 | 176 | 10.494–97 | 171 |
| 335 | 175 | 10.522–25 | 171 |
| 346–59 | 175 | 14.236 | 109 |
| 375–79 | 175–76 | 14.286 | 109 |
| 598–605 | 177–78 | 14.287 | 111 |
| 736–37 | 189n34 | 14.287–89 | 109–10 |
| 749–53 | 180 | 14.288–89 | 112 |
| 758–61 | 180–81 | 14.293–94 | 110 |
| 780–86 | 181 | 14.331–35 | 110 |
| 787–91 | 181–82 | 14.334–35 | 112 |
| 793–97 | 182 | 14.342–45 | 110–11 |
| 800–802 | 184 | 14.354–55 | 113 |
| 962–82 | 175n14 | 15.158–59 | 24 |

# GENERAL INDEX

| | |
|---:|:---|
| Compositor: | G & S Typesetters, Inc. |
| Text: | General, 10/15 Janson |
| | Greek, Hellenica |
| Display: | Janson |
| Printer and binder: | Thomson-Shore, Inc. |